HUMANITARIAN INTERVENTION AND THE UNITED NATIONS

Norrie MacQueen

EDINBURGH UNIVERSITY PRESS

As always, this book is for Betsy and Triona

Edinburgh University Press Ltd
22 George Square, Edinburgh
www.euppublishing.com

Reprinted 2012

Typeset in Sabon
by 3btype.com, and
printed and bound in Great Britain by
CPI Antony Rowe, Chippenham and Eastbourne

A CIP record for this book is available from the British Library

ISBN 978 0 7486 3696 9 (hardback)
ISBN 978 0 7486 3697 6 (paperback)

Contents

United Nations military interventions since 1948   iv

List of abbreviations and acronyms   vi

Preliminaries   xi

1   Evolution: intervention and humanitarianism from collective security to peacekeeping   1

2   After the cold war: a new world order?   42

3   Sovereignty and community: a 'responsibility to protect'?   67

4   Africa: post-colonial intervention amidst fragile statehood   94

5   Humanitarian intervention and coercive action: the Balkans   141

6   A model intervention? The birth of Timor Leste   177

7   Is it worth it? Success and failure in UN intervention   207

Further reading   228

Index   233

United Nations military interventions since 1948

1948–present	Palestine	UNTSO
1949–present	Kashmir	UNMOGIP
1956–1967	Suez	UNEF
1958	Lebanon	UNOGIL
1960–1964	Congo	ONUC
1962–1963	West New Guinea	UNTEA/UNSF
1963–1964	Yemen	UNYOM
1964–present	Cyprus	UNFICYP
1965–1966	India–Pakistan	UNIPOM
1965–1966	Dominican Republic	DOMREP
1973–1979	Sinai	UNEF-II
1974–present	Golan Heights	UNDOF
1978–present	Lebanon	UNIFIL
1988–1990	Afghanistan–Pakistan	UNGOMAP
1988–1991	Iran–Iraq	UNIIMOG
1988–1999	Angola	UNAVEM-I, II, III, MONUA
1989–1990	Namibia	UNTAG
1989–1992	Central America	ONUCA
1991–present	Western Sahara	MINURSO
1991–1993	Cambodia	UNTAC
1991–1995	El Salvador	ONUSAL
1991–2003	Iraq–Kuwait	UNIKOM
1992–1994	Mozambique	ONUMOZ
1992–1995	Somalia	UNOSOM-I, II
1992–1999	Macedonia	UNPROFOR, UNPREDEP
1992–2002	Bosnia	UNPROFOR
1992–2002	Croatia	UNPROFOR, UNCRO
1993–present	Georgia	UNOMIG
1993–1994	Uganda–Rwanda	UNOMUR
1993–1996	Rwanda	UNAMIR

1993–present	Haiti	UNMIH
1993–present	Liberia	UNMIL
1994	Chad–Libya	UNASOG
1994–2000	Tajikistan	UNMOT
1997	Guatemala	MINUGUA
1998–2000	CAR	MINURCA
1998–2005	Sierra Leone	UNAMSIL, UNOMSIL
1999–present	DR Congo	MONUC
1999–present	East Timor	UNAMET
1999–present	Kosovo	UNMIK
2000–2008	Ethiopia–Eritrea	UNMEE
2004–present	Côte d'Ivoire	UNOCI
2004–2006	Burundi	ONUB
2005–present	Sudan	UNMIS
2007–present	CAR–Chad	MINURCAT
2007–present	Darfur	UNAMID

Abbreviations and acronyms

AMIS	African Union Mission in Sudan
APODETI	Timorese Popular Democratic Association (*Associação Popular Democrática Timorense*)
ASEAN	Association of Southeast Asian Nations
AU	African Union
CAR	Central African Republic
CNN	Cable News Network
CNRT	National Council of East Timorese Resistance (*Conselho Nacional de Resistência Timorense*)
CSCE	Conference on Security and Cooperation in Europe
DDR	Disarmament, demobilisation and reintegration
DOMREP	United Nations Representative in Dominican Republic
DPKO	Department of Peacekeeping Operations
DRC	Democratic Republic of Congo
ECOMOG	Economic Community of West African States Military Observation Group
ECOWAS	Economic Community of West African States
ESDP	European Security and Defence Policy
EULEX	European Union Rule of Law Mission (Kosovo)
Falintil	National Liberation Forces of East Timor (*Forças Armadas da Libertação Nacional de Timor Leste*)
F-FDTL	Falintil-Defence Forces of Timor Leste (*Falintil-Forças de Defesa de Timor Leste*)
Frelimo	Front for the Liberation of Mozambique (*Frente para a Libertação de Moçambique*)
Fretilin	Revolutionary Front for an Independent East Timor (*Frente Revolucionária de Timor Leste Independente*)

ICC	International Criminal Court
ICJ	International Court of Justice
IDPs	Internally displaced persons
IFOR	Implementation Force (Bosnia)
ILC	International Law Commission
INTERFET	International Force for East Timor
JNA	Yugoslav National Army
KFOR	Kosovo Force
KLA	Kosovo Liberation Army
MFO	Multinational Force and Observers (Sinai)
MINUGUA	United Nations Verification Mission in Guatemala (*Misión de las Naciones Unidas en Guatemala*)
MINURCA	United Nations Mission in the Central African Republic (*Mission des Nations Unies en République Centrafricaine*)
MINURCAT	UN Mission in Central African Republic and Chad (*Mission des Nations Unies en République Centrafricaine et au Tchad*)
MINURSO	United Nations Mission for the Referendum in Western Sahara (*Mission des Nations Unies pour l'Organisation d'un Référendum au Sahara Occidental*)
MNF (I–II)	Multinational Force (Lebanon)
MONUA	United Nations Observation Mission in Angola (*Missão de Observação das Nações Unidas em Angola*)
MONUC	United Nations Organization Mission to the Congo (*Mission de la Organisation des Nations Unies au Congo*)
MPLA	Popular Movement for the Liberation of Angola (*Movimento Popular de Libertação de Angola*)
NATO	North Atlantic Treaty Organization
NCC	National Consultative Council (East Timor)
NFZ	No Fly Zone (Bosnia)
NGO	Non-governmental organisation
ONUB	United Nations Operation in Burundi (*Opération des Nations Unies au Burundi*)
ONUC	United Nations Operation in Congo (*Opération des Nations Unies au Congo*)

ONUCA	United Nations Observer Group in Central America (*Observadores de las Naciones Unidas en Centroamerica*)
ONUMOZ	United Nations Operation in Mozambique (*Operação das Nações Unidas em Moçambique*)
ONUSAL	United Nations Observation Mission in El Salvador (*Observadores de las Naciones Unidas en El Salvador*)
OSCE	Organization for Security and Co-operation in Europe
PDD25	Presidential Decision Directive No. 25 (US)
Renamo	Mozambican National Resistance Movement (*Resistência Nacional Moçambicana*)
RPF	Rwandan Patriotic Front
RtoP/R2P	Responsibility to protect
SNA	Somali National Alliance
SWAPO	South West African People's Organization (Namibia)
UDT	Timorese Democratic Union (União Democrática Timorense)
UMMISET	United Nations Mission of Support in East Timor
UMOSOM (I–II)	United Nations Operation in Somalia
UNAMET	United Nations Mission in East Timor
UNAMID	UN–AU Mission in Darfur
UNAMIR	United Nations Assistance Mission for Rwanda
UNAMSIL	United Nations Mission in Sierra Leone
UNASOG	United Nations Aouzou Strip Observer Group (Chad)
UNAVEM (I–III)	United Nations Angola Verification Mission
UNCIVPOL	United Nations Civilian Police
UNCRO	United Nations Confidence Creation Organization (Croatia)
UNDOF	United Nations Disengagement Observation Force (Golan Heights)
UNEF (I–II)	United Nations Emergency Force (Suez–Sinai)
UNFICYP	United Nations Force in Cyprus
UNGOMAP	United Nations Good Offices Mission in Afghanistan and Pakistan

UNHCR	United Nations High Commission for Refugees
UNIFIL	United Nations Interim Force in Lebanon
UNIIMOG	United Nations Iran–Iraq Observer Group
UNIKOM	United Nations Iraq–Kuwait Observer Mission
UNIPOM	United Nations India–Pakistan Observation Mission
UNITA	National Union for the Total Independence of Angola (*União Nacional para a Independência Total de Angola*)
UNITAF	Unified Task Force (Somalia)
UNMEE	United Nations Mission in Ethiopia and Eritrea
UNMIH	United Nations Mission in Haiti
UNMIK	United Nations Interim Administration in Kosovo
UNMIL	United Nations Mission in Liberia
UNMIS	United Nations Mission to Sudan
UNMOGIP	United Nations Military Observer Group in India and Pakistan
UNOCI	United Nations Operation in Côte d'Ivoire
UNOGIL	United Nations Observation Mission in Lebanon
UNOMIG	United Nations Observer Mission in Georgia
UNOMIL	United Nations Observer Mission in Liberia
UNOMSIL	United Nations Observer Mission in Sierra Leone
UNOMUR	United Nations Observer Mission Uganda–Rwanda
UNOSOM (I–II)	United Nations Operation in Somalia
UNOTIL	United Nations Office in Timor Leste
UNPREDEP	United Nations Preventive Deployment Force (Macedonia)
UNPROFOR	United Nations Protection Force (former Yugoslavia)
UNSF	United Nations Security Force (West New Guinea)
UNTAC	United Nations Transitional Authority in Cambodia
UNTAET	United Nations Transitional Administration in East Timor
UNTAG	United Nations Transition Assistance Group (Namibia)

UNTEA	United Nations Temporary Executive Authority (West New Guinea)
UNTSO	United Nations Truce Supervision Organization (Middle East)
UNYOM	United Nations Yemen Observer Mission
USC	United Somali Congress

Preliminaries

The concept of 'humanitarian intervention' by the United Nations that we explore in this book is, in different ways, both narrowly and broadly defined here.

Our focus is narrow in that we are concerned solely with the use of military (or, in a few cases, police) contingents to manage local conflicts. This is not to say that the UN does not also intervene with humanitarian objectives in a whole range of non-military ways. The entire architecture of the organisation's functional agencies, from the High Commission for Refugees to the Food and Agriculture Organization, is in a direct sense concerned with humanitarian action, whether aimed at immediate aid or long-term solutions. But here our concern is with the deployment of armed force (although ideally it is not directly exercised as such), as a means of pre-empting, controlling or preventing the recurrence of violent conflict. Over the years these military-based activities have increasingly involved liaison and co-operation with the UN's other non-military agencies in multifunctional operations dealing with complex emergencies. But our primary concern is with the particular problems, political and military, in the UN's deployment of armed force.

In another sense our focus is a wide one. While concentrating on military action the book embraces all such undertakings by the UN. Contemporary humanitarian intervention was not suddenly invented as an activity in the 1990s when the term first came into common use. The end of the cold war certainly had a huge quantitative impact on UN interventions. It ended the superpowers' determination to exclude other actors from their respective spheres of interest, and fanned into life long-suppressed conflicts in these. But the proposition that there was any fundamental qualitative change in the nature of UN interventions at this time is debatable (and debated in this book). Armed humanitarian intervention had long existed previously, though in the United Nations it was usually described as 'peacekeeping'.

The two terms are not entirely synonymous, of course. Traditional United Nations peacekeeping, as it developed from the late 1940s, was concerned with the interposition of military observers or forces between hostile national armies, usually in the aftermath of an international conflict. While this was obviously not as directly 'humanitarian' as the operations to deliver aid in Somalia or Bosnia in the 1990s, say, it had clear humanitarian ends in its aim of preventing further armed conflict. Otherwise, it could reasonably be asked, why was the United Nations doing this if not in pursuit of the fundamental aims of the organisation? The first objective set out in the preamble to the charter in 1945 was, after all, 'to save succeeding generations from the scourge of war, which twice in our lifetime has brought untold sorrow to mankind'. In this sense all interventions by armed forces either under the command of or formally legitimised by the United Nations are by definition humanitarian interventions.

Humanitarian intervention by the UN therefore is conceived here as part of the broad canvas of military involvement. But not only does the activity pre-date the term, it also pre-dates the United Nations itself. To fully comprehend contemporary humanitarian intervention it has to be set in a long historical narrative. This too is reflected here, particularly in the first chapter, which is concerned with the 'evolution' of intervention and which explores in some detail the precursors to UN military forces.

Similarly, while our concern is with humanitarian intervention as a United Nations 'project', actors other than the UN have engaged in (or sometimes just claimed to engage in) humanitarian intervention. Often these interventions will have had some semi-formal association with the United Nations. The French-led Operation Turquoise in Rwanda in 1994 and, more creditably, the Australian-led intervention force in East Timor in 1999 both had security council authorisation, though neither was a 'UN' operation in the full sense. Other interventions have taken place in some form of partnership with the United Nations. The UN-NATO 'dual key' arrangement in Bosnia in 1994–5 lies in this category, as does, in a rather different sense, the NATO enforcement operation in Kosovo in 1999 and the 'hybrid' operation with the African Union in Darfur established in 2007. All of these should be considered in the broad context of United Nations intervention and this is reflected in the scope of this book.

Much of the discussion of humanitarian intervention since the 1990s has related to a supposed change in the basic fabric of international politics. This goes much further than an acknowledgement of the impact of the end of cold war bipolarity, though that is seen as part of a larger picture. Put briefly, have we moved (or are we are at least moving) beyond the old 'rules' of international relations which are generally considered to have been in place since the Peace of Westphalia of 1648? The centrepiece of this 'Westphalian' international system has been the sovereign state. In this conception the political world consists of territorially defined units (states) which exercise absolute authority within their own borders. In the interests of peace and order, the sovereignty of each state has to be respected by all other states, regardless of differences in power and capacity (the idea of 'sovereign equality'). The constraints that such a system place on humanitarian intervention are obvious. In principle, even where there is a manifest need for outside intervention to relieve suffering and right wrongs, this cannot take place without the consent of the sovereign state within whose territory the suffering is taking place.

The general liberation of thought about international relations encouraged by the end of cold war rigidities, along with the apparent weakening of state power as a result of economic globalisation, has resulted in new critical approach to the idea of 'Westphalianism'. How far should human beings be bound by the old prohibitions around sovereignty when faced with humanitarian demands? Is sovereignty truly a 'right', or is it a responsibility which can only be exercised by a government after it has passed the 'qualification' of humanitarian responsibility towards its own people? Should those who fail this qualification forfeit the right to external respect for their sovereignty? In such a post-Westphalian world, humanitarian intervention would be a responsibility of the 'international community' which, morally, must be exercised, regardless of the willingness or unwillingness of the host state to accept it. Even in such a new, humanly responsible system, such interventions would need to be legitimised, however. What more appropriate source of this legitimisation could there be than the long-established, globally representative United Nations?

A problem in this line of thought tends to be the blurring of the line between prescription and description. Yes, most individuals with a progressive outlook on the world would agree that a post-Westphalian world would be a very good thing (at least as far as other states are concerned). But do we actually inhabit – or are we even moving towards – such a desirable international arrangement? Have the end of cold war bipolarity and a globalising world economy actually delivered us into a new world order in which humanitarian need takes precedence over national sovereignty? It is far from clear that they have.

And, even if we are in a post-Westphalian age with regard to sovereignty, is there any evidence that states accept the concomitant part of interventionism: the responsibility to do the intervening? Has there been a fundamental reformulation of the idea of national interest which makes UN member states more willing than in the past to intervene in conflicts with no obvious relevance to their own foreign policies? Are we now ready to spend blood and treasure on 'quarrels in far-away countries between people of whom we know nothing', as British prime minister Neville Chamberlain put it when responding to Nazi aggression in central Europe? Or, is there a large element of well-intentioned wishful thinking in such propositions?

This book is sceptical towards claims that the fundamental nature of the international system has changed in this way – or even that there is strong evidence of a shift in that direction. To misquote Mark Twain, 'reports of the demise of Westphalianism are greatly exaggerated'. The state remains a stubbornly assertive presence in international relations, both in its resistance to unwanted intervention within its territory and in its reluctance to incur costs in making such interventions in the territories of others. The United Nations itself, after all, is an intergovernmental organisation, not a supranational one. It takes only the lightest investigation of its history and politics to make clear that the pursuit of fairly narrow national interests is what its member states see as the purpose of their presence in the UN. The use of the United Nations as alibi or scapegoat is common enough. Thus it was the 'UN' that failed in Bosnia and the 'UN' that stood by as genocide was unleashed on Rwanda. In truth, though, it was no such thing. The United Nations there as elsewhere did no more or less than the five permanent members of its security council were prepared to permit and equip it to do.

And (maintaining the pessimistic tone) even when so permitted and equipped, the outcomes of the UN's humanitarian interventions will often be less than desired, whether by the subjects of the intervention themselves or the wider world. The idea that such 'failures' of intervention are always or even often the fault of the UN officials in New York or in the field is simply false. A hard lesson for the advocates of humanitarian intervention, but one which must be learned, is that some conflicts are just not amenable to resolution by external intervention. In short, success and failure are not always determined by political or military technique by UN personnel. Until the particular dynamics of a conflict have reached a stage where external intervention is appropriate, even the most creative forms of intervention will be unavailing. (The matched pair of Angola and Mozambique in the 1990s is offered in illustration of this.)

More fundamentally, what precisely is success in humanitarian intervention? The cessation of immediate violence? Deep and enduring peace and equity? A more stable international system? Each of these is a reasonable aspiration for UN operations. But not all will be achieved, and success in one might itself compromise the pursuit of another.

These considerations are explored here, both in broad terms and in relation to particular operations and regions. The first three chapters explore the generalities: the evolution of multinational intervention and humanitarianism in world politics; the impact of the end of cold war bipolarity; and the conceptual and theoretical considerations surrounding contemporary intervention. The practice of intervention is then examined in relation to a range of operations since the 1990s in sub-Saharan Africa, the Balkans and East Timor. These have been chosen because of their broader representativeness in the spectrum of humanitarian intervention as a UN 'project'. The final chapter attempts to tackle head-on the complicated and highly contested issue of the effectiveness of UN intervention.

While scepticism about some of the less realistic expectations and ambitions for humanitarian intervention is a feature of this book, its point of view is essentially supportive of the endeavour. Once all the necessary caveats about the enduringly conservative nature of world politics and the many political constraints on UN action have been entered, we are still left with an activity which, over the past six decades, has saved many thousands of lives and improved millions more. Beyond the compromises and half-measures which are an inevitable part of such a highly politicised activity lies an essentially noble project pursued by admirable individuals, both civilian and military. While we do its reputation no good by disregarding its limitations, ultimately it deserves to be celebrated as a fundamentally decent activity in an often far from decent world.

For some, the international community is not intervening enough; for others it is intervening much too often. For some the only issue is in ensuring that coercive interventions are effective; for others questions about legality, process and the possible misuse of precedent loom much larger. For some, the new interventions herald a new world in which human rights trumps state sovereignty; for others it ushers in a world in which big powers ride roughshod over the smaller ones, manipulating the rhetoric of humanitarianism and human rights. The controversy has laid bare basic divisions within the international community. In the interest of all those victims who suffer and die when leadership and institutions fail, it is crucial that these divisions be resolved.

The Responsibility to Protect: Report of the International Commission on Intervention and State Sovereignty (2001)

Chapter 1

Evolution: intervention and humanitarianism from collective security to peacekeeping

The origins of collective humanitarian intervention long pre-date the end of the cold war. Although the intensity of intervention and public awareness of it as a phenomenon have grown enormously, it has a protracted historical ancestry. At different times and in various places the collective and the humanitarian elements in military interventions may have been questionable. But in the eyes of those who have advocated such interventions over the centuries, as well as those who have carried them out, an ethical dimension has usually been at least claimed for them. What were the medieval crusades if not 'collective humanitarian interventions' at least in the justifications, and usually also somewhere in the consciences, of the crusaders themselves? Those who bore the brunt of those Christian onslaughts obviously did not see things quite in that light. But then, as now, such operations are defined differently when seen through different lenses.

There are also continuing arguments about not just what constitutes humanitarianism, but also the nature of 'intervention'. In one view the application of any sort of pressure on a state, whether it involves a military presence or not, would be intervention. Economic and diplomatic pressures, however mild and subtle, amount to intervention and when applied for humanitarian purposes these too would constitute humanitarian intervention. The United Nations itself is empowered by its charter to apply such pressures and has proved reasonably adept at doing so. The diplomatic isolation of errant states and the application of economic sanctions against them have long been weapons in the UN's non-military armoury. Often the UN will approach intervention in an incremental way, applying these milder tools before committing to military actions. While this book is mainly concerned with intervention by military personnel acting under mandates provided by the United Nations, we need to be aware at the outset that this is not the beginning and end of 'humanitarian intervention'. Nor, as we have noted, is it a uniquely UN activity. Its pedigree in world politics and history is long and complex.

The European beginnings: from Westphalia to the new imperialism

In truth, of course, pressing the medieval political and religious power-play of the crusades into the mould of contemporary humanitarian intervention is unlikely to produce a satisfactory model. For one thing, the forces of intervention, if that is what they were, came not from a collection of modern states acting as what would now be called a coalition of the willing, but from a varied and irregular set of feudal political entities in which power was neither territorially defined nor guided by fixed constitutional arrangements. Such a political setting for intervention did not come into existence until after the emergence of geographically delineated sovereign states somewhere around the seventeenth century. This period marked the beginnings of what we now refer to as the 'Westphalian' international system. The end of the thirty years war in 1648 came with the signing of the Treaty of Westphalia (in western Germany). In an effort to remove the causes of the long conflict, which had laid waste to much of central and northern continental Europe, the Treaty set out what would become the basic principles of international relations up to at least the end of the twentieth century.[1]

The new Westphalian state system replaced the remnants of the old idea of 'Christendom' in Europe, the basis of which had become increasingly uncertain with the passing of the political and economic system of the medieval period. The idea of an international order based on an overarching structure of religious authority and feudal loyalties had already become anachronistic by the beginning of the seventeenth century. By that time, the Protestant reformation in northern Europe had long posed a challenge to the idea of universal religious and political obedience to the Catholic Church. Meanwhile, dramatic social and economic changes had eroded the basis of the non-territorially defined power on which the feudal system was built.

The three central concepts of Westphalia were territoriality, sovereignty and autonomy. A new international political system now began to emerge founded on geographically fixed political states separated by permanent borders. The governments of these states would be sovereign in their control of internal political and legal power. Externally, none of them would have the right to interfere in the exercise of that power (and the enjoyment of sovereignty) by any other. The concept of intervention, whether humanitarian or of any other sort, therefore became fraught with philosophical and practical difficulties. There were now dilemmas confronting interventionist behaviour which had not existed to the same extent previously when European nations were bound together in what might be described as a 'supranational' notion of Christendom.

Over the centuries that followed Westphalia, a recognisably 'modern' way of doing international politics began to evolve. The practice of diplomacy, hitherto usually an *ad hoc* activity designed to meet immediate circumstances and requirements, became permanent and professionalised. International law, which so far as it had existed previously had drawn its legitimacy from the Church, became secularised in its authority and also increasingly codified in formal agreements. The status of international law was now based on the acceptance by states of conditions placed on the periphery of their sovereign status. These developments in both diplomacy and law were to a great degree driven by economic imperatives which came from the dramatic growth in international trade in the seventeenth and eighteenth centuries.

By the nineteenth century new elements were appearing which changed the texture of international relations at the European – or, perhaps more correctly now, the transatlantic – 'centre'. Economic imperatives remained important, but increasingly they were joined by culturally shaped forces as well.[2] Intervention in other parts of the world through the projection of national power came to be justified in the language of the civilising mission and the responsibilities of the white man's burden. Of course for many historians (often but not always Marxists), this coincidence of economic and cultural forces was not accidental; the latter legitimised the exploitation inherent in the former.

By the nineteenth century, western European States – and later the United States on its own behalf – had acquired a sense of their own unchallengeable superiority. European leaders saw their countries' economic progress (which had been dramatically accelerated by the industrial revolutions across the continent) along with their military, political and social 'advances' as unarguably better than any alternative anywhere else in the world. Christianity in all its sects and forms offered a doctrinal underpinning to these attitudes. The stage therefore was set for what might almost be described as a resumption of the crusades. Imperialism, long a competitive economic venture among the powers of western Europe, now acquired a 'humanitarian' gloss. Increasingly, the military interventions which were an essential part of the colonial process were justified accordingly. Such attitudes reached their apotheosis in the so-called 'new imperialism' which occupied so much European time and energy in the last decades of the nineteenth century. But the process had begun much earlier. British naval patrols policing the ban on the Atlantic slave trade began in the second decade of the century and later became 'multilateral' with the participation of France. In reality, this 'humanitarian intervention' came at little cost to the countries involved as both the British and French imperial economies were moving away from their dependence on the plantations of the Caribbean. This relatively consequence-free gesture, sceptics would argue, remained typical of humanitarian interventions into the twenty-first century.

Beyond the tropical frontiers of imperialism, the nineteenth century also saw significant changes in the way the European powers managed their own relationships within their own continent. The aftermath of the French Revolutionary and Napoleonic wars which straddled the end of the eighteenth and the beginning of the nineteenth centuries led, as the thirty years war had a century and a half earlier, to a new sense of how international relations should be conducted.

The concert of Europe arrangement which emerged after 1815 was, it is true, in most senses just an alliance of victors; it certainly was not an international organisation in the sense the term would come to be understood in the twentieth century. But it did involve a new level of self-interested co-operation in the collective management of the inter-national system of the time. It was an alliance infused with the new mindset of the nineteenth century. The 'humanitarian' concerns of the concert system were most evident in its support, military and political, for Christian populations under Muslim Ottoman rule, particularly in the Balkans. Here too, of course, the motives of the western states were mainly concerned with political advantage within a shifting balance of power, but the humanitarian element was nevertheless present as more than just a pretext.[3]

Between world wars: the age of the League of Nations

As in 1648 and then again in 1815, the year 1919 saw a further major advance in world leaders' attempts to regulate the international system in a more effective way. The end of the first world war resulted in the most elaborate and far-reaching venture to date in the form of the League of Nations. Reflecting the realities of the distribution of power at the end of the war, the League's principal architect was the American Democratic President Woodrow Wilson. Just as the humanitarianism of nineteenth-century international relations emerged from a west European cultural milieu, the new inter-war humanitarian sensibility was now heavily influenced by the American political worldview and American historical attitudes.

Wilson, the standard-bearer for these, personified a certain type of patrician moralism then associated with the north-eastern part of the United States. The son of a Presbyterian minister, before entering politics Wilson had been president of Princeton University. As the commander-in-chief who had taken the United States into the first world war, he presented, at the beginning of 1918, his famous Fourteen Points to the US Congress setting out America's war aims. These mainly looked back to the unresolved conflicts of the pre-war years. There was an insistence on self-determination for the peoples of the Balkans and eastern European countries which when the war began had been under the imperial rule of Austria-Hungary and Turkey. But in his speech Wilson also gestured forward to the new twentieth century. The final of the Fourteen Points set out the basis for the new age of international organisation. A 'general association of nations' was to be 'formed under specific covenants for the purpose of affording mutual guarantees of political independence and territorial integrity to great and small states alike'.[4]

The new League of Nations, which became the institutional embodiment of this aspiration, was in virtually all respects a radically new international entity. Whatever the ignominy of the League's eventual decline and collapse in the years before the second world war, it provided the template for virtually all the important international organisations since. In particular, the United Nations which emerged in 1945 as its successor was so similar, at least in its basic structure, as to appear in hindsight as a refinement of its predecessor rather than a distinctly new institution in its own right.

The League was built on a quasi-state structure. It had a basic constitution: the covenant. It had a 'parliamentary' organ – the assembly – on which all of its members states were represented. It had a 'cabinet'-type body at the top of its structure – the council, on which sat the great powers of the day. The League also had its own dedicated 'civil service', its secretariat, whose secretary-general and officials, in a wholly revolutionary way for the time, were required to be loyal first and last to the League and not to their states of origin. In another unprecedented development, the new League was to have its own permanent headquarters (in Geneva in Switzerland). Additionally, a judicial dimension was provided by the creation of a Permanent Court of International Justice (which would sit in the Hague in the Netherlands).

The fundamental purpose of the League was to substitute a system of collective security for the old national arrangements which had been based on confrontation between opposing alliance systems. These, in Wilson's view, had led inevitably to the outbreak of war in 1914. This view reflected an American image of the 'old' European world of *realpolitik* conducted by secret diplomacy with no reference to ethical or moral standards. Now, in the new world of the League of Nations, states would operate in an international environment in which security was to be jointly guaranteed for all by all. Those joining the League had to sign up to the principles of its covenant, one of which required them to accept an obligation 'not to resort to war'. National stocks of arms were to be reduced to 'the lowest point consistent with national safety and the enforcement by common action of international obligations'. These obligations were primarily the responsibilities attached to League membership. The League itself claimed the authority to 'take any action that may be deemed wise and effectual to safeguard the peace of nations'.[5]

Wilson was uniquely empowered by America's dominating strength in 1919 to impose his vision of the new world order on Europe. He had nevertheless set himself a uniquely difficult set of political and diplomatic problems and in the event he proved incapable of resolving these. Critically, the United States itself, which had provided the moral and cultural underpinnings for the new body, did not join the League. The political class in the United States had never been fully at one with the decision to enter the first world war. Now, after it had ended, an isolationist tendency began to reassert itself among important sections of Congress. The horrific conditions faced by American troops in Europe in 1917 and 1918 convinced many that the old Europe with its incorrigible tendency towards war and conflict was best left alone to deal with its own problems. Too close a relationship with it would merely infect the hitherto healthy American body politic. In many respects Wilson and his supporters saw the situation in similar terms. The essential difference was in their calculation of responsibilities and likely consequences. Would engagement with Europe and leadership of the League be good for the world and therefore the United States? Or would it simply be bad for the United States? The latter calculation won the day.

The withdrawal of the United States from the League project before it had even begun was obviously a major blow to the hopes for a global system of collective security. Such an ambitious and far-reaching framework could hardly operate in the absence of what was beyond question the strongest state in the system. But the American refusal to participate had another consequence. Without the driving vision of

Wilsonian morality, the pursuit of collective security was bereft of any real champion. Control of the League and responsibility for navigating it through the post-war international system now fell to the other victors in the war, Britain and France. Their instinct, now freed from the constraints of the new American morality, was to guide the organisation back to the precepts of the old concert system of the previous century. From this perspective, the purpose of the League was primarily to manage the balance of power in Europe and beyond as the best means of securing stability in the international system. This in itself, of course, was a form of moral behaviour, but of a highly pragmatic and self-interested type.

In truth, the departure of the United States, while significant, was probably not critical to the longer-term failure of collective security. For one thing, there was no guarantee that future American administrations would share Wilson's worldview, whether within the League of Nations or outside it. Indeed, the 1920 presidential election saw the Democrats defeated and a succession of essentially inward-looking administrations began, which lasted until the election of the Democrat Franklin D. Roosevelt in 1932. But more fundamentally, comprehensive and effective collective security would have demanded a major adjustment in the organising principles of international relations. It would have required nothing less than a shift away from the Westphalian benchmark of the untouchable state sovereignty and independence of nation-states. That this fundamental tenet of international relations may be changing as we move further into the twenty-first century is a proposition that is itself strongly contested, as we shall see. But there was certainly little prospect of such a change miraculously taking place in the first quarter of the twentieth century, with or without the exhortations of a fully engaged United States.

The first years of the League were ones of relative stability in world politics. Viewed in retrospect, though, this was not an achievement of the organisation itself. No new world order was initiated by the new international institution. The calm in international politics, it would soon become clear, was due to the inevitable period of wound-licking after the horrors of 1914–18. As the world began to recover from this collective post-war trauma, roughly when the 1920s gave way to the 1930s, aggressive power politics returned to centre stage. When they did the League was incapable of meeting the new challenges in any collective way; the old arts of high diplomacy favoured by those who now dominated it proved inadequate against the rising waves of aggressive militarism in both Europe and Asia.

A sequence of League 'failures' which would later be exhaustively recorded by those hostile to its basic ambitions now began. In 1931 Japanese military adventurism over Manchuria in the north of the chronically weak and politically fragmented China brought only the most inadequate League response. This conflict appeared remote from the mounting concerns of the European continent where the centre of gravity of the League now lay. Consequently Britain and France showed no inclination to confront Japanese behaviour from the platform of the League council. In 1935 Italy's invasion of the independent African state of Abyssinia (Ethiopia) commanded more attention because it related directly to European diplomacy. Here, though, Britain and France were anxious not to provoke Fascist Italy. They also harboured a long-standing mistrust of each other's intentions in this and other areas of foreign policy, which was typical of the old diplomacy the League had originally been designed to supplant. From this point in the narrative of the League of Nations, the appeasement of Nazi Germany seemed to follow naturally, though in reality the relevance of the League had diminished almost entirely as the next war approached in the late 1930s. Although formally wound up only in 1946, the League had ceased to have a significant role in world politics a full decade earlier.

The failure of the League to realise the high ambition of subordinating the international system of sovereign states to a new collective interventionism should not distract attention from its very real achievements. In reality, the ambitions for a comprehensive system of collective security were almost certainly unrealisable anyway. Workable collective security still remains unachieved, close to a century after the League was formed. The more modest but still considerable achievements of the League were shaped by the modernist global culture of the time. This was revealed in several areas of League policy even in the face of the tendency of the big European powers to look backwards to the nineteenth rather than forward into the twentieth century. The notion of rights was prominent in much of the discourse of the League. The creation of a so-called World Court (the Permanent Court of International Justice), for example, was evidence of this. It is important to see this in its proper context, however. In the first half of the twentieth century, 'rights' tended to be viewed as a collective good rather than an individual one. National self-determination was a driving aspiration of the post-1918 years as four historic empires – Hohenzollern Germany, Hapsburg Austria-Hungary, Ottoman Turkey, and Romanov Russia – were brought down and broken up. But this was an aspiration for the general rights of 'peoples' rather than the individual rights of the 'person'. Nevertheless, the involvement of the League in the pursuit of those rights was, in a sense, a form of political humanitarian intervention.

The post-war treaties signed at Versailles and elsewhere are often criticised for being punitive and politically brutal in a way that manufactured grievances which contributed to the outbreak of the second world war. But in many areas the victorious powers, acting as coalitions of the willing or through the agency of the League, went to considerable lengths to redraw the map of Europe with maximum sensitivity to the aspirations of the various populations concerned. Often this involved the deployment of multinational forces to oversee expressions of free choice in the form of plebiscites. In the early 1920s, from Denmark to the Baltic and down into the Balkans, a sequence of votes was organised and policed by international commissions. These usually produced clear results after peaceful, transparent and carefully managed processes which went a considerable distance in realigning personal identity with geopolitical fact.

Year	Area	International frontier	Multinational force
1920	Schleswig	Germany–Denmark	Britain, France
1920	Allenstein and Marienwerder	Germany–Poland	Britain, France, Italy
1920	Klagenfurt Basin	Austria–Yugoslavia	Britain, France, Italy
1921	Upper Silesia	Germany–Poland	Britain, France, Italy
1921	Vilna	Poland–Lithuania	Planned: Britain, France, Italy, Spain. To include later: Belgium, Denmark, Greece, Holland, Norway, Sweden

Table 1.1 Plebiscite management by the League of Nations and other multinational forces, 1920–1

Perhaps the most strikingly modern of the League's successes in this field was its management of the Saar territory in the years between 1920 and 1935. The Saarland, a coal-rich industrial centre positioned between France and Germany adjacent to Luxembourg, was ethnically German in population, though it had a small French minority. France, facing the daunting process of its own industrial reconstruction after the war-time destruction of its infrastructure, wished to exercise its right of conquest by annexing the Saar. The League intervened with a plan that would allow France to exploit the territory's natural resources and industrial capacity for a period of fifteen years from 1920. At the end of this a referendum would be held to determine the Saar's long-term future. Before this the territory would be governed essentially as a League of Nations protectorate. It was an arrangement which would become familiar many decades later with United Nations transitional administrations in West New Guinea, Cambodia, East Timor and Kosovo. The Saar referendum was duly held in 1935 amidst high political tension, policed by an international force composed of British, Italian, Dutch and Swedish contingents. Two years after the Nazis came to power in Germany, the government in Berlin was determined that there should be no question of anything but a resounding vote for a return to the fatherland. Interestingly, though, it was not a vote for union with France that concerned the Germans; this was never a likely outcome. The main worry in Berlin was a third option on the referendum voting paper which offered a long-term future to the territory as a League of Nations entity. In the event the vote for a return to Germany was overwhelming, but almost nine per cent of the population would have preferred the new status of citizen of the League of Nations.[6]

Beyond Europe too the League developed an interventionist policy. Another League administration was established in the Leticia region of the Amazon, in 1933–4. This was designed to provide a transitional period in the transfer of the territory, initially agreed then violently contested, from Peru to Colombia which was to provide the latter with commercially important access to the river. The League's involvement here and its use of protectorate powers amidst the tensions of the time and place may well have prevented a major South American war.

The League's main humanitarian contribution in the non-European world, however, was not in the form of direct intervention but in the 'mandate' principles applied to imperial rule. The nationalities of central and eastern Europe once freed from 'colonial' rule by the defeat of old empires were judged to merit self-determination as an immediate right. Prevailing racial attitudes as well as political realities on the ground meant however that a different approach had to be formulated for the non-European possessions of the defeated. These were in effect the German tropical colonies in Africa and the Pacific along with the Ottoman-ruled parts of the Middle East. Hitherto such territories would simply have been regarded as legitimate spoils of war and annexed by the victorious powers. But the new sensibility which shaped the League's approach replaced the idea of a simple change of colonial ruler with active preparation for self-rule. The colonies of the defeated were not to be gifted to the victors but administered by them under a mandate to prepare their peoples for independence. Mandated status was, in short, a stage on the way to independence and the primary duty of the 'mandatory' (the state responsible for the territory) was to prepare the population for this. The mandated territories included major countries of the contemporary Middle East removed from Turkish control. Iraq, Jordan and Palestine became British mandates and Syria and Lebanon became French responsibilities. In Africa modern-day Namibia passed to South African control and Tanzania to that of Britain. Belgium took responsibility for what would become Rwanda and Burundi, and Britain and France had joint responsibility for Togo and Cameroon in West Africa. With the demise of the League of Nations the remaining mandates became 'trusteeships' and were overseen by the United Nations Trusteeship Council.

Yet however successful these ventures may have been in re-framing the humanitarian debate around self-determination and colonialism, they counted for little amidst the collapse of the larger security project of the League of Nations. Whatever the humanitarian successes of the League, by 1939 there was little evidence of their balancing the sense that the vision of a truly collective system of security had been abandoned. There could be no clearer evidence of this than the outbreak of world war in 1939.

New ambitions: the beginnings of the United Nations

The lack of credit given to the League in political and public opinion did not mean that the fundamental ambition of peace through global organisation had been extinguished. On the contrary, the assumption that a new world institution would arise at the end of the war was evident quite early in the conflict. In the summer of 1941 Britain and the United States (which, still several months before the Japanese attack on Pearl Harbor, had yet to join the war) signed the Atlantic Charter. This insisted that the end of the war should bring 'the establishment of a . . . permanent system of general security'.[7] Aspiring to the collectivisation of security through multilateral arrangements was obviously an important element in a transatlantic relationship which was destined to become much closer and interdependent in the near future. Soon after the United States joined the war, the term 'United Nations' began to gain currency, though originally as a description of the anti-Axis alliance rather than the title of an international organisation.

Concrete planning for the new institution pre-figured in the Atlantic Charter accelerated as it became clear that these 'United Nations' were likely to win the war. In 1944 allied representatives met at Dumbarton Oaks near Washington to being work on the constitution that would define the structure and objectives of the new project. This new 'charter' would supersede the League covenant.

The ideas that emerged at Dumbarton Oaks were presented to the allied leaders, Franklin D. Roosevelt, Joseph Stalin and Winston Churchill, at the Yalta Conference in February 1945. Once again, the main impetus for the post-war organisation came from the United States – and again its allies did not fully share the American vision. Roosevelt, like Woodrow Wilson, was a liberal East Coast Democrat and this political background strongly influenced his political vision of the new organisation. But Roosevelt had perhaps a clearer sense of the possible than Wilson (he had the benefit, after all, of his predecessor's experience to build on). This more realistic mindset influenced both the international and the domestic pursuit of his plans. Throughout the negotiating process he was careful to bring the other leaders with him rather than exploit America's relative power at the end of the war to impose his own model of the new United Nations without consensus.[8] On various occasions, particularly at Yalta, he was driven to the point of exasperation by what he regarded as Stalin's unrealistic propositions. But he managed to build a fundamental agreement among his allies more successfully than Wilson had at Versailles. And, at home, Roosevelt took pains to keep the American Congress, if not unanimously behind him, then at least not actively opposed to his ideas for the new organisation and his view of America's central role within it.

As it took shape the new United Nations looked in many respects very much like the old League. There were some changes in nomenclature – from council to security council and from assembly to general assembly, for example. But the basic function of each part of the structure remained broadly similar. The difference, it was hoped, would lie in the political and legal framework within which these organs would work. The UN set out to be – and ultimately succeeded in becoming – much more universalist in its membership than the League. In the language of the charter, all 'peace-loving' were qualified to be members simply by virtue of *being* peace-loving and not according to any special status, quality or qualification. The League of Nations had been beset initially by problems caused by the exclusion of major powers; later it was critically weakened by abandonment by major powers. While it would take the UN some time to acquire a truly universal character, the assumption that this was the proper character of the organisation was present from the outset.

Like the League, the UN's central ambition was to create a global system of collective security. In contrast to the League, however, the obligations placed on the UN's membership in pursuit of this were both precise and onerous. The United States, the Soviet Union, Britain, France and China – the five most significant world states defined approximately by a mixture of political, military, economic and demographic factors – would constitute a group of 'policemen', as Roosevelt described them. As the five permanent members of the security council they were to be, according to the plan, united in the common cause of maintaining world peace and security with responsibilities set out in detail in the charter. The remainder of the membership, which made up the general assembly (or, if elected, the non-permanent membership of the security council), had their legal responsibilities fixed in the charter as well. When the council determined there had been, as chapter VII of the charter puts it, a 'breach of the peace, threat to the peace or act of aggression', article 43 required all members to: 'undertake to make available to the security council, on its call . . . armed forces, assistance and facilities'.[9] The terms of chapter VII will be discussed more fully in the next chapter but, in short, it followed that membership of the UN required states to accept a very significant qualification to their sovereign independence, one located in the central area of military capacity. Members accepted an obligation to intervene anywhere in the world if called on to do so. The new approach therefore attempted by means of legal formulation to make collective security succeed in the hands of the United Nations where it had failed in the much looser grip of the League.

None of this however was directly intended to enable the UN to carry out humanitarian interventions in the sense of that term understood today. That type of UN action was still some distance away at a later stage in the evolution of the organisation's use of military forces. Just as generals are accused of a tendency to fight the last war, the

UN's military outlook focused on the failure of international organisation to prevent the outbreak of the second world war rather than the requirements to deal with the new conditions which might threaten a third one. The starting point was a view of the world as a Westphalian system of sovereign states bound by a set of rules in which trouble would only arise when a state or states acted aggressively (and therefore 'illegally') towards another state or group of states. This of course had been the sequence of events which had led to the outbreak of war in 1939. At such a point the 'police' powers of the security council would be invoked and the UN would act collectively under the direction of the five permanent members to deal with the problem.

Even if this 'state-centric' view of conflict were a valid and realistic one (and we shall return to this question), the post-1945 world was simply not a friendly environment for this form of collective security. Before the charter had even been opened for signature in 1945, the division of the post-war world into opposing geographic and ideological blocs had already begun. Collective security on the UN model needs as its fundamental requirement a collectivity of view among the big powers on the security council. Despite having worked together in a reasonably cohesive alliance in the war against Germany and Japan, it soon became clear that with the end of it the world was taking on a bipolar structure between capitalist west and communist east. While the charter employed the word 'aggression' in its various articles, it did not define it. Consequently, there was no objective legal reference point in difficult cases.

It must be said, though, that even if a definition were to have been supplied, it is unlikely that it would have done much to prevent fundamentally different interpretations of particular events. A polarised international system will almost always result in polar-opposed determinations of guilt and innocence in any given conflict. Virtually from the beginning therefore the elaborate and far-reaching mechanisms that the United Nations sought to put in place to preserve world peace were simply unviable.

This threatened paralysis in the central military function of the UN and how the situation shaped the development of the organisation's concept of military intervention will be discussed in due course. But before that it is important to acknowledge that beyond the military sphere, the United Nations did represent and consolidate a fundamentally new emphasis on the humanitarian role of international organisation.

The UN and the development of humanitarian law and practice

An institutional awareness of humanitarian responsibilities was present in the United Nations from the outset. As we have seen, the League's humanitarian conscience, reflecting its times, tended to be refracted through a particular cultural lens. The underlying assumption had been that the process of national self-determination, once established as a global norm, would itself bring a natural end to humanitarian abuses. The key lay in the alignment of national identity with representative government. At the same time, though, the League did provide a general framework for practical humanitarianism in its provision of a home for the various specialised agencies like the Red Cross and the International Labour Office that had developed in the early twentieth century. But as well as taking over this organisational role, the UN's approach in contrast was to embrace humanitarian responsibilities directly as an institution in its own right.

This approach was a consequence of the global conflict from which the UN emerged. The strategic character of the first world war, based largely on national armies confronting each other over relatively limited geographic fronts, had involved a special hell for the foot soldiers of those armies; but the impact on the larger civilian populations of the belligerent countries involved was relatively limited. In contrast to this war of position, the second world war was very much a war of movement in its geographic diffuseness. It was also a 'total war' in the direct impact it had at all levels among most of the populations touched by it. From the aerial bombardment of cities to violent occupation and suppression of civil resistance, the war of 1939 to 1945 created humanitarian horrors on a scale beyond anything experienced earlier in the twentieth century. And, of course, there was the accompanying Holocaust which amounted to nothing less than a series of parallel genocides. Inevitably, therefore, the United Nations began with a particularly sharp sense of its humanitarian responsibilities.

This awareness was evident in different aspects of the UN's structures and activities in the early years. There was a distinctly legalistic tone to its approach here as well as in its particular model of collective security. The League's Permanent Court of International Justice was absorbed into the UN system, though it was now to be known as the International Court of Justice (ICJ). It was henceforward given a new prominence in the promotion and maintenance of international legal norms.

The constitutional basis of the ICJ is set out in chapter XIV (articles

92 to 96) of the UN charter and in an appended special statute.[10] The Court consists of fifteen judges effectively appointed by the security council and the general assembly on a more or less equitable geographic and political spread. Judges serve for nine-year terms, though they can be reappointed, and they elect a president from among their own number. The ICJ's responsibilities cover the gamut of public international law – along with the special function of acting as arbiter of the UN's own rules and regulations. The state-centric view of world politics that characterised the League's activities persisted, however. The ICJ can arbitrate only on issues raised by states, acting alone or as a group, which involve the behaviour of other states in respect of existing international law. No individual or any other non-state actor can either be brought to book by the Court or seek redress from it. Nevertheless, the ICJ is responsible for the oversight of the behaviour of governments in respect to the various aspects of international law which touched on humanitarian protection (such as the Geneva Conventions on the conduct of armed conflict). A great deal of its work has been involved in other areas, particularly in arbitrating in territorial disputes over frontiers and in the laws of the sea. While these may well have indirect humanitarian implications in particular cases, in general the ICJ is not concerned with humanitarian intervention in any obvious way.

The Court has another weakness in the view of many, in that compliance with its findings is largely voluntary: states are not bound by them. Despite this, some sixty-five states have agreed themselves to accept the compulsory jurisdiction of the Court in matters affecting them. The reasons for this counter-intuitive surrender of an element of state sovereignty are both intangible and strictly calculated. National prestige within the international system is an immensely powerful currency, though one the precise exchange rate of which is always difficult to calculate. It tends to accrue, however, to states that make public gestures of good world citizenship. More concretely, states will accept the ICJ's jurisdiction as the necessary price of reciprocity. The ICJ can only have any significant impact if can operate within a legal community of states willing to comply with its judgments. States therefore are impelled into an 'I-will-if-you-will' situation. It is sadly but clearly the case, however, that the minority (albeit a large one) of states willing to accept compulsory jurisdiction are not those most likely to be in breach of their humanitarian responsibilities.

Enforcement of international law in respect of the behaviour of individuals rather than states would have seemed to be the obvious way forward in order to strengthen humanitarian principles. In the first days of the United Nations the omens for were misleadingly strong. The Nuremberg trials of the major Nazi war criminals in 1945 and 1946 and similar tribunals in eastern Europe and Asia seemed to suggest a dramatic departure in this direction. The accusation that the Nuremberg process was no more than victors' justice could be countered by the argument that the existing structures of international law and its enforcement at the time that the war crimes trials were being planned were wholly inadequate for an essential task. A state-to-state approach to the crimes against humanity perpetrated by the Nazis was meaningless: the Nazi state no longer existed. And, as the final judgment at Nuremberg stated, 'crimes against international law are committed by men, not abstract entities, and only by punishing individuals who commit such crimes can the provisions of international law be enforced'.[11]

As time passed and cold war bipolarity deepened, the war crimes trials (at Nuremberg and elsewhere) appeared to be one-off events. Attempts to build on them to create a permanent new legal structure for the enforcement of humanitarian norms were unsuccessful. In 1948 the UN created the International Law Commission (ILC) to explore this and other ideas for the further development of international law but its deliberations, though lengthy, appeared to lead nowhere. Specifically, a mandate from the general assembly to explore 'the desirability and possibility of establishing an international judicial organ for the trial of persons charged with genocide . . .' appeared to run into the sand.[12] A draft statute for such a court was produced by the ILC in 1951, but failed to make the essential transition from the legal to the political realm.[13] Just as the polarisation of the international system had blocked any advance towards collective military security, the impossibility of bringing both poles to view humanitarian standards through a single lens ruled out such a court. Only with the end of the cold war could any advance be made here – and even then, it was to be far from a smooth or easy advance.

A new world of human rights?

Aside from these evident shortcomings in developing frameworks of accountability and enforcement, the new UN did lay down markers of a new international focus on the rights and well-being of the individual. The Genocide Convention of 1948, for example, was one of the organisation's first contributions to the onward development of international law even if the proposal for a court to enforce it failed. The Convention committed its signatories to take action – including by military intervention if necessary – to prevent or stop the crime of genocide wherever it took place.[14] This was a commitment which, much later, during the horror of Rwanda in 1994, would cause difficulties for the permanent members of the security council.

In December 1948 the general assembly proclaimed the Universal Declaration of Human Rights (UDHR) which, in the words of its preamble, was to serve 'as a common standard of achievement for all peoples and all nations'. Members of the UN were 'to cause it to be disseminated, displayed, read and expounded principally in schools and other educational institutions, without distinction based on the political status of countries or territories'. The Declaration was drafted by the UN Commission on Human Rights which had been set up in 1946 under the chairmanship of Eleanor Roosevelt, widow of President Roosevelt. The UDHR sets out in its thirty articles a range of rights now largely accepted as minimum norms in most democratic countries. They include the basic right to life, liberty and security of the person; freedom from slavery and torture; and family rights. The Declaration also sets basic political, legal and employment standards to which the individual should expect his or her government to adhere.[15]

Although the Declaration was adopted by the general assembly at the end of 1948 with no votes against, its ratification by governments was not so easily achieved. The difficulties underlying this national acceptance – and in achieving the universal implementation of its terms – touch directly on the contested idea of the universal applicability of norms worldwide. This in turn crosses over into more contemporary debates about the underlying principles of humanitarian intervention by the UN and other multilateral organisations. Put simply, are human rights ever truly universal? Or are all conceptions of rights culturally determined? Criticism of the UN Declaration over the years has focused on its essentially western cultural bases. Such 'rights', it can be argued, are rooted in the political liberalism of eighteenth-century western Europe and North America. The individual is the focus of this idea of rights, whereas other conceptions, for example those of twentieth-century European and Asian communism, would place a much stronger emphasis on collective rights. This is a view that has also been expressed by many non-communist leaders in the global south who have to confront massive problems of underdevelopment. How does an absolute right to freedom of expression weigh against the right to basic literacy – or even the right not to starve to death? In this view, the preoccupation should be on rights as 'freedoms from' (hunger, disease, and so on) for the community as a whole. Political theorists, following the philosopher Isaiah Berlin, refer to this category of rights as 'positive freedom'. It is 'negative freedom' (or 'freedom to') that predominates in the UN Declaration. Critically, of course, this is not merely a wrangle about priorities; 'freedoms to', it is argued, can actively operate against 'freedoms from'. The rights of the individual will frequently clash with the rights of the community.[16]

Countries whose political cultures are steeped in religious observance (states which might be described as 'theocracies') present another challenge to assumptions of universality. Where policies are influenced or even determined by religious requirements, some of the individual freedoms set out in the UN Declaration may simply not be recognised as such and may even be seen as heretical. Inconveniently for rights universalists, many such regimes enjoy widespread democratic support. From this perspective the imposition of supposedly universal norms can seem to be simply a form of cultural imperialism.

These complexities around the very notion of 'universal' rights have obvious implications for the wider debate about armed humanitarian intervention. But in the early years of the UN they were little thought about. With the end of the cold war and the evident defeat of communism in the early 1990s, however, the western character of universal norms became overt and unapologetic. The victory of western liberal values was now supposedly complete and the accompanying norms had now apparently become universal.

The failure of collective security and the rise of peacekeeping

This, though, moves the narrative of humanitarianism ahead of the history of armed intervention by the United Nations. We left the discussion of this at the point where the impossibility of an effective system of collective security in a polarised world was becoming clear. If final empirical proof of this were needed it was provided in 1950 with the outbreak of the Korean war. The end of the second world war in Asia had left the Korean Peninsula occupied by Soviet forces in the North and the United States army in the South. Reunification of Korea, which had been occupied by Japan, had been set as an objective by the wartime allies but in the years after 1945 both sides had consolidated their own favoured regimes in each part of the peninsula. In June 1950 communist North Korea attempted to force unification on its own terms by the simple expedient of invading the western-backed South.

The conflict was a classic illustration of the problem of guilt being assigned in different directions when seen through different ideological lenses. For the South and its American patrons, the North had committed a clear 'act of aggression' and was therefore subject to the security articles of the UN charter. North Korea, however, justified its actions – and was supported by the Soviet Union – on the grounds that the South by failing to cooperate in the process of reunification was in breach of its legal and moral responsibilities.

Taking advantage of a temporary Soviet boycott of the security council (in protest at the failure to transfer the Chinese seat to the Communist regime that now controlled the country), the United States was able to dictate the formal response of the UN to the crisis. The result was the creation of a supposedly 'United Nations' Unified Command which oversaw a multinational force to engage the North Korean army. In reality, however, this was simply a US-led alliance which fought the Korean war on behalf of the South. The fighting dragged on inconclusively for three years, embracing invasions and counter-invasions, threats of nuclear escalation and the involvement of Chinese communist forces as it did so. An armistice – not a peace settlement – in 1953 re-established the border between North and South Korea on its original position along the 38th parallel (or line of latitude).

The war left both the Korean peninsula and the United Nations organisation with confused identities. The co-option of the UN (or at least its name) by the United States seemed to bear out long-held Soviet suspicions. The organisation, far from constituting a genuine global forum, would always, Moscow believed, be subject to political manipulation by the western majority which made up its membership in the early 1950s. For a precarious period it appeared that the organisation would follow one of two equally bleak paths: it could become a mere extension of the western alliance system which the Soviet Union and its allies would eventually just abandon; alternatively, the frustrations and failures of trying to pursue multilateralist goals in a polarised system might eventually force it down the route already taken by the League of Nations into irrelevance and terminal decline.

In the event, a new role emerged which saw the UN undertaking military interventions – though of a type very different from that originally envisaged in the charter. The elements of this new 'peacekeeping' function were in fact already present even before the outbreak of the Korean war. In 1948 and 1949 the United Nations had established multinational military observation missions respectively in Palestine and Kashmir. Each followed regional wars which came, effectively, in the wake of flawed decolonisation processes. The United Nations Truce Supervision Organization (UNTSO) was formed to oversee the cease-fire between Israel and its Arab neighbours after the war which followed the end of the British Mandate in Palestine and the declaration of the new Israeli state. In south Asia the United Nations Military Observer Group (UNMOGIP) was deployed to supervise the mutual withdrawal of Indian and Pakistani forces after the war over Kashmir, which became a disputed territory following the partition which followed the end of British India.[17]

Neither operation was considered at the time an example of a distinctive practice called peacekeeping, however. While there is some evidence that the creation of UNTSO at least had been influenced by the League of Nations operations after the first world war, the term did not exist in the 1940s and the activity had not been envisaged in the UN charter.[18] The development of peacekeeping into a distinct concept with its own 'rules' and characteristics was for the future, but both UNTSO and UNMOGIP had features which would place them retrospectively in this new category of UN activity. Both missions were composed of military personnel from countries which were acceptable to the parties involved in the conflicts because of their perceived impartiality. Neither operation would have been undertaken without the consent of the opposing sides. The two missions followed mandates set for them by the security council and both operated on the basis of the moral and political authority thus bestowed on them. Although both UNTSO and UNMOGIP are still deployed today, they were not designed to be permanent presences and their mandates must be constantly renewed. Although 'military' in their tasks and personnel, there was an assumption that the question of force (used either against the observers or by them) simply did not arise. Politically, neither conflict, at least at the time of the first UN deployment, had any direct relevance to the deepening cold war; they were remnants of an earlier imperial history.

Although UNTSO and UNMOGIP were early harbingers, the principal impetus for the development of peacekeeping as an established UN activity came in 1956, three years after the end of the Korean war. In that year the Egyptian government of the radical Arab nationalist President Gammal Abdel Nasser nationalised the Suez canal. This followed American moves to block international financial support for the construction of the massive hydro-electric scheme at Aswan on the Nile. Britain, France and Israel, each with its own interests in keeping the canal out of direct Egyptian control and each for its own reasons hostile to the Nasser regime, plotted an invasion to seize the canal zone.

The conspirators were evidently unprepared for the storm of international controversy which their actions would provoke. The emerging Afro-Asian bloc in the UN was outraged at what seemed to be a shameless act of neo-colonial aggression. More seriously from the Anglo-French point of view, the United States was wholly unsympathetic. While Nasser was no more popular in Washington than he was in London or Paris, the Americans had been kept in the dark about their allies' plans and were appalled at the potential damage they could do to broader western interests in the world.

Into this storm of criticism and recrimination stepped a pivotal figure in the development of the UN's world role in the post-Korea years: Dag Hammarskjöld, the UN's Swedish second secretary-general. The son of a Swedish prime minister, Hammarskjöld had been brought up at the heart of his country's political class. His reputation as a highly competent but low-profile bureaucrat was particularly attractive to a security council which had been constantly buffeted by conflicts around the Korean war. Sweden's historical neutrality – which had been maintained while the other Scandinavian states had joined the North Atlantic alliance in 1949 – was also an important factor in his appointment.

Once in office Hammarskjöld showed himself to be much more of an activist than the security council which had appointed him originally expected. His particular concern was with the stresses and tensions generated by the two major international phenomena of the era: global bipolarity and the accelerating decolonisation process. Hammarskjöld's attitudes towards these challenges and how they should be met were inherently conservative, though characteristic of the time. His preoccupation was with the safe management of the established international system of states.[19]

Together with Lester Pearson, the foreign minister (and later prime minister) of Canada, and with the encouragement of the United States delegation at the UN, Hammarskjöld formulated a plan for a United Nations Emergency Force (UNEF) composed of contingents volunteered by UN members. This force would 'interpose' itself between the sides and oversee military disengagement in the canal zone. British and French vetos, however, prevented the security council taking the lead on the issue. It was therefore referred to the general assembly under the so-called 'Uniting for Peace' process which, ironically, had been introduced in 1950 as a means of circumventing Soviet obstruction over Korea.[20] The Suez crisis and the creation of UNEF therefore became the business of the assembly's first Emergency Special Session.

Although often described as the UN's first peacekeeping operation, UNEF was essentially a larger-scale version of the military observer missions already in place in Palestine and Kashmir.[21] While it would be a substantial force rather than just a monitoring mission (UNEF had a strength of 6,000 while typically UNTSO had fewer than 200 and UNMOGIP fewer than fifty), the underlying principles of neutral supervision and moral presence were the same. Crucially, UNEF took no position on the merits of the dispute over Suez. This was an early illustration of one of the main diplomatic functions of UN inter-

Operation	Typical strength	Duration
Truce Supervision Organization (Palestine): UNTSO	180	1948–present
Military Observer Group in India and Pakistan: UNMOGIP	45	1949–present
Emergency Force (Suez): UNEF	6,000	1956–67
Observation Group in Lebanon: UNOGIL	600	1958
Operation in the Congo: ONUC	20,000	1960–4
Temporary Executive Authority and Security Force (Irian Jaya): UNTEA/UNSF	1,600	1962–3
Yemen Observer Mission: UNYOM	200	1963–4
Force in Cyprus: UNFICYP	1,200	1964–present
India–Pakistan Observation Mission: UNIPOM	100	1965–6

Table 1.2 United Nations military interventions in the 'first' cold war, 1948–66

ventions. Their neutrality offers a blank canvas onto which each side in a conflict can apply its own gloss. For Egypt, the UN intervention provided public proof that the Anglo-French action had been both illegal and immoral. Meanwhile, Britain and France could present their military action as merely an essential first phase in a process of internationalisation made necessary by Egypt's behaviour. The second phase of this was, they implied, properly the role of the UN. Moreover, there was no expectation that UNEF would ever be required to use force. It could be deployed only with the consent of the parties. UNEF did not establish a presence on the Israeli side of the border, for example, because of the refusal of permission by the government. UNEF performed its role without serious incident for eleven years until, on the eve of the next Arab–Israeli conflict, the six days war of June 1967, the Egyptian government required it to withdraw.

The summary study and the rules of traditional peacekeeping

In 1958, two years into UNEF's deployment, Hammarskjöld produced a lengthy paper on the experience of UNEF which was designed to serve as a guide to future peacekeeping ventures.[22] In distillation, this 'summary study' asserted three fundamental principles of peacekeeping practice. These set out what became the essential characteristics of UN military intervention from the 1950s to the 1980s. They mark the fundamental differences between classical peacekeeping and coercive collective security on one side and later forms of humanitarian intervention. Sometimes described as a 'holy trinity', these defining principles are: consent; neutrality; and use of force only in self-defence.[23]

The fact that the first of these principles was usually expressed in terms of 'host state consent' is revealing of one of the features of traditional peacekeeping which tie it to a particular historical and political setting. The Hammarskjöldian view of peacekeeping was essentially a Westphalian one in the sense that it was concerned primarily with conflicts between sovereign states in the international system. There was a clue to this in Hammarskjöld's own characterisation of peacekeeping as part of a process of 'preventive diplomacy'. It was an inter-state activity that took place between responsible political entities which would normally be member states of the United Nations. To date the parties in the conflicts subject to UN military interventions had been Israel and the Arab states on its borders, India and Pakistan, and Britain, France, Israel and Egypt. All were member states of the UN. The limited value of this inter-state model would soon be exposed. The requirements of humanitarian intervention and the inadequacy of traditional peacekeeping methods in meeting them would confront the United Nations only a short time after the appearance of the summary study.

First, though, Hammarskjöld's model did have some post-Suez validation, once again in the Middle East. In 1958 an international crisis emerged when the Maronite Christian party of President Camille Chamoun of Lebanon complained of Syrian interference in Lebanese politics and military infiltration across the border in the mountainous region between the two countries. This was more than just a local spat, as Chamoun's conservative regime was regarded by the United States as a key friend in the region. Meanwhile Syria, along with Nasser's Egypt, was at the forefront of radical Arab nationalism which was spreading throughout the Middle East and which tended towards the Soviet Union in its ideological and diplomatic sympathies. By winning security council agreement to the deployment of a military observer mission on the border (the UN Observer Group in Lebanon – UNOGIL), Hammarskjöld was able to fence off the crisis from a dangerous entanglement with cold war rivalry.[24] Although an American force was sent to Lebanon it remained garrisoned around the capital, Beirut, while UNOGIL took up positions in the critical border area. The UN military observers reported that no significant Syrian activity was taking place there. This confirmed a widely held suspicion that the Lebanese government had been trying to manufacture an international crisis to distract attention from internal dissent and summon up western support. Like the Suez venture, the observation mission in Lebanon was a classic example of inter-state Westphalian peacekeeping on the model that formed the basis of the summary study. It was, however, to be one of a diminishing number of such exemplary operations.

The Congo: intra-state entanglement and the beginnings of humanitarian intervention

Two years later in July 1960 the UN embarked on what was to that date by far its largest military intervention. The United Nations Opération in the Congo ('ONUC' from the French acronym *Opération des Nations Unies au Congo*), which would eventually reach a strength of 20,000, followed the botched decolonisation of the Belgian Congo. The vast territory (today the Democratic Republic of Congo) was simply unprepared for independent statehood. Yet when confronted by the first signs of nationalist agitation, Belgium, itself a small, politically divided and far from rich country, chose to withdraw rather than embark on a proper, if belated, process of preparation. Within days of the transfer of power the new national army had mutinied. The ensuing attacks on Europeans brought Belgian troops (who remained by agreement in the country) back onto the streets. This led the Congolese president, Joseph Kasavubu, and the country's radical prime minister, Patrice Lumumba, to seek external support against what they saw as post-colonial aggression by Belgium. The crisis was vastly complicated by the simultaneous breakaway of the mineral-rich southern province of Katanga. This secession was supported and nurtured (and probably actively engineered) by European commercial interests acting with the tacit support of the Belgian government. Other parts of the huge country, suspicious on regional and ethnic grounds of the leadership in the capital, Kinshasa, then attempted to follow Katanga's example. The cumulative result was a multi-layered humanitarian crisis of the type that some decades later would be described as a 'complex emergency'.

The situation in the Congo was a clear challenge to the traditional peacekeeping model. The UN, however, proved slow to respond appropriately to this, clinging stubbornly to the holy trinity of peacekeeping principles even after they were exposed as wholly irrelevant to Congolese realities. The UN's engagement began, at least notionally, as an inter-state operation. From the perspective of the Congolese government, ONUC should have been an operation against 'Belgian aggression'. This, of course, was never the view of the majority of the five permanent members of the security council, three of which were formal allies of Belgium in NATO. The Soviet Union had its own view of the situation and this fundamental division in the council would later bring deep difficulties to the UN as a whole. But there was general agreement that UN personnel should 'interpose' themselves between the Congolese authorities and Belgian forces, allowing the latter to withdraw. Subsequently, the UN would undertake training of the Congolese armed forces.[25]

The pace of events in the Congo soon left these relatively modest ambitions behind. The Katanga secession and fighting in other provinces was quickly followed by the implosion of the central government. Two months after the arrival of UN troops, President Kasavubu, who was generally regarded as pro-western, and prime minister Lumumba, seen by the west as a pro-Soviet radical, dramatically turned on each other. Kasavubu managed to cling to power while Lumumba was forced, humiliatingly, to seek UN protection. At the beginning of 1961 Lumumba was captured by his enemies and transferred to Katanga where he was brutally murdered.

Now, not only was the UN facing a civil ('intra-state') emergency rather than an international conflict, but also the notion of 'host state consent' had become meaningless as the Congolese state collapsed. 'Neutrality' became impossible in a web of issues where even inactivity was a policy decision with consequences for one side or the other. The struggle for power between Kasavubu and Lumumba brought this home. Whatever ONUC did or did not do would objectively serve the interests of either the president or the prime minister against those of the other. A separate problem, but one which posed a similar dilemma, was that the UN's reluctance to try to end the secession of Katanga by force could also be interpreted as partiality towards the secessionists. Yet any action against Katanga could equally be seen as partisan. In this context the question of the use of force by UN personnel took on a much more politically charged character. Where did self-defence end and aggressive action begin? Did the UN have a responsibility to use force to defend others as well as themselves? In order to keep a larger peace, was it necessary to take military action, for example, against Katanga?

In the absence of any effective central state it fell to ONUC to deal as best it could with the inevitable population displacements and refugee movements taking place within the Congo and across its borders. Such a humanitarian role simply had not been envisaged for what was supposed to be a traditional peacekeeping intervention. But the operation had to be widened to meet the challenge and this was done reasonably effectively given the absence of any prior experience of this type of undertaking by UN forces.

At the institutional level the tangled complexity of the Congo crisis took a heavy toll on the United Nations. Its capacity for intervention during the remainder of the cold war would be affected as a result. Far from inoculating a regional conflict from larger bipolar rivalries, the UN involvement in the Congo instead aggravated hostilities in the security council. The Soviet Union, seeing an opportunity to seize the moral high ground against the west and gain favour with the emerging Afro-Asian bloc in the UN, denounced the failure to end the 'neo-colonial' secession of Katanga. ONUC was also accused of responsibility for, if not complicity in, the death of Lumumba. Hammarskjöld in person became a target, denounced for his pro-western bias. An elaborate plan developed by the Soviet leader Nikita Khrushchev for a fundamental reform of the UN to replace the office of secretary-general with a 'troika' of bloc appointments (eastern, western and Afro-Asian) was abandoned only when it became clear that it would not gain sufficient support from the general assembly. One long-term consequence of the Congo conflict was a disaffected Soviet Union: the whole idea of UN military invention had come to be seen in Moscow as merely a tool of western interests. More immediately, the crisis led directly to the death of Dag Hammarskjöld, in a plane crash during emergency negotiations in Africa over Katanga.[26]

The UN operation in the Congo ended in 1964. For a time the country seemed to have been stabilized. Katanga had returned to central government control after the collapse of the secession (to which the UN forces were eventually committed) and a working government existed in Kinshasa.[27] The internally displaced had begun to return to their homes (though thousands of refugees who had crossed the Congo's borders into neighbouring countries preferred to stay where they were). In the longer term the problems faced by the Congolese state and its peoples were not resolved by the UN intervention, however. A year and a half of political chaos followed the departure of the UN, with wild shifts in power and authority between different political and regional interests. Then, at the end of 1965, the army commander, Joseph Mobutu, seized power. Mobutu, who had remained close to the shifting centre of power throughout the Congo's post-independence troubles (and who had been instrumental in the murder of Lumumba in 1961), quickly established himself as 'president for life'. Restyling himself 'Mobutu Sése Séko' and changing the name of the country to Zaire, he remained president, if not for life, then very close to it. He died in September 1997 after fleeing into exile the previous May. Maintained in office for more than thirty years as a reliable anti-communist friend of the west, his usefulness diminished dramatically with the end of the cold war. Over his decades in power state resources were systematically plundered by his ruling clique and government; in the sense of the provision of basic services, these effectively ceased to exist. His end came when a long, slow-burning 'Lumumbist' insurgency was energised by support from neighbouring Rwanda whose army was in pursuit of the Hutu *génocidaires* who had sought refuge in Zaire after the horrors of 1994.

The end of Mobutu (and 'Zaire', which was renamed the Democratic Republic of Congo) did not bring any relief to the long drawn-out humanitarian disaster which had come virtually to define the country. The disintegration of the Mobutu regime brought what, viewed from a long historical perspective, was a reversion to the violent chaos that had preceded it. Now, though, there was a new and disastrous element deepening the humanitarian impact of that chaos: the Congo was at the

The Congo (Democratic Republic) today

centre of a region-wide international conflict. Once again, it fell to the UN to intervene – though this time with a more explicitly humanitarian role (see Chapter 4).

In the meantime, at the UN in the 1960s, the Congo experience put an end to any early complacency about the peacekeeping project as a whole. The model inter-state operations in Palestine, Kashmir, Suez and Lebanon, where the parties behaved more or less responsibly and where the UN's moral authority was fully respected, were now seen in a larger and less reassuring context generated by the trials of ONUC. A new wariness on the part of UN bureaucrats and among potential force contributors emerged. This was evident in 1964, the year the Congo operation ended, when a new force had to be assembled for Cyprus. This cut across the basic assumptions of traditional peacekeeping as it was another intra-state conflict, between Greek and Turkish Cypriot communities (though as this suggests, the crisis had obvious international implications). Paradoxically, its conduct would adhere closely to the basic rules of consent, neutrality and non-use of force, but there was little confidence among those approached to contribute troops for Cyprus at the outset that this would be the case. Although the

Cyprus conflict had clear humanitarian dimensions, principally because of the two-way movement of local ethnic minorities within the island, the UN force was largely an interposition presence along the ethnic dividing lines.

West New Guinea: 'anti-humanitarian intervention'?

Before Cyprus, while attention was focussed on the twists and turns of the Congo operation, the UN was involved in a venture which has been rather overlooked but which proved to be an augury of a later age of United Nations intervention. The UN transitional administration of 1962–3 in West New Guinea set the institutional precedent for the later creation of UN 'protectorates' of various types in Cambodia, East Timor and Kosovo. Simultaneously, it looked back to the League's quasi-state roles in the Saar and Leticia in the 1930s.

West New Guinea, known as Iran Jaya in Indonesia, comprises half of the huge island of New Guinea, the eastern part of which is formed by Papua New Guinea. The territory had marked the easternmost part of the Dutch East Indies. When Holland's imperial rule gave way to the new state of Indonesia after the second world war, the Netherlands refused to include West New Guinea in the decolonisation process. The Dutch position was that the territory was fundamentally different from the other islands making up the vast archipelago that became Indonesia. Its indigenous people were Melanesians (Papuans, as they now prefer to be called), living predominantly in tribal villages in the rugged mountainous interior. Socially, economically and in political organisation they had natural affinities with other Melanesian countries in the South Pacific like Papua New Guinea and the Solomon Islands. Like these other societies, the Dutch argued, West New Guinea needed to be further prepared for independence (the other Melanesian countries of the region did not become independent until well into the 1970s). Moreover, independence for West New Guinea when it came, according to the Dutch, should not involve absorption of the indigenous Melanesians into the alien Asian culture of Indonesia. Unsurprisingly, the radical nationalist regime of the Indonesian leader Sukarno did not agree. As the successor state to the Dutch empire in Asia, Indonesia was, he insisted, the proper political destination for Irian Jaya whose continued separation from the Indonesian nation was merely unfinished business of decolonisation.

While the focus of Afro-Asian attention became fixed on the Congo and the UN's efforts there in 1960 and 1961, the situation in

West New Guinea deteriorated rapidly. In parallel with Sukarno's diplomatic campaign to gain the territory for Indonesia, Indonesian paratroops were being infiltrated into the interior, where they engaged Dutch colonial forces.

The United Nations, from Indonesia's point of view anyway, was the obvious forum in which the issue should be pursued. The prevailing mood in the general assembly was powerfully anti-colonial. This was due partly to the growth of Afro-Asian influence as decolonisation brought a fundamental shift in the balance of forces in the assembly away from the global north. But anti-colonialism in the UN was also encouraged by an anxiety on the part of the leading states of the north to keep on the right side of this burgeoning new majority in the general assembly. Another significant factor was the identity of the new secretary-general who succeeded Hammarskjöld after his death in Africa in September 1961. U Thant of Burma was the first non-European to lead either the League of Nations or the UN. As an Asian he was more committed than his predecessor to a UN role in the resolution of the West New Guinea crisis. Under his overall supervision a settlement was agreed in August 1962 by which the Netherlands, which was finding its position untenable without the public support even of its European allies, effectively agreed to the transfer of the territory to Indonesia.

Simply to surrender to Sukarno's aggressive demands, though, would have involved an unacceptable loss of diplomatic face for Holland. Instead, the territory was to be handed over in the first instance to the UN. An Administrator appointed by the secretary-general would lead a Temporary Executive Authority (UNTEA) and this would be supported by a substantial Security Force (UNSF). This was to be formed mainly by Pakistani troops who, of course, were both Asian and Muslim like their Indonesian counterparts. Through the Temporary Executive Authority the UN exercised effective sovereignty over Irian Jaya for almost eight months from October 1962 until May 1963 after which the territory formally became part of Indonesia.

The amnesia that the West New Guinea operation has been subject to is probably due to a number of factors. For one thing, the affair was overshadowed by the much larger and infinitely more 'dangerous' contemporaneous commitment in the Congo. Politically too, it was less charged than the Congo operation. While the Congo at times appeared to threaten the very existence of the UN as then constituted, the West New Guinea mission did not even occupy the security council, being authorised and overseen by the general assembly.[28] As the institutional

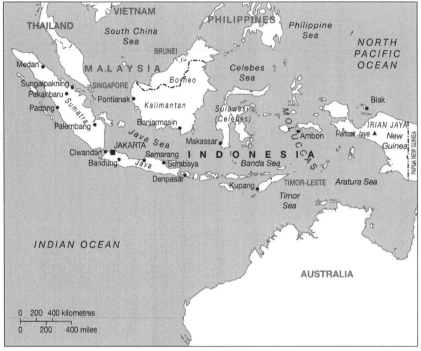

Indonesia (and Irian Jaya)

climate in the UN at this stage was one in which security council co-operation would have been extremely difficult to achieve, U Thant quietly shifted responsibility to the assembly. Also, West New Guinea appeared, at least beyond the Asia-Pacific region, to be extremely remote from what was still a predominantly transatlantic (if no longer strictly Eurocentric) international system. But it is possible too that the moral difficulties surrounding the West New Guinea venture made it difficult to confront by those fundamentally committed to the idea of UN interventionism. The mission was, in one sense, a textbook success. It was a simple inter-state operation with which both parties to the conflict fully cooperated. Its formal mandate was wholly fulfilled. Violence ceased and an agreed political process had been completed. The undertaking served the face-saving role of UN intervention already evident in the Suez operation. For Indonesia, the UN presence validated the claim over Irian Jaya and was a means by which it was fully met. For the Netherlands, it had become clear by 1962 that its position was becoming untenable. Passing the territory to the UN and not directly to Indonesia was therefore a means by which a diplomatic defeat could be presented as transfer of responsibility to the United Nations.

Yet if the UN action is to be judged as a humanitarian intervention rather than an act of traditional Westphalian peacekeeping, the picture becomes much murkier. Once in control of the territory the Indonesian government began what amounted to a systematic campaign of dispossession against its indigenous population. Melanesians were excluded from any significant level of political participation. Land rights, a central element in Melanesian culture, were trampled over and tenure transferred to colonists, mainly from Java, who arrived as part of Indonesia's internal transmigration programme. The rich mineral resources of the territory were parcelled out to foreign mining companies and most of the profits channelled to the non-Papuan military and political elite of Indonesia, All signs of political dissent were violently suppressed by Indonesian police and troops. A so-called 'act of free choice', which had been built into the 1962 agreement at the insistence of the Dutch as a means of safeguarding Papuan aspirations, proved to be little more than a farce. When finally held in 1969 it consisted of 'consultations' with supposedly 'representative councils' whose membership had been carefully selected by the Indonesian government.

In short, the humanitarian calamity predicted by the Dutch if Indonesia were to take control of Irian Jaya effectively came to pass. And it did so as a result of United Nations intervention. In this way, Irian Jaya points to a hard truth: there are UN interventions which are not humanitarian, and there may be UN interventions which in the longer term are actually 'anti-humanitarian'. The requirements of stabilising regional international relations (which were largely met by the UN operation in Irian Jaya) are not necessarily compatible with the longer-term ones of humanitarian protection. The venture was a pointer to the fact that the choices made by the UN will sometimes favour international stability over local justice.

UN intervention and the management of détente

In the years between the creation of the Cyprus force in 1964 and the end of the cold war in the late 1980s, such moral conundrums did not emerge to confound UN interventions. Subsequent operations by and large returned to the Westphalian norm in the sense that they were international undertakings designed to stabilise conflicts that might otherwise grow into larger international confrontations. They involved none of the ethnic and cultural complexities of West New Guinea. In part this was a consequence of the United Nations having been co-opted in the early 1970s by the superpowers in pursuit of the process of détente. The geopolitical location of these later interventions was the Middle East, and specifically on the borders between Israel and its neighbours. The logic of détente, pursued most vigorously by Henry Kissinger who was US national security advisor and then secretary of state at this time, was that in an age of nuclear 'mutually assured destruction' the superpowers had clear interests in common. It was to their own benefit now to cooperate in managing conflicts in the international system rather than exploit them for unilateral advantage. To this end they should pool and utilise their power to force the compliance of their client states on the ground.

In pursuit of this strategy Kissinger drew in both his Soviet counterpart, foreign minister Andrei Gromyko, and the UN secretary-general, the Austrian Kurt Waldheim who succeeded U Thant in 1972. The first major test of this triumvirate of interests came in October 1973 in the aftermath of the Arab states' unsuccessful war on Israel. Two UN operations were put in place. Immediately after the fighting finished, the second UN Emergency Force, UNEF-II (the first was the Suez force between 1956 and 1967), was deployed in the Sinai between the Egyptian and Israeli armies.[29] UNEF-II remained in place until the implementation of the Israel–Egypt Camp David peace agreement in 1979. The second operation, on Israel's other sensitive border, with Syria, was more difficult to negotiate and demanded all of Kissinger's skills in a process of shuttle diplomacy between Tel Aviv and Damascus. But the United Nations Disengagement Observation Force (UNDOF) was eventually deployed in the Golan Heights in June 1974, where it remains in place today.[30]

Operation	Typical strength	Duration
Second United Nations Emergency Force (Sinai): UNEF-II	7,000	1973–9
Observation Disengagement Force (Golan Heights): UNDOF	1,000	1974–present
Interim Force in Lebanon: UNIFIL	4,500	1978–present

Table 1.3 'Détente peacekeeping' by the UN

Israel and its neighbours

Neither of these undertakings had any direct humanitarian purpose beyond the obvious one of helping to prevent a recurrence of fighting. Each was a traditional interpositionary force between the armies of generally cooperative member states of the United Nations. In this sense these operations would have been immediately recognisable to Dag Hammarskjöld.

The next 'détente' operation had a larger humanitarian element to it and was altogether a more complex – and less successful – venture than either UNEF-II or UNDOF. This was in Lebanon. Although the UN observation mission on Lebanon's border with Syria in 1958 had been successful in carrying out its immediate and limited mandate, this intervention could do nothing to alter either the dangerous dynamics of Lebanon's ethnically divided politics or its precarious geostrategic location. The country's chronic political tensions had increased in the mid-1970s partly in response to the region-wide climate of conflict and more especially because of an influx into Lebanon of Palestinian refugees, and their political structures, after their expulsion from Jordan. The outbreak of what amounted to civil war in 1975 between Christian and Palestinian factions eventually provoked an Israeli invasion from the south, in March 1978.

To meet the threat to broader international relations that this posed, the United States supported the creation of a new UN force designed to guarantee Israel's border and help restore authority to Lebanon's weak central government. The difficulty, however, was that the superpower détente on which this sort of peacekeeping had depended for its success in recent years was already unravelling by 1978. US–Soviet relations had suffered after the communist victories in southeast Asia. Suspicion had also grown after the sudden collapse of the Portuguese empire in Africa in 1975 and its replacement by a collection of Afro-Marxist states across the continent. Détente had not ended altogether, though. It would take the Soviet invasion of Afghanistan at the end of 1979 and the simultaneous arrival of Ronald Reagan in the White House to finally bury it. In the meantime, there was enough momentum in the process to allow the creation of a UN Interim Force in Lebanon (UNIFIL). But there was not enough energy left in détente to secure the success of the operation in what was anyway an infinitely more difficult situation than that faced by UNEF-II and UNDOF.

The result for the UN was in some ways reminiscent of the experience in the Congo in that an overly optimistic mandate set at the outset was quickly overtaken by events.[31] The intention to interpose a traditional peacekeeping force as a buffer between hostile parties and then to use it to facilitate a return to 'normality' was simply unachievable. Uncooperative parties – whether armed Palestinian groupings, pro-Syrian factions, Israeli forces or the Israelis' local Christian clients in southern Lebanon – made sure of this. Moreover, the central government and army to which power was to be returned were incapable of assuming the responsibility even if the UN had been capable of delivering it to them. As in the Congo too, the necessary level of big power co-operation was absent. There was no longer sufficient momentum left in superpower co-operation to ensure the necessary pressure was placed on regional clients (by the Soviet Union on Syria and by the United States on Israel) for co-operation with the UN operation. In the meantime, the humanitarian consequences of the uncontained conflict in areas of high population density were left to the UN to deal with as best it could.

The UN Interim Force in Lebanon, despite its manifest shortcomings in the situations it has been required to operate in, continues in place. Since 1978 it has faced successive crises generated by external interventions, whether by Israel on one side or Syria on the other. Israeli invasions took place in 1982 and then again in 2006, each precipitating major humanitarian problems with which UNIFIL along with other UN humanitarian agencies had to deal. Syrian attempts to control Lebanese politics have also led to difficulties, though with less large-scale humanitarian damage. While the impact of UNIFIL on the underlying conflict dynamics in Lebanon has been minimal, its humanitarian role, largely unforeseen in its original mandate, has been considerable. The force has had a major role in particular in helping to deal with regular waves of internal refugees and in providing safe havens for civilians in its bases. (This has not always been successful, however: in 1996 over 100 died when Israel attacked the UNIFIL base at Qana.) In a sense UNIFIL has been a traditional peacekeeping force which has evolved into a humanitarian intervention. In this role, despite chronically limited resources from a divided security council, it has performed with a reasonable level of success not properly acknowledged by the various parties to the conflict.

Waiting for the new world order: UN intervention suspended

With the end of détente, the pattern of UN military interventions did not, as might have been expected, return to that of the earlier cold war. In fact, UN operations went into a state of dormancy. Existing commitments – in Cyprus, South Asia and the Middle East – continued, but no new involvements were approved by the security council. This may seem odd given the peculiarly dangerous conditions in the international system of the 1980s. The world was surely in special need of impartial intervention by the UN at exactly this time. There would appear to be a major paradox: when impartial intervention is most necessary it seems that it is least likely to take place.

To understand the role and potential of the United Nations in international politics, however, it is essential to appreciate that it is first and last an inter-governmental organisation. It can do precisely what its members – usually meaning its most powerful members – permit it to do. UN intervention has always taken place within this 'permissible zone'. In phases of high international tensions the zone will contract as UN politics become shaped by states' suspicions of the intentions of others. Traditional spheres of influence will be reasserted and will harden to exclude any outside intervention – including by the United Nations.

Conversely, in times of relative ease in international relations the permissible zone for intervention will expand. The big powers are more relaxed about where the irreducible core of their national interest lies. At such times the United Nations will be seen to offer a safe (and cheap) agent of intervention, and confidence in its impartiality will be high. This is clear from the exploitation of the UN's capacity for intervention by the superpowers during the years of détente. But an 'impermissible core' persisted even at the height of détente. Regardless of how relatively relaxed East–West relations may have been during the 1970s, UN intervention in either southeast Asia or eastern Europe was never a possibility even then.

During the so-called 'second cold war' of the 1980s which succeeded the era of détente, the depth of suspicion between the big powers was such that the permissible zone for UN intervention contracted virtually to nothing. Such new multilateral interventions that were launched during this period of enforced UN inactivity were alliance-based and therefore trustworthy in respect of big-power interests. In Sinai, between Israel and Egypt, one such mission was established after a now wary Soviet Union refused to sanction the continuation of UNEF-II after Camp David in 1979. The Multinational Force and Observers (MFO) which replaced the UN force was formed largely of NATO members and remains deployed today (though with limited functions in what is a largely peaceful area). In Lebanon, during the crisis following the Israeli invasion of 1982, rather than expand the geographical and operational mandate of UNIFIL, the United States encouraged and led the establishment of more 'reliable' Multinational Forces (MNFs) in and around Beirut. These particular non-UN ventures did not, though, have marked humanitarian roles. The MFO in Sinai was and remains a military observer mission deployed to verify Egyptian–Israeli disengagement. The MNFs in Lebanon were multilateral peacekeepers only in name, having a war-fighting potential quite alien to UN interventions. Their evidently partisan role in fact attracted a deadly hostile response.

By the mid-1980s, therefore, one might have concluded that the age of United Nations military intervention had passed. Existing operations could continue for a while and then, sooner or later, die on the vine either having completed their mandates or because these mandates were not renewed. At all events, it seemed new ones would no longer be created. UN interventions simply could not be established in the cockpit that was now the security council. But a dramatic transformation in the fortunes of the UN was imminent. The permissible zone for intervention, apparently now shut down completely, was about to be thrown open to an extent unimaginable hitherto.

Notes

1. The Treaty of Westphalia and its broader implications are dealt with comprehensively by Derek Croxton and Anushka Tischer in *The Peace of Westphalia: A Historical Dictionary* (Lanham MD: Greenwood Press, 2001).
2. For an account of the development of thought on humanitarian intervention from the early nineteenth century see Garry J. Bass, *Freedom's Battle: The Origins of Humanitarian Intervention* (New York: Knopf, 2008).
3. The distinguished theorist of empire, Immanuel Wallerstein, has located contemporary humanitarian intervention in the long narrative of this 'civilising' illusion of European imperialism. See his *European Universalism: The Rhetoric of Power* (New York: The New Press, 2006).
4. Wilson's Fourteen Points can be found at http://avalon.law.yale.edu/20th_century/wilson14.asp
5. The League Covenant in its entirety can be found at http://avalon.law.yale.edu/20th_century/leagcov.asp
6. On the status of the Saar and the referendum, see F. P. Walters, *A History of the League of Nations* (London: Oxford University Press, 1960), pp. 586–92. Walters had been an assistant secretary-general of the League.
7. The Atlantic Charter of 1941 can be found at http://avalon.law.yale.edu/wwii/atlantic.asp
8. The definitive account of the construction of the UN remains Ruth B. Russell's *A History of the United Nations Charter* (Washington DC: Brookings Institution, 1958).
9. Charter of the United Nations chapter VII, found at http://www.un.org/en/documents/charter/chapter7.shtml
10. Charter of the United Nations chapter XIV, found at http://www.un.org/en/documents/charter/chapter14.shtml
11. This passage was quoted in the landmark 1998 Rome Statute of the International Criminal Court by which responsibility under international law was finally extended systematically to individuals as well as states. Found at http://untreaty.un.org/cod/icc/general/overview.htm
12. General assembly resolution A/RES/260(III), 9 December 1948.
13. Draft Statute, found at http://untreaty.un.org/ilc/summaries/7_3.htm
14. Convention on the Prevention and Punishment of the Crime of Genocide, 1948. Text found at http://74.125.77.132/search?q=cache:U8loTrf95VoJ:www.un.org/millennium/law/iv-1.htm+genocide+convention&cd=3&hl=en&ct=clnk&gl=uk
15. Universal Declaration of Human Rights, 1948. Full text found at http://www.un.org/en/documents/udhr
16. Isaiah Berlin, *Liberty* (2nd ed., Oxford: Oxford University Press, 2002).
17. The operations were mandated by security council resolutions S/RES/47

(1948), 21 April 1948 (UNMOGIP) and S/RES/50(1948), 29 May 1948 (UNTSO).

18. At the beginning of 1948, the general assembly Palestine Commission, faced with Britain's announcement that it was relinquishing its League of Nations mandate over the territory, produced a paper, *Precedents Concerning the Creation of an International Force*, which drew on the experience of the 1920s and 1930s in considering a possible military role for the UN. General assembly document A/AC.21/W.18, 22 January 1948.

19. The fullest study of Hammarskjöld as secretary-general, though one largely uncritical in its assessment, remains that by his one-time assistant, the British international civil servant Brian Urquhart: *Hammarskjöld* (London: Bodley Head, 1973).

20. General assembly resolution A/RES/377(V), 3 November 1950.

21. UNEF was mandated by general assembly resolution A/RES/1000(ES-I), 5 November 1956.

22. *Summary Study of the Experience Derived from the Establishment of the United Nations Emergency Force*, general assembly document A/3943, 9 October 1958.

23. See Alex J. Bellamy and Paul D. Williams, *Understanding Peacekeeping* (2nd ed., Cambridge: Polity, 2010), p. 174.

24. The security council became actively involved after the failure of mediation by the Arab League. The mandate for the operation was set out in security council resolution S/RES/128(1958), 11 June 1958.

25. Hammarskjöld had used his powers under article 99 of the UN charter to bring the matter personally to the security council. ONUC's initial mandate was set out in security council resolution S/RES/143(1960), 14 July 1960.

26. For an account of the politics of the Congo in the security council at this time see Evan Luard, *A History of the United Nations, Volume 2: The Years of Decolonization, 1955–65* (London: Macmillan, 1989), pp. 217–316.

27. A strengthened mandate following the death of Hammarskjöld declared the secession of Katanga illegal and empowered ONUC through the secretary-general to take vigorous action, including the use of the requisite measure of force, to remove the foreign mercenary forces which were the mainstay of the secession. S/RES/169(1961), 24 November 1961.

28. The Temporary Executive Authority and Security Force were part of a bilateral agreement reached between the Netherlands and Indonesia. This was embodied in general assembly resolution A/RES/1752(XVII), 21 September 1962. The entire cost of the operation was met by the two states involved and the matter remained within the general assembly rather than the security council.

29. In the circumstances, the security council encountered no difficulty in

formalising the mandate for the force. Security council resolution S/RES/340(1973), 25 October 1973.

30. UNDOF was mandated by security council resolution S/RES/350(1974), 31 May 1974.

31. UNIFIL was established and mandated by S/RES/425(1978) and S/RES/426(1978), both adopted by the security council on 19 March 1978.

Chapter 2

After the cold war: a new world order?

As the final decade of the twentieth century began, the United Nations contemplated a new role in world politics. The end of the paralysis imposed by the bipolar system of the cold war appeared to have removed the constraints that had prevented the organisation from acting as an effective agent of global security. The idea of a 'new world order', a term famously used by US President George Bush, became pervasive. And, at that time, there was a real sense that this could be more than just rhetoric. The cold war had ended rapidly and dramatically, but relatively peacefully and with remarkably little reprisal or even recrimination within states of the one-time eastern bloc. (Admittedly, this was often because the post-communist elite had just a short time before been the communist elite, but however politically distasteful this may have been, it did make for a relatively non-violent transition.) The Soviet Union (as it remained until 1992) was led by genuine reformers who appeared initially to embrace the end of bipolarity as warmly as the nominal victors in the west. For a time Soviet president Mikhail Gorbachev seemed to be engaged in a fundamental reinvention of his country's place in the world. The route being tentatively followed by Gorbachev and his supporters appeared to be one from authoritarian superpower to progressive, north European liberal democracy on the model of the USSR's Nordic neighbours.

The end of the cold war seemed to accelerate the development of a new global sensibility in which the idea of humanitarian responsibility was much more prominent than in the past. This shifting worldview, at the level of public opinion and national politics alike, took time to work through into new formal structures in the United Nations. Paradoxically, this process was accelerated by some of the darker consequences of the end of the cold war and the brutal conflicts generated in the actual new world order. But whatever the driving forces, the end of bipolarity did act as a catalyst for a changed sense of the importance of humanitarianism in world politics.

The horrors of the former Yugoslavia and Rwanda in the 1990s led the UN, under pressure from member governments which were themselves responding to the demands of their citizens for new judicial processes, to punish those responsible for the violence against civilians. Special tribunals were established in the Hague (for the former Yugoslavia) and in Arusha in Tanzania (for Rwanda), and were the first such international courts of their type since the Nuremberg and related war-crimes trials after the second world war. In 2001 another similar temporary court was established in Sierra Leone at the end of the civil war there. Their existence and relative success reinvigorated the long-standing debate over the extension of the UN's judicial powers beyond the International Court of Justice to cover the actions of individuals and not just states. The result, after a protracted and difficult process, was the creation of a permanent International Criminal Court (ICC). Several countries, the United States prominent among them, were reluctant to accept that their citizens should be subject to international law in this way. However, after a long process of negotiation involving concessions and compromises which the more enthusiastic advocates of international justice feared might jeopardise the entire project, the Rome Statute came into effect in 2002. The new court would be composed of eighteen judges and would come into formal existence in the Hague the following year.[1]

The broader discourse of human rights was also given greater prominence in the United Nations in the post-cold war years for much the same reasons (see Chapter 1 for discussion of the political complexity of the fundamental concept of human rights). This had hampered developments after the initial launch of the Universal Declaration in 1948. Now, though, the passing of communism as a major force in world politics helped move debate on from basic arguments about individualism and collectivism. One concrete result of this was the elevation of the UN Commission on Human Rights in 2006 to a new Human Rights Council with the formal status of a principal organ of the United Nations.[2]

This is in part a product of a general shift in perceptions of 'security' in both national and international politics. Security as a narrowly conceived, essentially military or quasi-military concern has gradually given way in the post-cold war years to the more inclusive idea of 'human security' within which military considerations are at best contingent. In other words, 'security' is increasingly seen in the UN and other international forums not as something that is limited to the state and its stability and survival; rather it is primarily concerned with the wellbeing of the individual, and all else including the 'security of the state' is assumed to flow from that. Human security involves social and economic well-being, including respect of personal dignity and human rights.[3] If these elements are in place, the human security perspective suggests, then the states within which the individual lives becomes as a consequence 'secure'. In turn, just as human security generates state security, state security becomes the precondition for international security. This hierarchy of related priorities has obvious implications for debates about the purpose of and justification for humanitarian intervention. The human security viewpoint draws a direct line of causation between intervention to alleviate human suffering and global stability.

None of this, of course, amounted to the seismic 'end of history' famously announced by the American political philosopher Francis Fukuyama in his famous article in 1989.[4] The Soviet system had lost the cold war, but that did not mean, it soon became clear, an enduring historical victory for liberal democracy as he suggested. But Fukuyama did capture the zeitgeist of the early post-cold war years, and his thinking both shaped and reflected a wider body of ideas, even if some of it was perhaps at the subliminal level rather than actively articulated.

In the new diplomatic universe both the United States and the Soviet Union placed an emphasis on multilateral approaches to the management of the huge shifts in the dynamics of international politics which had come with the end of bipolarity. Europe, both as a region and as an organised political entity, was generally happy to enter this new order. Beyond the transatlantic world, in Tiananmen Square in 1989 the Chinese leadership had bloodily marked its rejection of the global wave of democratisation. But there was no sign that China's market reforms and its integration with the global economy were faltering. Understandably, therefore, many in and around the United Nations regarded this as a unique opportunity for the organisation. In particular there seemed to be a chance to revive – or perhaps, more correctly, belatedly inaugurate – the UN's founding ambition of collective security based on military enforcement.

Enforcement rediscovered?

The precise terms of this original ambition for a system of coercive collective security are set out in chapter VII (articles 39 to 51) of the UN charter, which is concerned with 'Action with Respect to Threats to the Peace, Breaches of the Peace and Acts of Aggression' and which we touched on briefly in the previous chapter when we discussed national obligations.[5] Article 39 places responsibility on the security council to 'determine the existence of any threat to the peace, breach of the peace, or act of aggression' after which it will 'decide what measures shall be taken . . . to maintain or restore' peace and security. The following articles comprise an escalating table of options if an aggressive state fails to comply with the security council. These begin in article 41 with non-military actions such as suspension of diplomatic relations, economic sanctions and physical blockades. If these measures fail to force compliance with the will of the UN, article 42 sets out military options which might involve '. . . such action by air, sea, or land forces as may be necessary . . .'

During the early planning of the United Nations the idea for a regular standing force was mooted. This would have comprised a military equivalent of the secretariat: a permanent body loyal first and last to the UN as an institution rather than to the home governments of the individuals involved. This, had it ever been formed, would have provided the means of enforcing action taken under article 42. The idea was not pursued, however, on the grounds of the wastefulness of such a level of preparedness in what, it was hoped, would be a fundamentally peaceful post-war world. In the absence of such a force, responsibility devolves to the armed forces of individual members as and when they might be necessary. The undertakings required of individual UN members to provide collective security are set out in article 43 (see Chapter 1). In principle the UN forms a global military alliance based on firm mutual obligations.

Despite having to provide the necessary armed forces on demand, the input of the mass of UN member states into the decision-making processes involved in deploying forces and in their strategic direction is limited under the charter. The permanent members of the security council are responsible for determining the need for military action. Then a global high command composed of their chiefs of staff issues the military orders. This Military Staff Committee is dealt with in article 47, which sets out its responsibility 'for the strategic direction of any armed forces placed at the disposal of the Security Council'.

These are clearly onerous demands to make on sovereign states. The commitments under article 43 which required states to participate in security council-determined actions were enough to keep Switzerland – which would generally be considered a model international citizen – out of the UN until 2002. To sign the UN charter and accept the obligations of chapter VII would have been incompatible with, successive Swiss governments decided, the country's long-standing policy of neutrality. As we will see when we explore the development of UN military intervention, the Swiss need not have worried. So far-reaching were the demands of the charter and so complex the politics of the cold war that chapter VII was never properly invoked.

By the beginning of the 1990s, the cold war had ended and all the apparent obstacles it had posed to the realisation of a system of collective security had been removed. With a new, unprecedentedly cooperative relationship developing between the two historic superpowers, was there perhaps a chance that this original vision of collective security could be realised?

The prospect of an answer to this question appeared almost on cue in 1990. In August of that year Saddam Hussein's Iraq invaded Kuwait, its southern neighbour. The UN's reaction, though demonstrating a high level of engagement with the crisis, fell short of a full-scale application of chapter VII. Four of the five permanent members of the security council agreed to legitimise military action by a coalition of the willing. The enabling resolution passed at the end of November 1990 'authorised' UN member states acting with the government of Kuwait to employ 'all necessary means' to enforce the implementation of earlier security council resolutions demanding Iraq's withdrawal if by mid-January 1991 the occupying forces had not taken this 'one final opportunity' to withdraw of their own volition.[6]

All but one of the permanent members of the council voted in favour, including the Soviet Union. Critically, while China abstained from this commitment and expressed opposition to military action, it did not vote against the others' commitment of support for armed force against Iraq and therefore no veto was imposed. The coalition was carefully constructed to demonstrate the maximum global engagement. It involved thirty-four countries altogether, including all of the then members of the NATO alliance, the pro-western southern Arab states and representatives from Asia, Africa and Latin America. Three of the five permanent members of the security council formed the largest individual components of the military coalition: the United States, Britain and France in that order.

The narrative leading up to military action closely followed the sequence set out in chapter VII. First there was a security council condemnation of Iraq and a demand for its withdrawal. When this did not take place, economic sanctions followed and then a transport blockade.[7] Only when it became clear that none of these non-military measures would succeed did the security council authorise the use of force. But at this point the council's actions began to depart from the charter script. Strong as the 'authorisation' of military action may have been, it fell short of the security council taking action on its own behalf. There was no question either of UN member states being required to participate in the campaign under article 43, nor of the Military Staff Committee directing it in line with article 47. In some respects the arrangements put in place resembled the American-led war against North Korea in the early 1950s which had also been legitimised, at least initially, by the UN (see Chapter 1).

But the circumstances in the security council in 1990 were utterly different from those of 1950. The Gulf war took place in a wholly altered international context. Though Soviet and Chinese troops may not have played an active part in the anti-Iraq coalition during the Gulf war, in Korea both had effectively been the 'enemy' of the UN-authorised operation. To that extent, therefore, the omens for the emergence of a new interventionist United Nations appeared favourable, even if Operation Desert Storm was undertaken by a free-standing military coalition rather than the UN as an institution. To expect the full-scale application of chapter VII with the construction of a UN-directed army under the command of a Military Staff Committee of all five permanent members would have been unrealistic in 1991. The world and the UN had after all only just emerged from four-and-a-half decades of cold war. But, as a first stage, Operation Desert Storm seemed far from disappointing at the time, and might just have been a possible first step towards a genuine system of UN enforcement.

Yet there were serious questions concerning the objectives of the anti-Iraq coalition and the extent to which humanitarian motives had truly dictated their intervention. These questions would prove significant for both the development of UN military action and for the west's attitude towards Iraq and the broader Middle East in the future. American dominance of the fighting and its strategic direction in 1991 was plain. There was widely expressed scepticism about US motives in leading the coalition. Were these really founded on humanitarian concern and a commitment to maintaining the rule of law in the new world order? Or was Washington simply self-interested in its engagement with the crisis and primarily concerned with the implications for the stability of the Middle East, of western influence there and of the security of the region's oil production? Beyond the United States and its western allies, the continued acquiescence of the other members of the security council was far from guaranteed. It is unclear how long Russian agreement to the military action would have been maintained had the fighting been more protracted. Early in the crisis Moscow had used its historically close bilateral relations with Iraq to seek a peace settlement outside of the UN process. This had been received unenthusiastically by the United States. And it is possible too that Chinese concerns over the extent of UN validation of the military action might soon have hardened into the security council veto which had been avoided in November 1990.

Moreover, the realist Westphalian character of the intervention was underlined by the coalition's response to the humanitarian crisis its actions had provoked in Iraq in the aftermath of the war. Saddam's regime remained in power in Baghdad even though, in purely military terms, the coalition could have successfully pressed its initiative, pursued his retreating forces into Iraq and established an occupation. Diplomatically, however, this was not considered a wise option. For one thing, the status of such an action in international law would have been unclear. The carefully constructed consensus in the United Nations behind military action to liberate Kuwait would have been threatened and divisions in the security council would certainly have widened. Coalition military forces, particularly aircrew, had qualms about the carnage they were being asked to inflict on a largely defenceless Iraqi army in full retreat.

Instead, the coalition attempted to engineer the destruction of the regime from the inside. The Kurds of northern Iraq and the Shia of the south, both long hostile to the Sunni minority which dominated the regime, were consequently encouraged to rebel. The uprisings were brutally suppressed by Saddam and the coalition did not deliver the desperately needed – and expected if not actually promised – military aid from the coalition. Although the imposition of a no-fly zone by the allies over Iraqi Kurdistan eventually allowed a *de facto* Kurdish secession, the fate of the Shia majority in the south at the hands of the Sunni-dominated regime was grim. The realist calculations of global politics, however, prevented any intervention to meet the humanitarian disaster that had been created by the war and the brutal politics of its aftermath.

The Gulf war then, coming in the immediate wake of the end of the cold war, did not deliver a new world order of genuine UN collective security and humanitarian interventionism through military enforcement. But peacekeeping – which had emerged in part in response to the impossibility of that collective security at the other end of the cold war in the 1940s and 1950s – not only remained an option for the UN, but was also becoming an increasingly important one. In the event, it was from this strand of the UN's military possibilities that the new humanitarian interventionism emerged, rather than from that of enforcement.

The new vitality of UN peacekeeping was in fact underlined by its use in the management of the post-war settlement on the Iraqi border. The increasingly precarious Desert Storm coalition, as the war ended, pointed to a deeper UN involvement in the aftermath of the fighting. The legitimacy of the war itself might have been compromised had there been a protracted extension of the coalition in order to secure the border. As this task would not involve actual military enforcement, there was an opportunity for the UN to exercise direct responsibility under its peacekeeping hat. The result was the Iraq–Kuwait Observation Mission (UNIKOM) which was mandated in April 1991 to supervise the demilitarised strip along the border. Although there was a direct reference to chapter VII of the charter in its mandate, UNIKOM was very much a classic observation and interposition operation.[8] As such, it was not a 'humanitarian intervention' in the sense of confronting an immediate humanitarian challenge, but it was part of a growing momentum in the use of UN forces in the post-bipolar world that was gradually embracing objectives and techniques unfamiliar to the Hammarskjöldian tradition.

Even a glance at the numbers and timing of new UN military operations gives an indication of the extent of the surge in intervention that followed the end of the cold war. In the first thirty years of peacekeeping, between 1948 and 1977, twelve operations were established. In the following ten years – the decade dominated by the post-détente 'second cold war' – only one new force was created. During the next ten years, from 1988 to 1997, thirty-three new missions were mandated. The end of the cold war dramatically extended what in the previous chapter we described as the 'permissible zone' for UN intervention.

This, though, was not an unalloyed good. It was not just that the UN was allowed access to conflicts in areas where it had been denied hitherto. The end of the cold war also generated conflicts that had previously either not existed or had been managed by the superpowers themselves. The UN would never in the past have been involved in regions like Transcaucasia or Central Asia when they formed integral parts of the Soviet Union. But the conflicts in these places which brought UN involvement in the 1990s would most likely not have existed when they were part of the Soviet Union. Similarly, the long, tortuous and ultimately unsuccessful UN involvement in Somalia in the early 1990s began with the collapse of the regime of Siad Barre which had held power only because of external support provided in the context of cold war geopolitics. The end of his government then led, not to orderly regime change, but to the disintegration of Somalia as a territorial state. The terrible political vacuum which ensued and which it fell to the UN to manage was in a very real sense a product of the end of the cold war (see Chapter 4). Therefore not only did the cold war superpowers now admit the UN to new areas, but these areas were also subject to new conflicts generated by the end of the cold war. The former global rivals were no longer so concerned with spheres of influence which during the cold war they would have fought to preserve, nor were they concerned with the local conflicts which this removal of interest had helped provoke.

Boutros-Ghali's *Agenda for Peace*

Threatening as these darker consequences of the end of the cold war may have been, the UN embraced the new situation as an opportunity. The organisation now had the prospect of a much larger and more significant place in the international system than it could have achieved before. Undeniably, though, the political pressures and those on resources that this new role brought came at a cost. In response, in 1992 the secretary-general, Boutros Boutros-Ghali, produced a major report on the state of peacekeeping. This was *An Agenda for Peace: Preventive Diplomacy, Peacemaking and Peacekeeping*.[9] It was the first major report on the state of UN military intervention and its future prospects since Hammarsjköld's summary study of 1958. The *Agenda* was a much more accessible and widely distributed document than the earlier one, however, as it was designed to engage a wider public in the discussion of UN military intervention and its future. While the summary study was essentially an internal general assembly document, the *Agenda* in contrast was published in booklet form and made widely available in the few years before it could be accessed on the internet.

The preoccupations of *An Agenda for Peace* were very much those of the early 1990s. They also reflected the particular perspectives of the secretary-general himself. Boutros-Ghali was the UN's first secretary-general whose term of office, between 1992 and 1996, took place wholly within the post-cold war era. He proved to be one of the organisation's more controversial leaders. Initially he was seen in the security council and beyond as a rather inspired choice for the post. He was an Egyptian Christian and part of the country's westernised elite, who had risen from a career as an academic international lawyer to become deputy prime minister in the government of Anwar Sadat. In Boutros-Ghali, therefore, the UN had appointed a secretary-general of the global south; one moreover from an important Muslim country, and one who would not be expected to generate any uncomfortable political waves. But from the outset he showed a particular interest in the UN's interventionist role and this would bring him into close contact – and ultimately conflict – with the American administration of President Bill Clinton during the years of controversy over Somalia, Bosnia and Rwanda. As a result, in 1996, despite support elsewhere in the security council, Boutros-Ghali became the first UN secretary-general to be denied a customary second five-year term in office.[10]

The *Agenda* grew out of a summit of security council heads of state and government in January 1992. The tone of this meeting and of the secretary-general's report which followed was distinctly upbeat. For Boutros-Ghali a moment of unprecedented promise had arrived and the UN had to seize it. 'In the course of the past few years the immense ideological barrier that for decades gave rise to distrust and hostility – and the terrible tools of destruction that were their inseparable companions – has collapsed'. In consequence: '. . . a conviction has grown that an opportunity has been regained to achieve the great objectives of the charter – a United Nations capable of maintaining international peace and security, of securing justice and human rights and promoting, in the words of the charter, "social progress and better standards of life in larger freedom"'.[11]

Boutros-Ghali was not suggesting that conditions were right for any significant move beyond the Westphalian in the UN's approach to intervention. The 'foundation stone' was 'and must remain the state'. Yet, the idea of absolute sovereignty was, he suggested, never a reality and was now subject to the requirements of 'an ever more interdependent world'.[12] So far as this interdependency touched on post-cold war military intervention by the UN, *An Agenda for Peace* highlighted four principal areas for development: preventive deployment; the reinvigoration of the enforcement powers of chapter VII of the charter; new 'peace-enforcement units'; and the development of post-conflict peace-building.

Hitherto, UN interventions had taken place only after a conflict had occurred. In some circumstances, however, conflict could be pre-empted by the presence of UN forces before the point of violence was reached. This preventive deployment would not necessarily be restricted to inter-position between antagonists in the traditional peacekeeping mode:

> Humanitarian assistance, impartially provided, could be of critical importance; assistance in maintaining security whether through military, police or civilian personnel, could save lives and develop conditions of safety in which negotiations can be held; the United Nations could also help in conciliation efforts if this should be the wish of the parties. In certain

circumstances the United Nations may well need to draw upon the specialized skills and resources of various parts of the United Nations system; such operations may also on occasion require the participation of non-governmental organizations.[13]

His description of this departure more or less encapsulated the principles of the emerging forms of multifunctional humanitarian intervention.

An Agenda for Peace approached the never-used coercive military powers of the UN with some diffidence. Nevertheless, under 'the political circumstances that now exist for the first time since the charter was adopted, the long-standing obstacles to the conclusion of special agreements [to provide resources for coercive enforcement] should no longer prevail'.[14] Such forces may never be adequate to deal with major world conflicts, but they could have a role in enforcing outcomes determined by the security council in conflicts involving lesser powers. To give effect to such arrangements, Boutros-Ghali proposed, the original Military Staff Committee based on the chiefs of staff of the permanent members should finally be brought to life.

Enforcement as an extension of peacekeeping rather than full-scale collective security was also explored in *An Agenda for Peace*. The UN should consider the creation of so-called 'peace-enforcement units' which would have a specific mandate in particular circumstances.[15] An increasingly common scenario with which the UN was required to engage in the post-cold war world involved interventions designed to supervise peace agreements reached between antagonists. On occasion, one or more of these parties would then renege on undertakings made, bring the peace process to a halt and leave UN forces struggling with a now unachievable mandate. One of the more disastrous examples of this was taking place in Angola even as Boutros-Ghali was preparing his report. There the UNITA rebel movement, facing defeat in the electoral process which was the central part of the civil war peace settlement agreed with the Angolan government, simply decided to abandon its undertakings and resume fighting. In such circumstances, he suggested, the UN should be empowered to enforce compliance with previously accepted undertakings. Such operations would not, however, be part of the formal machinery of chapter VII enforcement, not least, presumably, because they would usually involve intra-state conflicts rather than the international ones originally envisaged in the charter.

An Agenda for Peace broached, though only tentatively, another aspect of the charter which had been rendered moribund by the cold war. Chapter VIII, which immediately follows the enforcement articles, deals with 'regional arrangements' in support of collective security.

The security council was given authority either to enlist or to legitimise regional organisations and alliances in pursuit of its ends, including in the military sphere. Clearly the cold war alliances could never fulfil this role. The North Atlantic Treaty of 1949 which forms the basis of the NATO alliance makes reference to the supremacy of the United Nations in security matters but also emphasises the right to self-defence under article 51 of the UN charter rather than the terms of chapter VIII as the legal justification for the existence of the alliance.[16] Now though the possibility existed of UN–regional partnerships at least in the area of peace operations even if the coercive aspects of the original charter provisions remained out of the equation. Security council authorisation for a regional organisation 'to take the lead in addressing a crisis within its region . . . could serve to lend the weight of the United Nations to the validity of the regional effort'.[17] The *Agenda* was no more explicit than this, however. No reference was made at this point to the regionalisation of peace operations as a means of reducing the burden on UN resources. This, though, was a concern that would become more explicit as in the 1990s demands for intervention grew.

Just as preventive deployment was designed to pre-empt the break-out of violent conflict, the process of post-conflict peace-building, which had a prominent place in *An Agenda for Peace*, was seen as a crucial means of consolidating peace after fighting had ended. Peace-building involved, according to Boutros-Ghali, 'comprehensive efforts to identify and support structures which will tend to consolidate peace and advance a sense of confidence and well-being among people'.[18] It might also include more specific military functions such as the disarmament of fighters, the destruction of weapons stocks, election supervision and military training. Beyond this, peace-building was a political process as much as a military one, embracing the advancement and protection of human rights, the reform of government institutions and the development of political participation. Here as in the other areas of innovation proposed in *An Agenda for Peace*, there was a new and explicit focus on multi-agency, multi-purpose engagement that took the idea of UN intervention far beyond Hammarskjöld's original notion of interposition and observation. Traditional peacekeeping, in other words, was giving way to novel multifaceted forms of humanitarian intervention.

The importance of *An Agenda for Peace*, it must be acknowledged, lay in its identification of new problems around military intervention in the post-cold war era rather than in the immediate implementation of new solutions. This was probably not Boutros-Ghali's intention; he evidently saw the exercise as an opportunity to put UN military intervention on a new footing and to expand the organisation's role in the post-cold war world. But it is difficult to locate specific examples of where Boutros-Ghali's prescriptions were applied during the remainder of the 1990s. Preventive deployment did take place once, in the form of the UN Preventive Deployment Force (UNPREDEP) in Macedonia, created in 1995 and designed to keep the new state which had broken from Yugoslavia in 1991 free from any spillover of the fighting still going on beyond its borders. This new form of intervention did not become widespread, however. There was an understandable if ultimately short-sighted reluctance on the part of potential contributing states to commit resources to situations where fighting had not yet broken out. Beyond this, no progress was made on the reinvigoration of the coercive powers which had formed the centrepiece of the original charter in 1945. The Gulf war of 1991 had come and gone and nothing had been done to build on the apparent promise of the, admittedly fragile, security council consensus that had enabled it.

The end of the cold war did not in itself, it seemed, generate sufficient like-mindedness between the permanent members to permit this. In fact, the Gulf war and the appearance of *An Agenda for Peace* the following year probably marked the high-water mark of post-cold war goodwill between the old superpowers. Henceforward, new national rivalries and suspicions would begin to fill the space vacated by the ideological battle between east and west. The distance still to be travelled to arrive at effective collective security would be clearly mapped a decade later when the permanent membership fragmented over the approach to be taken in the next confrontation with the Iraq regime of Saddam Hussein. In this later episode, American unilateralism won out against the more cautious collectivism on offer at the United Nations. The consequence was the US-led invasion and occupation of 2003 carried out without security council approval and in the face of criticism from secretary-general Kofi Annan.

Nor was there sufficient commitment to realise even the lesser ambition for peace enforcement units. The hard fact was that few if any states would be willing (or politically confident enough of their own citizens' reaction) to put their forces in harm's way to enforce peace agreements between unknown parties in far-distant countries. This was a reality which remained unchanged even after the horrors of the Rwanda genocide in 1994, which had grown directly from just the type of abandoned peace settlement that Boutros-Ghali had in mind for the proposed new, robust approach to intervention.

An Agenda for Peace proved to have more relevance with regard to the realities of post-cold war intervention in its focus on post-conflict peace-building. Since the mid-1990s peace operations have almost invariably involved commitments going beyond the point at which the UN's military forces have been drawn down. These commitments have focused on the nurturing of the institutions identified as key to maintaining the cessation of violence and preventing its recurrence. This, of course, has been a feature primarily of civilian operations undertaken by a variety of UN agencies and our primary concern here is with intervention by military or police personnel acting directly under mandates provided by the United Nations. But peace-building has become an important part of larger interventions in countries in which political violence is most obviously a consequence of their social and political institutions and processes. Peace-building offices have been established by the UN not only in the direct aftermath of a successful military intervention. They have been important in this – as for example in Mozambique in the mid-1990s – but peace-building has also been a feature of post-conflict situations where military intervention by the UN has been unsuccessful, such as in Angola in the late 1990s. Indeed peace-building enterprises are not always undertaken in the context of military involvement, successful or unsuccessful. Even where UN forces have not been deployed, peace-building offices may be put in place. One example of this can be seen in yet another Portuguese-speaking African state, Guinea-Bissau, where an office has functioned, admittedly with only limited success, since the end of a civil war there in 1999.

Supplementing *An Agenda for Peace*: a new realism?

At the beginning of 1995, Boutros-Ghali issued a *Supplement to An Agenda for Peace*. The intervening period had not been a happy one for United Nations interventionism. The relative optimism of 1992 had been dissipated by a series of apparently unsuccessful operations. In Africa the UN had been ineffectual in its attempts to manage the end of the Angolan civil war. The situation in Somalia had passed, under the oversight of the UN, from humanitarian crisis to general chaos. Most shockingly, 800,000 people had been killed in the Rwandan genocide of 1994 under the eyes of an impossibly inadequate UN force. In Europe, the conflicts in the former Yugoslavia, particularly in Bosnia, continued and UN forces were regularly humiliated by unresponsive local forces in their attempts to make any significant impact on the situation. There had, of course, been some successes for intervention, most notably, perhaps, in Mozambique. But in general the panorama was a dismal one and this was reflected in the tone of the secretary-general's *Supplement*. The problems of certain peace operations, he even suggested, were threatening to drag down the standing of the United Nations system as a whole. Intense media interest 'all too often focused on only one or two of the many peace-keeping operations in which [the UN was] engaged', 'overshadowing other major operations and its vast effort in the economic, social and other fields'. 'Hard decisions' beckoned for UN members.[19]

The problems were both quantitative and qualitative. There had been a huge increase in the number of military interventions the UN had been required to undertake: this 'increased volume of activity would have strained the Organization even if the nature of the activity had remained unchanged', Boutros-Ghali observed. It 'has not remained unchanged, however, there have been qualitative changes even more significant that the quantitative ones'. Most importantly, 'so many of today's conflicts are within states rather than between states'.[20] Five operations were in place at the beginning of 1988 of which four had been deployed to deal with inter-state conflicts. Since then, of the twenty-one new operations that had begun, thirteen were either wholly or mainly concerned with intra-state crises. These brought problems for the UN such as had not been encountered since the Congo operation in the early 1960s. Unaccountable armed groups, whether semi-formal militias or just armed civilians, were now confronting UN forces. There were no clear geographic lines of separation in many of these conflicts. Even earlier intra-state conflicts, such as that in Cyprus, had opposing forces with terms of engagement that were relatively simple and which were international in their essential characteristics. This was no longer the case.

UN interventions, Boutros-Ghali noted, were increasingly 'humanitarian' in nature as civilians were 'the main victims and often the main targets'.[21] Now twice the number of refugees was recorded by the UN High Commission for refugees (UNHCR) – 26 million – than had been in 1987, and the increase in the number of internally displaced people (IDPs) aside from cross-border refugees was even greater. Simultaneously, civil chaos tended to bring the disintegration of state institutions and services, which not only meant even greater humanitarian suffering, but also a general collapse in law and order. UN interventions now, therefore, 'must extend beyond military and humanitarian tasks and must include the promotion of national reconciliation and the re-establishment of effective government'.[22] In other words, post-conflict peace-building had now become not merely a desirable adjunct to military intervention, but an essential task in its own right.

The new demand for intervention in civil conflict in turn led to a new range of operational responsibilities. One of these, which had become all too familiar by the mid-1990s, was the use of UN forces to protect humanitarian relief operations. This had only featured on the margins of very few UN interventions in the past, such as that in the Congo. Now it had become a major – and extremely problematic – role. Humanitarian aid was obviously difficult to distribute under war conditions, but this was not the only problem. Aid, particularly food aid, had itself become a weapon to be deployed by the parties in conflicts, who would attempt to divert it to their own areas of support and deny it to those of its enemies. The first UN operation in Somalia (UNOSOM-I), in April 1992, had as the centrepiece of its mandate the role of enforcing aid distribution throughout the territory on the basis of need. Its failure to do so successfully had led to the United States taking over the role the following December in the form of the Unified Task Force (UNITAF). An almost identical situation was faced in Bosnia where the UN Protection Force (UNPROFOR) failed to secure the distribution of winter aid to remote Bosnian Muslim areas in the face of Serb and Bosnian Serb obstruction in pursuit of their own war aims. In the former Yugoslavia another novel and problematic aspect of UN intervention had developed. In both Bosnia and in Croatia before it the UN had established protected areas designed to ensure the safety of threatened ethnic populations.

One major shift in UN responsibilities since the end of the cold war – and one which Boutros-Ghali had already highlighted in *An Agenda for Peace* – involved peace agreements reached by the parties to a civil conflict which required third-party help to implement. This help might be relatively easy to provide in the form, for example, of the monitoring of electoral processes. More often, however, the responsibility would be much more onerous, involving cease-fire supervision and the disarming, demobilisation and social reintegration of combatants (the so-called 'DDR' process). UN forces would also often work with other agencies such as the UNHCR in helping with the repatriation of refugees and the return of IDPs. It could also involve the actual organisation of elections rather than just their monitoring, as well as the provision of security during them.

By 1995 operations of this sort had been carried out by the UN across the world from Namibia, Angola, Mozambique and Rwanda in Africa, to El Salvador in Latin America and Cambodia in southeast Asia. These operations met with very different degrees of success and failure. Often, as in the cases of Angola and Rwanda, the peace processes would simply collapse. This might be due to enduring mistrust between the parties or unforeseen events. Sometimes, though, it might just be due to the fact that the settlement itself, which the UN usually had no direct role in negotiating, was simply unviable. Failure therefore would be no fault of the United Nations or its forces on the ground, but this did not prevent the finger of blame being pointed in their direction, whether as a result of political calculation or simple ignorance.

By the middle of the 1990s all of these new factors – beginning with the increasingly intra-state character of UN missions and the new range of tasks required of forces on the ground – had fed the impression of a crisis in intervention. The *Supplement to An Agenda for Peace* was essentially an attempt to address the sources of this perception. To this extent it constituted less an updating of the original report than a new and notably less optimistic overview of the UN's record and assessment of its capacity for military intervention. In contrast to the 1992 report, the *Supplement* was not about seizing the historical moment to expand the UN's role; it was about measures which might allow the UN to maintain its interventionist responsibility in a global environment that had become resistant to multilateral solutions. Accordingly, Boutros-Ghali's proposals were workmanlike rather than ambitious, and focused on the day-to-day management of operations, rather than, as the original *Agenda* had, on the expansion of their range and significance.

The increasingly close involvement of the security council in the management of peacekeeping operations was noted by the secretary-general, though in his view this was largely to be welcomed. Commanders on the ground might bridle at the threat to their autonomy of micro-management by a politicised security council, but Boutros-Ghali's view seemed to be that the closer the permanent members of the council could be tied to specific operations, the greater the likelihood of appropriate mandates being set and of the necessary support being provided to complete them. To this end, direct communication with the security council would be increased. At the same time, countries contributing contingents to forces would also be kept more fully informed of developments as they were answerable to their own parliaments and publics.[23] Once again, this closer involvement by contributing states would be expected to commit them more closely to pursuing the successful outcome of even hazardous missions and reduce the possibility of precipitating withdrawal of forces.

This last point notwithstanding, Boutros-Ghali warned against a trend which had been emerging in recent operations: the tendency of UN command to be compromised by arbitrary interference by contributing states in the running of operations. There must always be a clear unity of command and in UN operations it must the UN's responsibility to provide it. There must be no 'attempt by troop-contributing Governments to provide guidance, let alone give orders, to their contingents on operational matters. To do so creates division within the force, adds to the difficulties already inherent in a multinational operation and increases the risk of casualties'.[24] In the secretary-general's mind here was Somalia, with its complex chain of command of an intervention the control of which was divided between the United Nations and the United States, often pulling in different directions. In Somalia too there was a suspicion among the UN command that the Italian contingent was taking direction from Rome as well as New York in a complex post-colonial political geometry (Somalia having been an Italian colony until the second world war).[25] But Boutros-Ghali may also have had the experience of Rwanda in mind. The previous year, Belgium (also the ex-colonial power) had attempted to set the UN's agenda after the death of its soldiers at the beginning of the genocide.[26]

In *An Agenda for Peace* Boutros-Ghali had approached with care the possibility of engaging with the UN's yet-to-be-invoked powers of coercive enforcement. But the fact that he did so at all was suggestive of the mood of the time. His proposal, it will be recalled, was that as a first stage the Military Staff Committee of the permanent members of the security council should be reconstituted. Now, in the *Supplement*, his view was that however desirable such wide-ranging enforcement powers might be in principle, it would be 'folly' to attempt to put them in place at the present time when the UN was 'resource starved and hard pressed to handle the less demanding peacemaking and peace-keeping responsibilities entrusted to it'.[27] Even the limited enforcement role he had proposed in the *Agenda* in the form of 'peace enforcement units' to ensure adherence to agreed peace settlements seemed to have been abandoned. Such situations, he now thought, needed time rather than arms, with coordinated programmes 'over a number of years and in various fields, to ensure that the original causes of war are eradicated'.[28] The relatively quick fix provided by the surgical enforcement of agreements had now given way to an enlarged view of post-conflict peace-building as a mechanism for managing disaffection over previously agreed outcomes.

In a similar vein, the idea of enlisting regional groupings in peace operations which had featured in the *Agenda* was cast in the more negative light of the times. There was still value in the idea, but there was also danger. States 'may claim international legitimacy and approval for forceful actions that were not in fact envisaged by the security council when it gave its authorization to them'.[29] This and other dangers in so-called 'inter-agency' interventions would become increasingly evident over the coming years in both Africa and Europe.

A 'new peacekeeping'?

The contrasting tone and proposals of *An Agenda for Peace* in 1992 and its *Supplement* in 1995, which were both published over the signature of the same UN secretary-general, speak clearly of the rapid decline in post-cold war optimism during these few years. Yet both reports had in common the starting point that military intervention by the United Nations had fundamentally changed in character since the end of the cold war. Or, as analysts began to express it, the UN was now engaged in a 'new peacekeeping' which was basically different from that first conceptualised in the 1950s. This peacekeeping was arguably 'new' in four senses: the nature of the conflicts involved; their geo-political location; the character of the mandates under which they operated; and the operational techniques employed.

Firstly and most obviously, the new peacekeeping supposedly differs from the traditional variety because it is deployed in domestic rather than international conflicts. That is to say, it is intra-state rather than inter-state. As Boutros Boutros-Ghali pointed out in his *Supplement to An Agenda for Peace*, by 1995 the large majority of post-cold war operations were concerned with conflicts within countries. It would be wrong to create a false before-and-after dichotomy in this regard, however. It is certainly true that over the twentieth century as a whole, internal conflicts have become relatively much more destructive and deadly than international ones. At the beginning of the century intra-state fighting accounted for about 10 per cent of deaths in armed conflicts; by its end the figure was 90 per cent. But this shift was probably a mid- rather than late-century phenomenon. That is to say, the shift in the balance of damage caused by internal as opposed to external conflicts began at the outset of the cold war rather than at its end. In fact, almost all UN interventions, whether during or since the cold war, have been in conflicts with both domestic and international dimensions.

The early observer missions established in Palestine and Kashmir in the late 1940s and the Emergency Force which followed the Suez crisis in 1956 were certainly predominantly international in their concerns. After Suez, however, the bases of the conflicts which brought UN intervention were much more ambiguous. The UN Observer Group which was deployed in Lebanon in 1958 itself determined that the crisis which had brought intervention was primarily a domestic rather than an international one. The massive Congo operation which began two years later was, beyond any question, a domestic operation, though one with clear international implications both in terms of cold war politics and Europe's post-colonial relationships. The intervention in West New Guinea in 1962–3 was outwardly concerned with a bilateral conflict between the Netherlands and Indonesia. But, as we have seen, the UN's choices and actions in the crisis would have far-reaching consequences for the internal politics and stability of the Indonesian state after it was enlarged by the annexation of West New Guinea. The Cyprus conflict which followed in 1964 was quite plainly intra-state in nature, the consequence of an imperfect post-colonial settlement. Equally plainly, though, it had international implications for relations between Greece and Turkey and, more widely, the cohesion of the NATO alliance. Of the two other operations which the UN mounted in the 1960s, one, which was another observer mission between India and Pakistan, was in essence an international one. The other, however, an observer mission on the borders of Yemen, was called into being by a civil war which, although it had drawn in competing interest from Egypt and Saudi Arabia, was still fundamentally a civil war. In the 1970s the two operations on Israel's borders respectively with Egypt and Syria were wholly inter-state missions. This status is emphasised by our characterisation of them in the previous chapter as 'détente peacekeeping'. But, it will be recalled, military interventions by the UN in the détente period ended with the Interim Force in Lebanon which was necessitated by a civil war, though obviously one with critical international aspects.

By the same token, few of the civil conflicts which have brought about UN humanitarian interventions since the end of the cold war have been free of important international implications. The return of UN forces to the Congo in 1999 was ostensibly an intervention in a civil war. But the conflict was region-wide, involving delicate international relationships which embraced all of Congo's neighbours in central Africa, many of whom had sent their forces into the country. Indeed the Congo disaster was closely tied to the Rwanda genocide; it was in many respects a consequence of it. The sequence of UN interventions in West Africa – in Liberia, Sierra Leone and Côte d'Ivoire – confronted crises which fed off of each other and which had major cross-border dimensions. And what of the former Yugoslavia? Were the UN forces deployed in Croatia, Bosnia and Macedonia dealing with a civil conflict amidst the disintegration of a unified state? Or were they missions to newly independent countries in conflict with their neighbours in an emerging new international region? The answer, clearly, is that they were both.

The second defining characteristic of the 'new peacekeeping' – its global range – is less ambiguous. Here we return to the model of an expanding and contracting 'permissible zone' in which UN interventions have traditionally taken place. The end of the cold war automatically expanded the geopolitical possibilities for UN intervention. The spheres of influence which were an inevitable part of a polarised international system had more or less dissolved. There were no longer the same 'impermissible cores' guarded by east and west alike and off-limits to external intervention. Between 1988 and 1994, UN operations were deployed across the world in these previously jealously protected areas. A UN military observer mission was placed on Afghanistan's borders following the withdrawal of Soviet forces after their disastrous occupation. Across Central America, which had hitherto been the carefully guarded backyard of the United States, UN missions eased the end of civil wars and the transition to democracy. This new region of activity was particularly significant because the controlling interest of the United States here long predated even the cold war, stretching back to the Monroe doctrine laid down in the 1820s.

Then in 1992 the UN began a landmark engagement in southeast Asia by establishing a Transitional Authority in Cambodia. This was a colossal undertaking in itself, involving the creation of a temporary administration on the lines of that in West New Guinea but in an even more complicated and particularly lethal political setting. But the UN commitment here was also significant because it was concerned with the reconstruction of an international region laid low by America's wars of the 1960s and 1970s. Over the longer term the end of the cold war did not mean the absolute expansion of the UN's permissible zone across the world – great power politics would re-emerge in the future along with the spheres of influence which are its essential currency. But there would be no return to the 'impermissibility' of the years of rigid bipolarity.

The two final markers of the new interventionism which supposedly distinguish it from the classic peacekeeping – mandates and operational tactics – are inseparable from each other: the mandate given to any mission will obviously determine the techniques used on the ground.

The widened range of responsibilities that UN interventions had to meet after the cold war has already been explored. The principal ones include the safeguarding, and on occasion the delivery, of humanitarian supplies, the oversight of peace agreements, the disarming and demobilising of fighters, and protection of civilian safe areas. Mandates which cover these activities obviously demand operational techniques going far beyond the interposition and observation associated with the Hammarskjöldian model of intervention. But how far did that model ever adequately represent UN military tactics during the cold war? Here too the Congo operation in the early 1960s marked a dramatic departure from the precedents of the late 1940s and the 1950s. Initially, in July 1960, ONUC was required to fulfil a sequence of fundamentally different mandates during its four years in existence. These began with a commitment to provide military assistance and training until Congolese national forces were capable of fulfilling their responsibilities. Within a few months, in February 1961 after the murder of Lumumba, the force was mandated to 'take immediately all appropriate measures' to end civil conflict in the Congo including 'the use of force, if necessary, in the last resort'. By the beginning of 1961 ONUC was

	January 1988	January 1992	December 1994
Security council resolutions in previous year	15	53	78
UN operations underway	5	11	17
Military personnel involved	9,750	11,495	73,393
Number of countries contributing personnel	26	56	76
UN peacekeeping budget (US$m)	230.4	1689.6	3610.0

Table 2.1 Key statistics on UN interventions pre/post-cold war
(Source: *Supplement to An Agenda for Peace*)

instructed 'to take vigorous action, including the use of the requisite measure of force' against armed elements not under UN command.[30] There was no essential difference between these shifting and escalating mandates and those associated with the 'new peacekeeping' after the cold war. Certainly, ONUC was authorised to behave in a way that went far beyond the traditional peacekeeping concept recently set out in Hammarskjöld's summary study. While subsequent UN operations in the 1960s and 1970s did tend to revert to the earlier model, the notion of UN military intervention as proactive, and in certain circumstances coercive, was hardly a novelty in the 1990s.

Viewed in historical perspective, therefore, it may seem that the novelty of the 'new peacekeeping' lay in the quantity of operations rather than their inherent qualities. As table 2.1 suggests, the sheer number of new commitments undertaken by the UN after the cold war inevitably widened the range of activities required of its forces. But did these operations involve anything which was essentially 'new' in the sense of mandates or techniques? The borderline between interposition and observation on one side and enforcement on the other had been approached and crossed in the Congo thirty years before the fighting in Somalia. The UN had assumed the trappings of a temporary state in West New Guinea three decades before its involvement in Cambodia. Indeed the League of Nations had already done this on a much more elaborate and protracted scale in the Saar even before the UN was thought of.

Any shift from the traditional model was not universally seen as desirable. Even Boutros-Ghali, who was patently a champion of expanded UN intervention, was concerned that a departure from the rules of traditional peacekeeping threatened to be counter-productive. Consent, impartiality and the use of force only in self-defence – the Hammarsjköldian holy trinity – were, he argued, normally prerequisites to the success of interventions. In the *Supplement to An Agenda for Peace* he noted that analysis of 'recent successes and failures shows that in all the successes those principles were respected and in most of the less successful operations one or other of them was not'.[31] In other words, if there were a new interventionism it was a consequence of the changed nature of conflict and not of a considered change in the intervention policies of the United Nations international policy changes. Moreover, this fortuitous departure from the traditional model, the secretary-general suggested, could well be to the detriment of the future and the success of UN interventionism.

Notes

1. The Rome Statue of the International Criminal Court can be found at http://www.un.org/icc/romestat.htm
2. The Human Rights Council was established by general assembly resolution GA/RES/60/251, 3 April 2006. See the Council website at http://www2.ohchr.org/english/bodies/hrcouncil/
3. See Mary Kaldor, *Human Security* (Cambridge: Polity, 2007); Neil MacFarlane and Yeng Foong Khong, *Human Security and the United Nations* (Bloomington: Indiana University Press, 2006).
4. Francis Fukuyama, 'The End of History?', *The National Interest*, (summer 1989).
5. United Nations charter chapter VII, found at http://www.un.org/en/documents/charter/chapter7.shtml
6. Security council resolution S/RES/678(1990), 29 November 1990. Beyond the Chinese abstention only Cuba and Yemen, then non-permanent members, voted against the resolution.
7. The initial resolution condemning the invasion and calling for Iraq's withdrawal was S/RES/660, 2 August 1990, which was passed within hours of the invasion. A further resolution a few days later, S/RES/661, 6 August 1990, imposed an economic blockade on Iraq. At the end of September this hardened into a ban on all air travel to or from Iraq and Kuwait: S/RES/670, 25 September 1990.
8. UNIKOM's basic mandate was set by security council resolution S/RES/689(1991), 9 April 1991. Originally a traditional military observation mission, its power – and its size – were dramatically increased two years later by security council resolution S/RES/806(1993), 5 February 1993, which it mandated to take military action against (Iraqi) provocations. UNIKOM was rendered redundant and drawn down after the US-led invasion of Iraq in 2003.
9. *An Agenda for Peace: Preventive Diplomacy, Peacemaking and Peacekeeping* (United Nations document A/47/277-S/24111,17 June 1992). Found at http://www.un.org/Docs/SG/agpeace.html
10. Boutros-Ghali wrote his own, suggestively titled, memoir of his time in office and his relationship with Washington: *Unvanquished: A US–UN Saga* (New York: Random House, 1999).
11. *An Agenda for Peace*, paragraph 8; paragraph 3. The quotation is from the preamble to the charter.
12. Ibid., paragraph 17.
13. Ibid., paragraph 29.
14. Ibid., paragraph 43.
15. Ibid., paragraphs 44–5.
16. See preamble, article 1 and article 5 of the North Atlantic Treaty (1949). Found at: http://www.nato.int/docu/basictxt/treaty.htm

17. *An Agenda for Peace*, paragraphs 60–5.
18. Ibid., paragraphs 55–9.
19. *Supplement to An Agenda for Peace: Position Paper of the Secretary-General on the Occasion of the Fiftieth Anniversary of the United Nations* (UN Document A/50/60-S/1995/1, 3 January 1995), paragraphs 4 and 104. Found at http://www.un.org/Docs/SG/agsupp.html 20. Ibid., paragraphs 9 and 10.
21. Ibid., paragraph 12.
22. Ibid., paragraph 13.
23. Ibid., paragraphs 39–40.
24. Ibid., paragraph 41.
25. Boutros-Ghali pointed to suspicions in the UN that the Italian contingent in Somalia had been leaking intelligence to favoured local factions, *Unvanquished*, pp. 96–7.
26. Some sense of Boutros-Ghali's jaundiced attitude towards the United States can be gleaned from his attack on Belgium's attempt to engineer a withdrawal of the UN force from Rwanda as the genocide was underway. This was the 'American syndrome': a tendency to withdraw when difficulties arose. Ibid., p. 132.
27. *Supplement to An Agenda for Peace*, paragraph 77.
28. Ibid., paragraph 22.
29. Ibid., paragraph 80.
30. These changing mandates were contained in, respectively, security council resolutions S/RES/143(1960), 14 July 1960; S/RES/161(1961), 21 February 1961; SC/RES/169, 24 November 1961.
31. *Supplement to An Agenda for Peace*, paragraph 33.

Chapter 3

Sovereignty and community: a 'responsibility to protect'?

Closely associated with the notion of a 'new peacekeeping' having emerged in the post-cold war period is the suggestion that UN interventions have become increasingly 'post-Westphalian' in nature. Not only have interventions changed in their location, mandates and tactics, but they have now also a new underlying function. The argument here is that the objectives of interventions are increasingly humanitarian and 'political' in the sense that they are focused primarily on improving conditions inside countries rather than on managing the (Westphalian) system of states of which they form part. UN military forces therefore should be and are concerned with the implantation of human rights and pluralist democracy in the countries in which they are deployed. These are now ends in themselves, according to those who both discern the emergence of a post-Westphalian world and actively welcome it.[1] In contrast, as we have seen, traditional peacekeeping is essentially about containing international violence and therefore is fundamentally Westphalian in nature.

The prospect of 'post-Westphalian' intervention

The proposition that we are in a post-Westphalian age of intervention is justified on the grounds that UN operations are now usually intra-state rather than inter-state activities. We have already suggested, of course, that the claim that intra-state engagement is somehow novel does not stand close historical examination. But even putting this aside, there are further questions to pose about the idea of a post-Westphalian shift.

For one thing, are interventions in civil conflicts necessarily by their nature post-Westphalian? It could equally be argued that to achieve an efficient and stable international state system the starting point must be the efficiency and stability of the basic units – the states – that make up the system. It would be quite wrong to suggest that the UN's intervention in Somalia in the early 1990s did not have genuine

67

humanitarian objectives. But beyond these lay the fact that the Somali state had more or less ceased to exist as a unit of the (Westphalian) system. This had obvious implications for the entire north-east African region. The subsequent interventions by Somalia's neighbours in the country's continuing civil conflict is a clear indication of this. Ethiopia did not become involved in Somalia because of humanitarian concern *per se* (though this may play a significant role): it sent troops into Somalia partly because more powerful actors in the international system, notably the United States, wanted it to for their own 'systemic' purposes and partly because it has a pressing concern with the stability of its own region, the Horn of Africa. After 11 September 2001 the danger to the broader international system of tolerating a violent unregulated space where a sovereign state should be became all too clear in the west. Further south, in sub-Saharan Africa, the ambiguity of the UN's humanitarian intervention in the Democratic Republic of Congo is also apparent. Again, there can be no question that humanitarian motivations have been important in UN decision-making on the Congo. But the danger of such a massive territory in such a delicate geopolitical location fragmenting and disappearing from the international state system must clearly be a major consideration in this decision-making as well.

Moving beyond the 'requirement' for the basic existence of the territorial state in an international state system, the political and social nature of that state is arguably also as important to the health of the Westphalian system as it is for the ethics of post-Westphalian humanitarianism. There is a strong case to be made in favour of human rights and democracy as necessary attributes of successful and cooperative Westphalian units. In recent years 'democratic peace theory' has proposed on the basis of historical analysis that liberal democracies do not go to war with other liberal democracies.[2] This claim has its origins in the work of the eighteenth-century German philosopher Immanuel Kant, who argued that the citizens of a democratic republic would simply not vote for war.[3] The idea, though, can also be linked to the broader canvass of Fukuyama's 'end of history thesis' which we touched on briefly in the last chapter. If liberal democracy had won the great historical struggle for world dominance, then history – defined as movement through conflict between overarching ideas – had indeed ended. If the greatest threat to the stability of the international state system is, as the experience of the twentieth century seemed to affirm, breakdown through general war, then it is surely good 'Westphalian' sense to ensure that the internal character of states does not increase that threat. To this extent, therefore, the dichotomy between supposed

Westphalian peacekeeping and post-Westphalian humanitarian intervention is perhaps a false one. Westphalian objectives may require post-Westphalian techniques. But similarly, post-Westphalian benefits may be a product of Westphalian motives. In other words, to preserve the fundamental structure of a system based on territorial sovereignty it may be necessary to qualify or even disregard that sovereignty in particular places when circumstances demand.

Beyond sovereignty: globalisation and cosmopolitanism

In parallel with this debate about the fundamental purposes of intervention, a growing body of theory concerned with underlying practical and ethical considerations around sovereignty and its limits has emerged in recent years.

One focus of interest has been the impact of globalisation. Globalisation in both its economic and cultural forms has fundamentally changed the nature of the international system. This has been a long-term process, of course, but it has been accelerated by the end of the cold war, which seemed to confirm the failure of any alternative economic and social models to liberal capitalism. The power of the state has been dramatically eroded (or 'hollowed-out' in the terminology of globalisation studies) by a worldwide process which might be affected by but cannot be prevented by national governments. Rapid changes in technology have also had a major and adverse impact on the traditional power of the sovereign state. New forms of internet-based communication which are largely beyond the power of the state to control have made geographical 'territoriality', historically a defining characteristic of statehood, much less significant in the real social and political world.[4]

The processes of globalisation have usually been seen from a left-wing or even just a humanitarian perspective as fundamentally malign. They cast the poor and weak – whether countries or individuals – to the mercy of brutal market forces. But these same forces, in their erosion of state power, can also be seen to hold out a promise of a new global morality. Globalisation in this sense offers the prospect of a new world politics based not on an 'international system' of unaccountable state units, but instead one built on an increasingly integrated and self-accountable 'international community'. In this new community, sovereign statehood and all the violence – both international and domestic – associated with it would be supplanted by new mechanisms of 'global governance' directed by a clear, consensually accepted, moral compass. This would not, at least in the first instance, amount to anything that could be described a 'world government'. National entities would persist, but they would no longer be contained within the bounds of unaccountable state structures. The obvious legitimising source of the new elements of this global governance would be the – already available – United Nations. Responsibility for the spread and application of the new norms and structures of governance would also be expected to fall to the UN. When required, this would involve military intervention against those determined to transgress them.

Globalisation might facilitate the growth in effectiveness of global governance, but the fundamental idea of such a post-Westphalian departure has developed within a quite distinct ethical construction. This lies in the theoretical framework of 'cosmopolitanism'. Cosmopolitanism – meaning, literally, 'universal polity' – is based on the proposition that humanity as a whole shares a set of universal values. This is not to say that all humans are the same. Cosmopolitanists (or 'cosmopolites', as these theorists are sometimes called) see respect for cultural differences – or 'otherness' – as a universal value in itself. For this reason world government, as opposed to global governance, is not necessarily a desirable destination of cosmopolitanism. While the further development of the International Criminal Court, for example, is to be welcomed, a potentially coercive global 'state' is not. Nevertheless, cosmopolitanism is a philosophy of moral universalism as it insists there are irreducible shared human values. These values, concerned with fairness, equity, altruism and justice, are also of course 'humanitarian'.[5]

While a global state may not be desirable in the cosmopolitan view, a sense of global citizenship plainly is. Everyone, whether as individuals or acting in the context of their various nations and states, has moral and ethical responsibilities to other individuals. These responsibilities apply without distinction. They relate equally to those 'others' within one's own immediate community and those beyond it. The implications of cosmopolitanism for state sovereignty are therefore clear. Universal human values take priority over the political claims of states and the governments that control them. Sovereignty therefore can never be absolute. By extension, the implications for intervention by the United Nations are equally clear. As the most legitimate vehicle for the transmission and defence of those universal values, the UN must not be constrained by a legalistic adherence to the doctrine of absolute sovereignty. It has a higher responsibility to intervene wherever and whenever universal human/humanitarian values are disregarded or even just at threat.

Legally and morally this relationship between cosmopolitan values and sovereign rights has been a difficult circle to square for the United Nations. Created as an avowedly inter-governmental organisation, the UN as an institution is itself in a sense rooted in the concept of national sovereignty. Its role, from this historical perspective, is to provide a forum for the accommodation of diverse sovereignties rather than a mechanism to undermine them. Only when a state grossly assaults the sovereignty of another – in a 'threat to the peace, breach of the peace or act of aggression' as the charter describes it – should the immunity from interference conferred by its own sovereignty be called into question. In the absence of such large-scale inter-state issues, freedom from interference by the UN appears to be absolutely guaranteed by the charter. Article 2 insists that 'nothing . . . shall authorize the United Nations to intervene in matters which are essentially within the domestic jurisdiction of any state . . .'[6] There would appear to be little legal wriggle-room in this statement of the limits of UN power. Indeed, this part of the charter goes some way to explaining the special significance of the holy trinity of consent, impartiality and force only in self-defence set out as the basic rules of traditional peacekeeping. Only adherence to all three of these principles would appear to keep UN military intervention on the right side of the organisation's own constitution.

The problems involved in infusing UN military intervention with cosmopolitan precepts are not merely legal. The moral universalism of cosmopolitanism is obviously at odds with the moral relativism of those who see the world and its various cultures in more 'pluralist' and less 'solidarist' terms. Respect for national sovereignty, from a pluralist perspective, is a means by which distinctive and different worldviews may be protected. In this view, while some universal values may indeed exist, they are not so extensive as to justify the interference of the citizens of one nation in the social and political make-up of other nations. This would hold equally for government and for international organisations. In this pluralist view different cultural, ethnic and religious values are not only inherent in different nation states, but often provide their defining character. If there is such a thing as an 'international community', critics of cosmopolitanism would suggest, it is one constructed from a plurality of beliefs and values. Such a community must embrace different attitudes to rights, attitudes which are ultimately all as 'legitimate' as each other. To follow the cosmopolitan road, pluralists argue, may involve the fatal mistake of confusing dominant (or just one's own) values for universal ones.

In the first decade or so after the end of the cold war, the arbiters of values within the UN security council tended to be the western powers. But they were in a position to do so principally because they had won the battle with communism. And, as we have already suggested, the 'end of history' triumphalism of the early 1990s was, to say the least, overstated. Since the beginning of the new century it has become clear that the notion of a universal set of moral tenets is at least premature and possibly just wrong. From the time of the Kosovo intervention in 1999 there has been a growing sense of a re-emergence of competing views in the security council about the basis on which interventions are decided and mandated. This does not amount, as some have suggested, to a new cold war.[7] But the consensus that surrounded the UN's actions in the Gulf in 1990 and 1991 has long dissolved. The Iraq which followed the invasion of 2003 obviously deepened Russian and Chinese suspicions about the west's proclivities for military intervention. The long and complex wrangle over the UN's proper role in Darfur has illustrated this changed climate. China, and to an extent Russia too, has seen intervention there as a slight to Sudanese sovereignty and has invoked the non-interference principle of article 2 of the charter in its support. For Sudan and its considerable body of supporters elsewhere in the global south, the implicit imposition of moral standards by the UN represents a species of western neo-colonialism rather than a defence of universal norms.

Prior to this new resistance to solidarist ideas of intervention there had in fact been some signs that cosmopolitan ideas were beginning to reach into UN policies and practices. Amidst all the political, philosophical and ethical debate around different values and the 'right' of intervention, by the late 1990s it was clear that a new public opinion about military action by the United Nations was developing, at least in the west. This emerging attitude derived from a variety of sources, but a major impetus was probably guilt. The previous decade had seen loss of life on a massive scale in conflicts across the world where the UN had evidently 'failed' to act decisively. The Rwanda genocide of 1994, the massacres in the former Yugoslavia and the man-made famines of Somalia were the most shocking – and most thoroughly reported – examples of this. There was a growing sense, at least at the level of what might be called informed public opinion, that the UN had failed to act because governments had failed to enable it to do so. In turn, governments had failed in this respect because their citizens had not pressed hard enough. In September 1999 secretary-general Kofi Annan caught the mood of the moment in an article published in *The Economist*. Annan was writing on the eve of the opening of that year's general assembly. He did so against the background of a period of crises and interventions in which the UN's role had been secondary rather than central. In March, when peace talks over Kosovo broke down, NATO began a military campaign against Serbia. This was undertaken with little more than token reference to the UN. Then, in September, an Australian-led intervention began in East Timor amidst the violence that surrounded the referendum there on the territory's separation from Indonesia. Here the UN's role was more prominent in that it formally legitimised and authorised Australia's action, but it did not itself initiate it.

Annan now called for a redoubled effort to set down the principles of UN intervention which would reflect a fundamental shift in public attitudes. The always thorny issue of sovereignty lay at the centre of the problem but, according to Annan, its status was changing:

> State sovereignty, in its most basic sense, is being redefined – not least by the forces of globalisation and international co-operation. States are now widely understood to be instruments at the service of their peoples, and not vice versa. At the same time individual sovereignty – by which I mean the fundamental freedom of each individual, enshrined in the charter of the UN and subsequent international treaties – has been enhanced by a renewed and spreading consciousness of individual rights. When we read the charter today, we are more than ever conscious that its aim is to protect individual human beings, not to protect those who abuse them.

The idea of 'human sovereignty' was, he suggested, beginning to replace that of state sovereignty, and this obviously posed special challenges to the United Nations in its approach to military intervention. The shift in attitude was not, he acknowledged, universal:

> This developing international norm in favour of intervention to protect civilians from wholesale slaughter will no doubt continue to pose profound challenges to the international community. In some quarters it will arouse distrust, scepticism, even hostility. But I believe on balance we should welcome it. Why? Because, despite all the difficulties of putting it into practice, it does show that humankind today is less willing than in the past to tolerate suffering in its midst, and more willing to do something about it.[8]

The following year, the first of the new century, in his keynote Millennium Report which took stock of the role of the UN at that symbolic juncture, Annan challenged member states to resolve the contradiction of their rhetorical commitment to humanitarian intervention and their tendency to cling to the formal constructs of sovereignty. 'If humanitarian intervention is, indeed, an unacceptable assault on sovereignty', he asked, 'how should we respond to a Rwanda, to a Srebrenica, to gross and systematic violation of human rights that offend every precept of our common humanity?'[9] Two landmark reports emerged from this climate of self-examination in the UN. At the end of 2001 *The Responsibility to Protect* was published. This was the product of a Canadian initiative, the International Commission on Intervention and State Sovereignty. First, though, the Brahimi Report – *The Report of the Panel on United Nations Peace Operations* – was published in 2000.

A new agenda for peace: The Brahimi Report

In March 2000, some months before his Millennium Report was published, Kofi Annan had commissioned his under-secretary-general, the Algerian diplomat Lakhdar Brahimi, to produce a report and recommendations on all significant aspects of UN peace operations. A panel of ten diplomats and military officers subsequently presented a 'comprehensive review of the whole question of peacekeeping operations in all their aspects'. Brahimi approached the future of UN intervention in a way that evoked many of the dilemmas of the past, though he did not explicitly acknowledge the longer historical narrative of peace operations in his report. In fact, Brahimi's own perspective on peacekeeping saw it as a historically youthful '50-year-old enterprise', in other words an explicitly UN project, rather than a long-evolving international activity.[10]

Much of the panel's attention was given to the continuing importance of the traditional issues of consent, impartiality and use of force. It acknowledged implicitly that the terminology of 'peacekeeping' was now more or less inappropriate as contemporary operations 'do not deploy into post-conflict situations so much as they deploy to create such situations'.[11] This obviously raised major issues for the traditional tripartite criteria and underlined the point made persistently by Boutros-Ghali in the early 1990s that traditional peacekeeping increasingly must be blended with post-conflict peace-building. At the same time, Brahimi engaged (as had Boutros-Ghali as well) with the 'other end' of the sequence of conflict. Just as in the 1950s Dag Hammarskjöld had placed peacekeeping in the larger context of what he described as preventive diplomacy, so Brahimi urged greater attention to what he described as conflict prevention. The change in terminology, of course, reflected the fact that most of this preventive action would now take place not in the diplomatic milieu of state-to-state negotiation but at the level of factions within states.

On the first of the holy trinity of criteria for traditional UN peace-keeping – the consent of the parties – Brahimi laid out the hard reality of intervention in civil conflicts. While the idea of 'host state consent' in traditional peacekeeping – in the Middle East, for example – was a matter of public diplomacy and therefore relatively easy to achieve, the intra-state environment of intervention in domestic crises was much more complex. In such situations consent to a UN intervention 'may be manipulated in many ways by the local parties'.[12] This problem lay at the root of Boutros-Ghali's call for the creation of 'peace-enforcement units' in *An Agenda for Peace*, which were supposed to ensure continued compliance with agreements made earlier by the parties to a conflict, even when the development of the situation appeared not to favour one or other of them. The long drawn-out civil war in Angola which continued throughout the 1990s despite the presence of UN forces was a case in point. Rwanda had presented a similar situation, where a peace process had been agreed as a preliminary to UN intervention but where 'consent' to this became meaningless amidst the genocide. While consent should remain an important criterion for intervention, according to Brahimi, it could not be an absolute condition. Commitments could not simply be abandoned because one actor had a change of mind. Returning to the rationale of Boutros-Ghali's earlier proposal for a more effective response to these situations, Brahimi argued that, once deployed, UN forces have a larger responsibility to the international community which agreed their mandates in the first place and they should not be prevented from carrying out these mandates by the calculation or petulance of local factions.

This important condition on the principle of consent leads logically in the report to the other two traditional concerns of UN intervention: impartiality and the use of force. Brahimi differentiated between the idea of 'neutrality' and that of 'impartiality'. The insistence on the supposed neutrality of UN interventions from Bosnia to Rwanda had in effect facilitated crimes against humanity when international forces on the ground failed to prevent mass murder. 'Impartiality' should rightly involve respect for the UN charter and the terms of an operation's mandate as the guiding sources of even-handed behaviour. But this is not the same as 'neutrality' if this is taken to mean 'equal treatment of all parties in all cases for all time, which can amount to a policy of appeasement'. Some interventions take place in situations where the parties 'consist not of moral equals but of obvious aggressors and victims, and peacekeepers may not only be operationally justified in using force but morally compelled to do so'.[13] To this end, UN forces must be both legally supported by security council mandates and physically equipped to take the initiative in safeguarding not just themselves, but also those who should reasonably be able to look to them for protection.

Brahimi raised these crucial points about the extent of the UN's powers and responsibility to intervene with evident feeling and considerable eloquence. But in doing so he was entering waters which, though all too familiar, the United Nations had not succeeded in navigating successfully in the past. On one side were the cliffs of an ineffectual presence unable to take the initiative as violence developed. On the other side were the reefs of 'enforcement', properly the concern of the sort of coercive collective security the UN had never effectively applied. The problem was not that the UN was routinely faced with situations where it was tempted to act to enforce an outcome in favour of one or other side in a conflict – such situations were rare. But in many operations (perhaps the majority of post-cold war interventions), use or non-use of force was not about political outcomes but about the immediate protection of those at risk of violence. Did the UN have an inherent humanitarian 'responsibility to protect' such people? If so, in what circumstances and to what extent could and should UN personnel use force to do so? While Brahimi asserted the moral imperative of protection, it was not the function of his report to explore the full range of implications, legal, political and moral, associated with that position. This was provided by the other landmark publication, which followed in 2001.

A 'responsibility to protect'?

The Responsibility to Protect was produced by the International Commission on Intervention and State Sovereignty. Although not a formal United Nations venture, the report was commissioned by the Canadian government as a direct response to the challenges set out in Kofi Annan's Millennium Report. It was co-chaired by two of the international great and good: the former Australian foreign minister Gareth Evans and Mohamad Sahnoun, who had been close to some of the UN's most fraught humanitarian interventions as the secretary-general's representative in both Somalia and in the Great Lakes region of Central Africa. There were ten further commissioners, all of whom had either close experience of UN operations in the field or had been prominent in public discussion of the issues around intervention. Their collective task was to explore the moral, legal and political issues surrounding international 'action taken against a state or its leaders, without its or their consent, for purposes which are claimed to be humanitarian or protective'.[14] Having done so, the Commission was to make appropriate practical recommendations to the United Nations.

The Commission did not emphasise the long-running and unresolved arguments about the bases of national sovereignty and its absolute inviolability or otherwise. There had been anyway, the report argued, a 're-characterisation' of the concept in recent years, driven by the greater focus on human rights and human security. This shift had been 'from sovereignty as control to sovereignty as responsibility in both internal functions and external duties'.[15] Consequently the Commission would 'prefer to talk not of a "right to intervene" but of a "responsibility to protect"'.[16] The legal bases of intervention were obviously important. Intervention could be legitimised by the authority of the UN security council under the charter. Intervention could also be justified by specific state obligations under international law such as the commitments implicit in the Genocide Convention. There was also an emerging practice of intervention (such 'customary practice' being a recognised source of international law) among the membership of regional organisations. But more important than legal 'rights' of intervention, in the Commission's view, was the nature of intervention.

Following both Boutros-Ghali a decade before and the Brahimi Report of the previous year, the Commission placed great emphasis on the tripartite nature of the intervention process. The 'responsibility to protect' (a term which immediately spawned a number of acronyms from the functional 'RtoP' to the text-speak 'r2p') comprised three composite obligations. There was first of all a 'responsibility to prevent'. Only if, for whatever reason, this failed was there then a 'responsibility to react', which might be by military means. Following this the 'responsibility to rebuild' would apply. Inevitably, the main focus of the report was on the most problematic of these three obligations: the 'responsibility to react' by military means. However much the report might strain to place this in the larger context of humanitarian action, it was the principal concern behind the creation of the Commission and by far the greatest focus of interest on the part of those who would read its report.

The main contribution of the Commission lay in defining the grounds on which international involvement in a conflict could reasonably be justified. It then set out criteria to be met by military intervention in such situations and identified the proper agencies to be responsible for it. On this last point, the Commission was clear that the primary responsibility for humanitarian action remained always with the state in which a crisis was occurring. Only when that state was unwilling or unable to take the necessary action, or where the state itself was the author of the crisis, should the international community become involved. When it did, the Commission was unequivocal in its view that the UN security council was the obvious locus of legal and political authority. 'There is no better or more appropriate body than the United Nations Security Council to authorize military intervention for human protection purposes. The task is not to find alternatives . . . but to make the Security Council work better than it has'.[17] To this end, the five permanent members should make special efforts to co-operate with each other when issues requiring humanitarian intervention were brought to them. Specifically, they should disavow the use of the veto in such cases when their own vital national interests were not involved because it was 'unconscionable that one veto can over-ride the rest of humanity on matters of grave humanitarian concern'.[18] Action by the general assembly in the event of a deadlocked security council would be a possibility under the Uniting for Peace process introduced in 1950 to circumnavigate deadlock over Korea (see Chapter 1). Intervention by regional organisations was also a possibility, though only if undertaken under the terms of the UN charter which permits such action if authorised by the security council.[19] But either of these would be poor and questionable substitutes for interventions mandated and directed by the security council itself.

Before the security council or any other international agency considered intervention, however, the nature of the crisis would have to be such as to fully justify military action. Even then, military intervention could not be an option in any and every conflict where humanitarian issues were at stake. Intervention should be restricted to only two situations: where there was large-scale loss of life or when there was large-scale ethnic cleansing.[20] Specifically, the Commission ruled out international intervention in circumstances where it was simply a situation in which human rights were denied either universally or to specific groups or ethnicities within the state. Nor could intervention take place to implant or restore democratic government. According to this framework, therefore, intervention would not have been appropriate, say, in the case of apartheid South Africa. Nor, despite the obvious humanitarian abuses of the regimes there, would it be justified in either Zimbabwe or Burma. What the precise start point of 'large-scale' killing or ethnic cleansing would be was not provided in the report. But the implication was that it would have to meet the levels of previous interventions like Somalia, Bosnia or Rwanda, where victims ran into the many thousands.

Even once a crisis met the threshold conditions for military intervention, the report proposed that four 'precautionary conditions' should be met.[21] Firstly, there must be 'right intention' in the sense that the purpose of the intervention must be clearly and unequivocally humanitarian. In other words, there must be no ulterior motives. In this respect a multilateral – ideally UN – intervention would always be 'safer' that a unilateral one which may be more about the pursuit of national interests by the intervening power than the well-being of the humanitarian victims. This, the Commission reported, was a major concern of those from which it took evidence in various parts of the world. Military intervention even then could only be a last resort, undertaken after all other non-military means had been explored and exhausted. Then, when military action was taken it had to be proportionate in scale, duration and intensity. Not only, therefore, would force be a final resort, but it would also be minimal. Finally, none of this should take place at all unless after due analysis there was a reasonable prospect of the intervention achieving its humanitarian ends. Quixotic action, in other words, must be avoided. Practical outcomes were what was important. In general terms, the report insisted that what it described as the 'Hippocratic principle' should apply to any intervention: 'first do no harm'.[22]

The Commission concluded by presenting a series of recommendations for various parts of the UN system.[23] The general assembly was invited to incorporate the key findings of the report into a declaratory resolution. This would affirm the idea of sovereignty as responsibility rather than power; assert the tripartite process of humanitarian intervention (prevention, reaction and rebuilding); and set out the threshold for military intervention (large-scale loss of life and/or ethnic cleansing). It would also articulate the precautionary principles for intervention (right intention, last resort, proportionality and reasonable prospects). The security council for its part should adopt a set of guidelines based on the report which would govern its collective response in cases where humanitarian intervention was in prospect. Additionally, the five permanent members should seek to agree to forego use of the veto in matters of humanitarian intervention. The secretary-general should adopt a coordinating role in pursuing these objectives.

Little of this came to pass. Secretary-general Kofi Annan dutifully pursued the objective of implementation of both the responsibility to protect agenda and the recommendations of the earlier Brahimi

Report. He had considerable rhetorical support in the general assembly in doing so, but at the level of the security council, where both reports agreed the only significant authority lay, there was little movement. There were both immediate and more profound reasons for this, and these go the very heart of the humanitarian project.

The new millennium and the shifting tectonics of global politics

The appearance of the Responsibility to Protect Report coincided almost exactly with the terrorist attacks of 11 September 2001 on New York and Washington. The report itself makes some tentative reference to this in an attempt to bolster the idea of the interconnectedness of world events and the need for multilateral responses. In reality, however, the new security order which emerged in the wake of 9/11 was not friendly to the idea of humanitarian intervention as presented in the report. The administration of George W. Bush was never destined to be a natural ally of those calling for a firmer commitment to multilateral humanitarian action. American governments of whatever ideological stripe were likely to approach this much more cautiously after the Somalia debacle of the early 1990s and other high-profile failures of intervention.

Participation in the Kosovo operation of 1999 had been urged on the Democratic administration of Bill Clinton by the British prime minister Tony Blair who genuinely saw the Kosovo venture as a humanitarian intervention. American participation, though, was probably only secured by the fact that it was in most respects a conventional act of 'enforcement' undertaken by the NATO alliance. It was not a UN venture. With the accession of George W. Bush to office, even this residual and conditional commitment to humanitarian intervention was lacking. The right-wing, neo-conservative-influenced administration, even before the terrorist attacks, was inherently suspicious of the UN and all its works. Now, in the utterly changed political landscape post-9/11, the worldview of the United States administration was ever more unilateralist and increasingly focused on what became known as 'homeland security'.

Foreign interventions by the United States, whether in Afghanistan at the end of 2001 or Iraq in 2003, might on occasion be dressed in the rhetoric of humanitarian intervention, but they were essentially acts of old-fashioned *realpolitik*. The effect of both the Afghanistan and more especially Iraq invasions was to devalue the currency of humanitarian intervention and undermine the credibility of those who advocated it.

This was the fate of the British Labour government in particular: Britain's humanitarian military actions in Kosovo in 1999 and Sierra Leone the following year were relatively pure in intent, but after its participation in the invasion of Iraq, the moral high ground slipped away.

Simultaneously, the outlook of the Russian government changed as the twentieth century turned to the twenty-first. As suggested in the previous chapter, at the beginning of the 1990s the new post-cold war Soviet Union (as it then still was) appeared to be in search of a renewed international identity. Gorbachev and his reforming foreign minister Eduard Shevardnadze seemed to be leading the country towards a type of Nordic 'middle power' stance. Commitment to multilateralism in general and the UN in particular appeared to be strong and growing. But the end of the Soviet Union and the subsequent years of painful economic and social readjustment in Russia helped forge, by the end of the decade, a new assertive nationalism. This hardly presaged another cold war, but it did produce an attitude to the outside world which was far less accommodating to anything that could be interpreted as western aggrandisement. There was a special sensitivity in Moscow towards the eastward expansion of NATO, especially after Vladimir Putin was elected president in 2000. This wariness had begun earlier, though, and was clearly in evidence after the NATO intervention in Kosovo and the air war against Serbia in 1999. After this, any attempt, actual or perceived, by the west to use the United Nations for its own ends under the guise of multilateralism provoked Russian suspicions and at times outright opposition.

In many respects, of course, this was not a new departure in Russian foreign policy. It could more realistically be described as a resumption of a long-standing habit, broken only during unusual times in the late 1980s and early 1990s. Now, though, Russia had if not an ally exactly, then a like-minded colleague in China. The end of the cold war helped bring – and at the same time distracted attention from – another fundamental realignment in world politics: the effective end of the Sino-Soviet conflict which had dominated world communist relations since the early 1960s. Although the two countries retained many differences and still harboured various rivalries, the ideological steam had been released from their relationship. China, like Russia, was fundamentally wary of United Nations interventionism. Moreover, its constitutional power as a permanent member of the security council was by the end of the 1990s complemented by a dizzying growth in its global economic power.

The consequence of these shifts and realignments in world politics was a security council in which much of the immediate post-cold war consensus had begun to break down. It was also one in which a majority of the five permanent members were fundamentally suspicious of any extension to the capacity of the organisation to behave as an autonomous actor, particularly in the area of military intervention. The predictable hostility of large authoritarian states to any dilution of national sovereignty was, moreover, deepened by the specifics of time and place. Both Russia and China had objections to particular multilateral interventions. Deep-rooted pan-Slav sentiment added force to Russia's natural hostility to NATO's war against Serbia over Kosovo, for example. Similarly, China, which was carefully crafting a new economic foreign policy towards sub-Saharan Africa at the beginning of the new century, was opposed to the anti-Sudanese government drift of UN policy on Darfur. The world into which both the Brahimi and the Responsibility to Protect reports were launched, therefore, was simply not a propitious one for the implementation of their recommendations.

Lying beneath particular historical circumstances at the start of the twenty-first century were other perhaps more profound and enduring features of international relations. States' concern with defending their sovereignty, whether it takes the form of the 'right' to preside over the mistreatment of their own citizens or their 'right' to ignore such mis-treatment elsewhere in the world, cannot be conjured away by simple declaration. The RtoP Commission may have 'preferred' to talk of a responsibility to protect rather than a right to intervene, but unless that preference is shared by a critical mass of states in the international system it will mean very little. Sadly, contrary to the Commission's assertion, there is indeed still such a thing as 'a faraway country of which we know little' and, more sadly still, many people and many governments would be happier to know even less. These are particu-larly unfortunate truths not least because both Brahimi and the RtoP reports were thoughtful, measured and relatively cautious in their recommendations. But they are truths nonetheless. Similarly, while the academic and theoretical discourse on security has certainly expanded in a way that foregrounds the idea of 'human security' rather than conventional 'national security', it is unclear how far this shift truly extends into the calculations on which governments base their policies. The stock-in-trade of government, after all, has traditionally been national security. While the rhetoric of national delegations at the United Nations may give the impression of a new political sensibility, there is little tangible evidence that this has permeated state policies.

The idea of human security has been given scant prominence in the pursuit of the so-called war on terror, for example. In these circumstances then, the RtoP Commission's hope to 'shift the terms of the debate' in a direction which would further facilitate military humanitarian intervention by the UN was always perhaps been rather a forlorn one.

Mobilising public opinion: a 'CNN effect'?

The state then, as a self-interested institution, may naturally resist any shift in the terms of the debate about intervention which would implicate a reduction in its own power. Yet the post-cold war years have without doubt seen a change in public perceptions of humanitarian need. This has been driven partly by technological developments, but post-bipolar world politics has also been a factor. New communications technologies, both at the levels of sophistication of apparatus and efficiency of diffusion, have brought images of conflict and its consequences into the homes of citizens of countries in far-distant parts of the world. Simultaneously, the end of bipolarity has removed much of the state control over news gathering and its dissemination which affected earlier periods of conflict. While Vietnam may have been the 'first television war' and American policy may have been shaped as a result, Soviet citizens remained largely in ignorance of events in Afghanistan until made aware of them on an individual basis as a result of personal loss. The end of the cold war changed these unequal rules of media engagement and saw the range and immediacy of news events increase across the board. The general shift, most obviously in central and east Europe but more widely as well, towards forms of government which were accountable to and required to respond to public opinion, also had tangible policy outcomes.

The impact of the new techniques and increased influence of the media on humanitarian interventions was acknowledged relatively early by the UN. In the *Supplement to An Agenda for Peace*, written in the aftermath of both the Somalia and Rwanda failures, Boutros-Ghali regretted the 'intense media interest, often laudatory, more often critical' focused on UN operations.[24] Five years later, the RtoP report noted that the 'revolution in information technology has made global communications instantaneous and provided unprecedented access to information worldwide. The result has been an enormously heightened awareness of conflicts wherever they may be occurring, combined with immediate and often very compelling visual images of the resultant suffering on television and in other mass media'.[25] There are important questions here about the effect of the media on humanitarian interventions which are difficult to fully resolve. One is, simply, does media power in this area truly exist? The answer, on even a cursory examination of the interplay between the media and state policy-makers, is that it certainly does, though assessing the extent of its impact is more problematic. Perhaps the more interesting question, however, emerges from this. If the media does play a role in determining policy, is it a positive one in support of effective humanitarian intervention? This is not so easily answered.

The term 'CNN effect' used to describe this new media prominence came into common usage when the United States deployed its Unified Task Force (UNITAF) in Somalia in 1992. The phenomenon it describes, though – the policy impact of public opinion formed and mobilised by the availability of instant graphic news coverage of events anywhere in the world at any hour – was already evident during the Gulf war the previous year. The expression is, of course, a figure of speech in that the actual CNN – the US-based Cable News Network – is taken as representative of the plethora of news outlets using the most up-to-date satellite and digital technology and broadcasting twenty-four hours a day.

In the case of Somalia the CNN effect was multi-layered, and this illustrates an important aspect of news coverage of humanitarian interventions. If a CNN effect does indeed operate on policy-makers, it does so in more than one direction. Not only does the media have the capacity to encourage intervention, but it can also inhibit intervention or indeed bring it to an end. In Somalia the impact at the outset came from images of the desperate consequences of the famine caused by the conflict. This engendered public pressure in the global north for 'something to be done'. The 'dance' between the media and policy-makers continued with the carefully staged initial American landings at Mogadishu. These were choreographed in such a way as to give the best possible media impression of the venture to the home audience. This phase of the coverage, it was hoped, would consolidate the initial spurt of public engagement with the undertaking. Ideally, of course, it would also have a generally beneficial effect of the administration's broader image among the American public. The final expression of the CNN effect was in the coverage of the abuse of the bodies of American soldiers killed in fighting in October 1993 which led rapidly to the withdrawal of US – and consequently UN – forces from Somalia. As one American journalist expressed it at the time, '(w)e went into Somalia because of horrible television images; we will leave Somalia because of horrible television images'.[26] This complexity has led one writer to speak in terms of a 'CNN curve' rather than a CNN effect.[27] The impact of media coverage of a humanitarian crisis may 'bend' in different directions and consequently exert quite different pressures on governments as events unfold.

The actual extent to which graphic news coverage as such determines states' willingness to participate in UN interventions is extremely difficult to assess. Undeniably, the nature of the reporting of humanitarian crises has changed dramatically over recent years but its precise impact on governments' behaviour is much less clear. It is a great oversimplification to suggest that governments would allow their foreign and security policies to be determined by news organisations. But in certain circumstances particularly striking media coverage will have a greater or lesser influence over action. When, for example, there is no prior policy towards a particular situation in place, media coverage will have a much greater role in forming opinions unshaped by previous debate. The policy vacuum might then be filled by this opinion and government forced to respond. Where national policies have already been formulated, however, governments will be in a better position to resist extraneous pressures. In 1994, the year following the Somalia debacle, the permanent members of the security council individually and collectively were utterly resistant to pressures for decisive UN intervention in the genocide then taking place in Rwanda. The news coverage of the violence in Rwanda was ubiquitous and graphic, but the 'negative' CNN effect of the previous year in Somalia tended to counteract any new pressure for positive action.

Governments may themselves exploit media coverage for their own purposes. It is likely, for example, that the Australian government had a clear view of the importance to its own national interests of a stable independent East Timor. When chaos descended on the territory after the referendum on separation from Indonesia in 1999, the images of mayhem and destruction were an important aid to the Australian government in gaining public support for its leadership of the initial coalition of the willing which intervened in East Timor. A similar process of media exploitation was undertaken by the British government the following year to rally support for its (non-UN) intervention in Sierra Leone. This began ostensibly as an action to protect foreign nationals in the country by securing the international airport. Gradually, however, it became clear that the intervention had much larger objectives and was designed to bolster the Sierra Leone government against a rebel onslaught on the capital. This objective revealed itself in pace with media coverage of the depredations of the rebel forces.

Apparent acquiescence to the CNN effect can also be used to divert public attention to 'easier' interventions, away from other crises where intervention would be at least as justified in humanitarian terms but which would present more difficult political or operational problems. This technique was outlined in a revealing contribution to a Brookings Institution–Harvard seminar by Lawrence Eagleburger in 2002. Eagleburger was assistant US Secretary of State in 1992 and had been a strong advocate of intervention in Somalia. Military intervention in Somalia, he admitted, was a means of distracting attention from Bosnia where the US was under mounting pressure to intervene: 'here were two cases where there was a humanitarian need. In one of them [Bosnia], the consequences of becoming directly involved were at best totally unpredictable and could probably lead to serious consequences. In the Somali case a much clearer opportunity [existed] to do something right and get the hell out'. Moreover 'the television, the press, the whole thing gave us an opportunity to make a choice which to some degree . . . took pressure off the constant drumbeat that the Bush [senior] Administration didn't give a damn about human rights'.[28] The attraction of intervention in Somalia was that the US could 'feed and get out'. It was the failure of the successor US administration of Bill Clinton, according to Eagleburger, that it did not do this but instead remained and became ever more deeply involved in the conflict.

Media pressure for action, even if it does affect government policy-making, is not regarded as an unalloyed good even by the strongest advocates of wider humanitarian intervention. News coverage and the emotions it fashions cannot always be managed for the most desirable ends. This goes beyond the negative impact on attitudes to interventions which are underway and the manipulation of media coverage by governments for their own ends that we have just discussed. An inherent problem of the CNN effect is that, like much media activity, it focuses public attention on the dramatic rather than the essential. As secretary-general Kofi Annan observed, the 'CNN factor tends to mobilise pressure at the peak of the problem – which is to say, at the very moment when effective intervention is most costly, most dangerous and least likely to succeed'.[29] As one analyst has put it, by 'ignoring conflicts during the pre- and post-violence phases and by being highly selective in its coverage of conflicts in the violence phase, the media helps to shift focus and funds from more cost-effective efforts directed at preventing violent conflict and re-building war-torn societies'.[30] That is to say, both the preventive and post-conflict peace-building phases of intervention, whose importance have been consistently emphasised in UN reports from *An Agenda for Peace* onwards, are pushed to the background. Focusing more attention on Somalia's difficulties at the point at which the central state began to disintegrate – long before the violence produced the hideous consequences of 1992 – would have served a greater good than the drama of the US Operation Restore Hope in 1992. Similarly, confronting the basic flaws in Rwanda's supposed peace agreement signed the year before the genocide, and at least attempting to rectify them, could possibly have saved many lives.

It is likely, then, that a CNN effect does exist. The difficulty, as this discussion suggests, comes in assessing the extent and nature of its impact on policy-makers. Or in gauging their impact on the CNN effect, for that matter, because it is essentially a two-way relationship. Whatever that impact may be, it is far from clear that it is a positive one for the larger aims of humanitarian intervention.

Sovereignty and intervention: new world order or wishful thinking?

As historical distance from the end of the cold war grows, the more optimistic assumptions about the nature of any new world order have come under increasing scrutiny. Prominent among the issues involved in this is the proposition that state sovereignty has become framed within a new discourse. The 'optimistic' view is that sovereignty is no longer an absolute attribute of the state. Sovereignty now implies – and is dependent on – responsibilities to individuals, specifically in the sense of their physical well-being and respect for their (universal) rights. Failure to meet these responsibilities, it is suggested, might both justify and demand intervention from the larger 'international community'. And the will of this community has its most legitimate expression through the agency of the United Nations. Interventions by the UN with the purpose of imposing this will, it is argued, are now essentially post-Westphalian in nature. Their objectives are humanitarian rather than driven by political expedience. In the new global disposition such interventions usually take place within states rather than between them, as was the case with traditional UN peacekeeping.

The pertinent questions in an interrogation of these propositions relate to the symbiotic relationship between the behaviour of states and the attitudes of individuals. Has state behaviour changed in any fundamental ways in the past decades? Is there a new sense of extended responsibility among individuals? If so, how does the latter affect the former?

States are now required to operate in a public arena in a way that they did not previously. Inevitably, governments have acquired particular skills and strategies to meet this situation. As a result, it is probably more difficult than in the past to separate a country's rhetorical position on issues of sovereignty and intervention from its actual intentions. There is, in other words, a script that governments will follow to present themselves in the best light as committed members of the international community. The United Nations as an institution has established certain norms of multilateral behaviour and states will wish at least to appear to have adopted them. The question then is whether there has been an observable change in state behaviour or whether states are just more adept at suggesting they have embraced such a change.

In truth it is difficult to locate evidence to suggest any substantive change in state behaviour in relation to sovereignty – either in respect of their own or that of other states. It is possible that there was what might be called a 'multilateralist moment' in the immediate aftermath of the cold war. This window was perhaps framed loosely by the first Gulf war in 1991 and the disintegration of the Soviet Union the following year. At this point the attitudes of the major powers were more than usually favourable to higher levels of joint action and, implicitly, multilateral interventionism. If such a phase did exist, it did not survive the brutal realities of the 1990s when various regions of the world underwent violent readjustment. Then, as we have suggested, an economically stricken Russia struggled to reconstruct itself, not on new, progressive 'Nordic' lines, but on a political foundation of defensive nationalism. Ironically, this nationalism was fed in part by the west's avowed humanitarian interventions against Serbia. Next, the terrorist attacks of September 2001 on the United States accelerated what was already a retreat by the administration of George W. Bush from the relatively positive approach to multilateralism of the administrations of both his predecessor Bill Clinton and that of his own father before that. The invasion of Iraq in 2003, conceived and led by the United States against the clear will of the United Nations membership as a whole, was a dramatic measure of the changed international climate. But it was not a sudden event; the direction of travel had been set long previously.

The hard truth was that the great anomaly lay not in this retreat from multilateralism, but in the earlier, momentary embrace of it. Ultimately, state sovereignty remained the organising principle of the international system. Generally speaking, those countries which had already established traditions of 'world citizenship' during and before the cold war – such as Sweden, Norway and Canada – maintained their commitment to interventionism. Those which had seemingly acquired new instincts in this direction – like the United States and the Soviet Union in the early 1990s – appeared to lose them just as quickly as they had adopted them

The fact that UN interventions after the end of the cold war were predominantly in intra-state conflicts rather than international ones does not in itself indicate a move to a new post-Westphalian sensibility. The important judgement here is not about the precise location of UN interventions, but about the underlying motivations driving them. While it would be quite wrong to disregard the humanitarian impulse behind UN operations in Africa, Asia and Europe, it would also be foolhardy to conclude that this was the only or even the dominant motivation. The health of the Westphalian state system is dependent on the health of the state units within it, and intra-state interventions by the UN were at least as concerned with this aspect of the commitment.

There is, moreover, another point about the nature of state behaviour which is often overlooked by many who analyse and assess apparent shifts in state conduct and attitudes. The focus of these analyses is essentially restricted to the transatlantic world, broadly defined. Beyond Europe, North America and a few culturally related states, the idea of a new approach to sovereignty is largely misplaced. The inescapable fact is that the majority of states in the world remain in thrall to the principle of sovereign equality and have been largely untouched by debates about post-Westphalianism and conditional sovereignty. They have shown little inclination to extend their own capacity for genuine humanitarian intervention in other countries. By the same token, they have not accepted the principle that their own sovereignty might be set aside if the UN or another 'legitimate' agency determines that they have failed to meet some externally imposed standard of behaviour. In short, the world remains some distance from forming the sort of international community which might be subject to new forms of global governance.

There are similar questions to be posed at the level of the individual as well as that of governments. How far have cosmopolitan ideas truly taken root among western populations? (Once again it is to the 'west' that, realistically, these questions must be restricted.) Yes, it may be possible, as the RtoP Commission suggests, to appeal to the public on the basis of a kind of extended national interest. There is plainly a danger that crises in distant parts of the world could, in the absence of intervention, engender greater levels of international terrorism or crime or create refugee flows which might eventually reach the shores of the west. This can certainly be deployed as a case for 'self-interested' humanitarian intervention.[31] But if these arguments do resonate with public opinion, they do not do so on the basis of cosmopolitan inclusiveness. Yes, there might be a growing awareness in western countries of individual human rights as a general principle, but to an extent this may be a side-effect of a general growth in individualism. If so, it is far from being a marker of a deepening global community. There may, in other words, be a heightened awareness of human rights on a self-referential basis, but this does not necessarily translate into a willingness to seek or protect them for others elsewhere in the world.

Here Francis Fukuyama's proposition – that we have reached the end of history in a world which is rapidly adopting liberal democratic principles of government and capitalist economics – can be posed against an equally celebrated contrary view. Also writing in the early 1990s, the American political scientist Samuel Huntington spoke of the new world order being characterised by a 'clash of civilizations'. Huntington's world is not one moving in the direction of ever-deepening integration: it is an increasingly fragmented one in which the parts, regionally and culturally defined, do not share universal norms but struggle to protect their own against threats, real or imagined, from others.[32] Widely derided by progressive opinion in the 1990s, Huntington's views inevitably attracted more sympathetic examination after 11 September 2001.

Two decades after the end of the cold war and despite the intervening upheavals of the so-called war on terror and the invasion of Iraq, neither Fukuyama's nor Huntington's competing grand narrative has been validated. In many respects the texture of world politics suggests continuity rather than the sort of radical change these overarching theses propose.

Yet the tally of UN military ventures in 2011 is much larger than in 1989. UN members continue to respond positively to regular calls from the secretary-general for troops contributions and they do so largely free of public opposition in their various countries. The motivations of governments for making these contributions are complex and vary from country to country. The influence of cosmopolitan thought is no doubt present somewhere among these. But there is little evidence to suggest that this – or any fundamentally challenging view of sovereignty – is more prominent than in the 1940s and 1950s when UN military interventions began. Beyond altruism, other considerations will be present in the calculations of states contributing forces for UN interventions, in varying proportions. Long-term, long-distance assessments of national self-interest will often feature (on the lines suggested in the RtoP report), but this is plainly derived from a traditional Westphalian perspective in which the fundamental stability of the international state system is important to everyone's national security. States will also commit forces to UN interventions for less tangible but never to be underestimated considerations of national prestige on the international stage. Countries like Canada, Sweden and Ireland have placed their UN role at the centre of their foreign policies over the long term and have greatly enhanced their international standing as a result. More practical motives such as opportunities for operational experience otherwise unavailable to national armies can also be important. In the case of a few smaller and poorer countries like Bangladesh, Nepal and Fiji, financial returns from the UN feature in national decisions to provide contingents for military interventions. Overall then, national self-interest is at least as prominent in the calculations of policy-makers in deciding to participate in UN interventions. This range of motivations is essentially no different from that in play during the age of 'traditional' peacekeeping. But while there may be little to suggest that a new global enthusiasm for humanitarian intervention has emerged in recent times, there remains, whatever the complexity of the motives in play, a general commitment to intervention in both the UN as an organisation and among its member states.

Notes

1. Two books by partisans of post-Westphalianism give an overview of the moral and political elements involved in the perspective. The first, which is by the well-known American liberal writer on international relations Richard Falk, focuses particularly on the United Nations: *Law in an Emerging Global Village: A Post-Westphalian Perspective* (Amsterdam: Hotei-Brill, 1998). The other is by the British-based academic Andrew Linklater: *The Transformation of Political Community: Ethical Foundations of the Post-Westphalian Era* (Columbia SC: University of South Carolina Press, 1999).
2. For explorations of democratic peace theory, see Bruce M. Russett, *Grasping the Democratic Peace* (Princeton NJ: Princeton University Press, 1994); and Paul K. Huth et al., *The Democratic Peace and Territorial Conflict in the Twentieth Century* (Cambridge: Cambridge University Press, 2003).
3. Immanuel Kant, *Perpetual Peace* (New York: Cosimo Classics, 2005). The original essay dates from 1795.

4. The literature on globalisation is of course dauntingly large. One of the best general introductions is to be found in Jan Aart Scholte, *Globalization: A Critical Introduction* (2nd ed., London: Palgrave, 2005).

5. The study of cosmopolitanism has grown rapidly since the end of the cold war. Its basic tenets are well captured in Kwame Anthony Appiah, *Cosmopolitanism: Ethics in a World of Strangers* (London: Allen Lane, 2006). Some of its most prominent theorists, including Richard Falk and David Held, contribute to the discussion in Daniele Archibugi (ed.), *Debating Cosmopolitanism* (London: Verso, 2003).

6. Chapter I of the United Nations charter, found at: http://www.un.org/en/documents/charter/chapter1.shtm

7. There is a viewpoint that we have indeed reverted to another phase of bipolarity. See, for example, Edward Lucas, *The New Cold War* (London: Bloomsbury, 2009).

8. 'Two Concepts of Sovereignty', *The Economist*, 18 September 1999.

9. Kofi Annan, '*We the Peoples': The Role of the United Nations in the 21st Century* (New York: United Nations, 2000), p. 48.

10. Report of the Panel on United Nations Peace Operations, issued as United Nations Documents A/55/305 (general assembly); S/2000/809 (security council), 21 August 2000, paragraph 12. Found at http://www.un.org/peace/reports/peace_operations

11. Ibid., paragraph 20.

12. Ibid., paragraph 48.

13. Ibid., paragraph 50.

14. Report of the International Commission on Intervention and State Sovereignty (December 2001), paragraph 1.38. Found at http://www.iciss.ca/report-en.asp

15. Ibid., paragraph 2.14.

16. Ibid., paragraph 2.4.

17. Ibid., paragraph 6.14.

18. Ibid., paragraph 6.20.

19. See chapter VIII of the UN charter: Regional Arrangements. Found at http://www.un.org/en/documents/charter/chapter8.shtml

20. Report of the International Commission on Intervention and State Sovereignty, paragraph 4.19.

21. Ibid., paragraphs 4.33–4.43

22. Ibid., paragraph 4.12.

23. Ibid., paragraphs 8.28–8.30.

24. *Supplement to An Agenda for Peace: Position Paper of the Secretary-General on the Occasion of the Fiftieth Anniversary of the United Nations* (UN Document A/50/60-S/1995/1, 3 January 1995), paragraph 4. Found at http://www.un.org/Docs/SG/agsupp.html

25. Report of the International Commission on Intervention and State Sovereignty, paragraph 1.29.

26. Marianne Means quoted in transcript of Brookings/Harvard Forum 'The CNN effect': How 24-Hour News Coverage Affects Government Decisions and Public Opinion, 23 January 2002. Found at: http://www. brookings. edu/events/2002/0123media_journalism.aspx

27. Johanna Neuman, *Lights, Camera, War: Is Media Technology Driving International Politics?* (New York: St. Martin's Press, 1996), pp. 15–16.

28. Brookings/Harvard Forum 'The CNN effect'.

29. Quoted in Philip Wilkinson, 'Sharpening the Weapons of Peace: Peace Support Operations and Complex Emergencies', *International Peacekeeping* 7(1) (2000), p. 76.

30. Peter Viggo Jakobsen, 'Focus on the CNN Effect Misses the Point; the Real Media Impact on Conflict Management is Invisible and Indirect', *Journal of Peace Research* 37(5) (2000), p. 132.

31. Report of the International Commission on Intervention and State Sovereignty, paragraph 8.15.

32. Samuel P. Huntington, *The Clash of Civilizations and the Remaking of the Modern World* (New York: Simon and Schuster, 1996). Huntington presented his thesis originally in an article in the influential American journal *Foreign Affairs* in 1993 as a riposte to Fukuyama's ideas.

Chapter 4

Africa: post-colonial intervention amidst fragile statehood

Since its first military intervention in the Congo in 1960, the UN has deployed military personnel in twenty-five operations to eighteen African countries. Of these, twenty-two missions in seventeen countries have begun since 1990. In some respects this is surprising. The stresses of the decolonisation process and its aftermath throughout the 1960s and 1970s certainly created situations which would have seemed to call out for UN military intervention. Yet, as we have seen, UN military activity was primarily focused on the Middle East and Asia during this time.[1] There were perhaps three reasons for this relative disregard of Africa's problems by the UN in this period, at least as far as military intervention was concerned.

Firstly, during the 1960s when decolonisation was at its most intense, external 'responsibility' for Africa was considered to remain properly with the former imperial powers. To this end, post-colonial security relationships were developed across the continent by both Britain and France. At the political level the Commonwealth and *francophonie* respectively tended to tie the foreign policies of the new states to those of their former colonial powers. The effect was to narrow the entry for third parties like the United Nations. This was evident in international reaction to the Nigerian civil war in the 1960s which followed the attempted secession of the province of Biafra. Three decades later a UN intervention in a conflict of that sort would have been virtually automatic, but in its time the Biafran crisis was still seen in essence as something which fell within a British sphere of influence. For its part, France seemed more than ready to deploy its own forces, typically in the form of the Foreign Legion, to manage crises across Francophone Africa, usually consolidating French national interests in the process.

Secondly, it is probably true to say that the experience of the one sub-Saharan African operation that the UN did undertake in the 1960s left both the UN as an institution and potential force contributors wary of further engagements. The Congo operation, as we have seen, departed dramatically and in many ways disastrously from the traditional peacekeeping script. A sense emerged that the 'African' character of the crisis in the Congo was both very difficult to deal with and typical of what would be experienced elsewhere in the continent. The multi-layered and ever-shifting complexity of the Congo crisis meant that this mission was of a fundamentally different order from earlier UN missions in the Middle East and South Asia, which were clearly inter-state in character. Africa's conflicts tended to be over-whelmingly ones rooted in internal problems of the state involving hugely complicated humanitarian issues.

Overt international conflict has in fact been extremely rare in Africa since independence. This might be thought surprising for a continent composed of a dense patchwork of sovereignties which for the most part share land frontiers. At the time of independence African states and organisations generally agreed that the colonial frontiers, however imperfect, were best left as they were. The alternative – a wholesale re-ordering of the political geography of the continent with all the chaos and conflict that would involve – simply did not bear thinking about. With some few exceptions, notably the conflict between Somalia and Ethiopia in the 1960s, the invasion of Uganda by Tanzania in the late 1970s and the war which began in 1998 between Ethiopia and Eritrea, borders have not proved to be a major source of serious conflict.

Thirdly, by the late 1970s when the outstanding issues of de-colonisation – or more correctly non-decolonisation – might have appeared to demand multilateral intervention, UN military activities had entered their state of post-détente suspension. There were no new UN operations anywhere during this period. The result was that the persisting running sores of late imperialism in the continent were approached only tentatively by the United Nations. The white minority regime in Southern Rhodesia which had broken away from Britain in 1965 therefore remained largely untouched during the most destructive phase of its liberation war in the 1970s by anything beyond (widely breached) UN sanctions. Rhodesia's eventual transformation into independent Zimbabwe in 1980 was brokered, not by the United Nations, but by Britain and the Commonwealth. By the mid-1960s Portugal was fighting three guerilla wars in three different African territories (Angola, Mozambique and Guinea-Bissau), but as Portugal's African wars approached their end in the early 1970s, Portuguese Africa formed part of the 'impermissible core', as we described it, where UN intervention was simply not to be considered. Portugal, a NATO member, was fighting pro-Soviet Marxist movements, and its allies, though often despairing of Lisbon's intransigence and refusal to engage with political reality, were not inclined to open up the matter to the United Nations.

Perhaps most discreditable though was the attitude in the UN towards Namibia (or 'South West Africa' as its South African overlords persisted in calling it). Namibia was in a very direct sense a United Nations responsibility. As German South West Africa it had become subject to the League of Nations mandate system after the first world war. The obvious 'mandatory' had been the neighbouring Union of South Africa. South Africa was one of the victors in the war and its prime minister, Jan Smuts, had been a prominent and progressive voice in the planning of the new League. With the arrival of the United Nations after the second world war, South West Africa in common with the other League mandates still in existence became a Trusteeship and remained under South African control. As South Africa adopted the ever-more extreme racist policies of apartheid in the 1950s and 1960s, it became clear that not only was South West Africa not being prepared for independence as its Trusteeship status required, but also that South Africa was planning quietly but determinedly to formally annex it. Throughout the 1960s and 1970s, pressure for action grew in a UN general assembly now dominated by post-colonial states of the global south. The security council, which had ultimate responsibility for forcing Trustee states to comply with their responsibilities under the charter, was in a politically delicate position on the issue. By the mid-1970s South Africa had become increasingly beleaguered in Namibia where a liberation movement, the South West African People's Organization (SWAPO), was gaining in strength. But simultaneously South Africa had a new reason to be obstructive. The sudden end of the Portuguese empire had seen power in Angola, Namibia's northern neighbour, pass to a revolutionary Marxist government.

The impasse over Namibia was not broken until the late 1980s. The decisive event was the beginning of the end of the cold war. This had an impact on the situation in Namibia in two separate but linked ways. Firstly, although the west had always held South Africa at arm's length and with noses pinched, its obvious geostrategic position along with its fiercely anti-communist stance were clearly useful. Consequently, external pressure over both apartheid and Namibia had always been less than wholehearted. This situation no longer pertained as the end of the cold war came in sight: South Africa now became much more vulnerable to outside pressure. Secondly, the end of the cold war removed the barriers placed on UN military intervention, not only in Africa, but also elsewhere since the collapse of détente in the late 1970s. The result was one of the UN's most clearly successful military interventions in Africa. In 1989 the security council created both the Transition Assistance Group (UNTAG), a large-scale military force which was deployed in Namibia and, simultaneously, the Verification Mission for Angola (UNAVEM).[2] The former policed and supervised a tense and occasionally violent electoral process in Namibia. This produced a SWAPO-dominated government which took power when Namibia became formally independent in March 1990. The Angolan side of the equation was crucial to South Africa's acceptance of this process.[3] UNAVEM, which consisted of military observers, oversaw the total withdrawal of the Cuban forces that had helped maintain Angola's Marxist government in power virtually since independence in 1975.[4]

The UN's military intervention in Namibia was to be the first of the wave of post-cold war deployments in sub-Saharan Africa. Some of these operations have been created to meet different problems in the same country at different times. The 1960 to 1964 Congo operation was deployed to meet specific problems associated with a botched de-colonisation. In 1999 the UN returned to confront a civil war which had drawn in forces from adjacent states. In Angola the success of UNAVEM in supervising the withdrawal of Cuban troops was followed by a sequence of much less successful interventions throughout the 1990s which were designed to help end Angola's civil war. UN troops were deployed in the Central African Republic (CAR) in 1998 and then again in 2007 to engage with a quite different crisis. The first intervention had been launched to manage a violent challenge to the legitimacy of the incumbent regime; the second was concerned with the spill-over of fighting from the Darfur region of Sudan into both the CAR and Chad. The Darfur conflict is itself subject to a UN intervention, but that is quite separate from another operation in southern Sudan.

Of all the UN's military interventions in Africa, only two can be said to conform to the model of traditional inter-state peacekeeping. In 1994 a small military observer mission (UNASOG) oversaw the withdrawal of Libyan officials and forces from the Aouzou Strip which, following an International Court of Justice ruling, Libya had agreed to transfer to its southern neighbour Chad. The operation was fully supported by each side and was carried out without incident. The area in question was largely unpopulated inhospitable desert and there were no significant humanitarian issues involved in the transfer. More complex and dangerous was the interposition force (UNMEE) deployed by the UN between Eritrea and Ethiopia from 2000 to 2008 following the 1998 war between the two countries. This too was a conflict over borders, but it was not easily or amicably resolved and the UN force was withdrawn after eight years in which no significant progress had been made towards a permanent resolution of the dispute.

Conflict and the African state

UNASOG and UNMEE formed a small and very untypical minority of the UN's interventions in Africa. For the most part these have been in intra-state conflicts, as we have observed. Some have been ostensibly inter-state operations but in reality have only been deployed as a result of internal conflicts in neighbouring states. The Uganda–Rwanda observer mission in 1993–4 and the Central African Republic–Chad mission in place since 2007 fall into this category. They existed because of the civil war in Rwanda and the Darfur conflict respectively. By far the greatest part of the UN's interventionism in Africa has been concerned with the humanitarian consequences of deep-rooted conflicts within states. The problems faced by the post-colonial state in Africa have been varied and profound. Although, as we have seen, the new states that emerged after the departure of the European imperialists opted to retain the existing colonial borders, this went only so far in creating conditions for a stable future. The African state sub-system, as we might describe it, was secured by this pragmatic approach but the new states that came to occupy the spaces left by colonial rule were in many cases extremely fragile. Various reasons have been adduced for this. Lack of proper preparation for independence and a consequent absence of necessary administrative skills is one the UN encountered early with the Congo operation. But if the problems of the state in Africa had been a result solely or even mainly of this technical shortcoming, time and properly directed post-independence aid programmes should have remedied them. Inescapably, there have been more profound problems facing many if not all new African states. Where the emphasis is placed among these problems tends to reflect the political perspective of those describing the situation.

Although it may have been the lesser of evils to retain existing territorial frontiers, it has often been argued that these have perpetuated mismatches between ethnicity and territorial statehood. Rival ethnic and/or regional groupings have been placed uncomfortably inside state frontiers and often violent competition between them for political control has followed. The Hutu–Tutsi relationship in Rwanda (and Burundi as well) would be an obvious example. A variation of this involved the distribution of one ethnic group across the borders of more than one state, creating a level of instability in each of them. The Bakongo people spread between southern Congo and northern Angola or the Jola who populate the frontier areas of Senegal, Gambia and Guinea-Bissau would be two of many examples of this.

Such problems are often blamed on the imperialists' 'straight lines on maps' approach during the scramble for Africa in the late nineteenth century. In this view, the European imperial powers sought first and foremost land and resources in competition with each other. Africa was therefore divided crudely and arbitrarily without any regard for the ethnic identity of the peoples whose land and resources were being seized. Those peoples were then left to suffer the inevitable political consequences when the imperialists departed. This is an apparently compelling argument but it must be treated with caution. It may be true that the interests, long or short term, of local populations were not uppermost in the minds of imperial planners, whatever 'civilising mission' rhetoric they may have used. But sheer practicality meant that few of Africa's colonial frontiers were in reality delimited by straight lines on the map, other than across barely populated deserts. There was a certain human logic to most colonial borders because they were usually determined by geographical features – large rivers, mountain ranges – that had already shaped the ethnic distribution of local populations. The imperial arrogance underlying colonial frontier agreements therefore can only be one element in a larger story.

Another explanation for the fragility of the African state and the conflicts thus engendered, one which refuses to 'blame the victim', – relates to neo-colonialism. The independence of most African states, according to this position, amounted to no more than 'flag decolonisation'. There may have been a change in the visible symbols and institutional structures of the post-colonies, but the exploitation of the new countries by their former colonial masters and later by multinational companies continued. The economic objectives of imperialism – export markets, cheap labour, raw materials – continue to be pursued as before, but without the expensive encumbrance of formal colonial rule. Decolonisation, in other words, is simply the starting point of neo-colonisation. Relative underdevelopment, a condition for successful neo-colonial exploitation, not only persists, but in Africa it worsened after independence. The new, supposedly independent state, these dependency (or world system) theories suggest, now becomes controlled by a national government. But this is both weak – because of its dependence on the support of the foreign neo-colonialists – and increasingly violent, as it attempts to suppress popular anger at the deepening deprivation and widening inequality between the governing elite (which acts on behalf of the neo-colonialists) and the impoverished masses.[5]

There are other critiques of the African state and explanations of its weakness and propensity to conflict which are less forgiving of (or just more attentive to) inherently local factors. African political culture has been described in some theoretical constructions as 'neo-patrimonial'. The underlying structures of politics, it is argued, leaves African states ill-adapted to the prevailing system of territorial statehood and militates towards political conflict. In outline, this perspective characterises the pre-colonial Africa states as 'patrimonial'. This was based on the delicate network of relations between patrons (who were effectively the political leaders) and their clients who constituted the mass of the people. These networks were usually based on affective relationships within ethnic or religious groups. Territoriality and fixed political borders had only a secondary role in delimiting the 'nation' in this structure. This was usually a very practical and effective form of social and political organisation. The irruption of European imperialism destroyed these structures, however, replacing them with a centralised, geographically defined colonial state based on the imperialists' own precepts. At independence it was this European model that was adopted by the new national rulers as the only one capable of allowing the new country entry to the broader international state system. But the underlying patrimonial culture had not in fact been destroyed by imperialism; it had merely been suppressed at the formal political level. Patrimonial attitudes and assumptions persisted at the social level and re-emerged to shape the new, post-independence political culture. The structural setting was fundamentally different now, however, as the outward forms of politics were based on the centralised territorial state. Thus patrimonialism becomes neo-patrimonialism.

The dynamics here are in fact similar to the contending dependency theory view of the mutation of colonialism into neo-colonialism. Both perspectives claim that formal institutions change while underlying dynamics remain in place. In the neo-patrimonial view, African states are now, at one level, 'modern' entities, based on the inclusion of the entire national population in the obligations and benefits of citizenship. But the politics that drove these new states, whatever its outward form, was a politics of patrimonialism in which the resources of the state were disbursed by patrons to their selected (usually ethnically or regionally defined) clients to the exclusion of other groups. Conflict between these groups – locked together in the new territorial state – was inevitable and the state was weakened by the very strategies (of dispensing patrimony) that it deployed to secure its position.[6]

None of these contending viewpoints provides a wholly comprehensive explanation of the weakness of African states and the consequent propensity for conflict and violence within them. All probably
have some contribution to make to an overall understanding. What is
less open to debate is the plain fact that in the post-independence decades,
the African state has been particularly vulnerable to failure and collapse
in comparison with states in other regions of the world. For a number
of reasons, by the 1990s this vulnerability had reached a particularly
critical point and its consequences made the need for external humanitarian intervention obvious. By the last decade of the twentieth century
most African countries had existed as independent states for about thirty
years. The process of state failure in vulnerable countries was consequently well advanced. Three decades after independence too, post-
colonial political and security relationships with former imperial powers,
whether Britain, France, Belgium or Portugal, had become less close

Location	Duration	Location	Duration
Western Sahara	1991–present	Central African Republic	1998–2000
Angola (3 operations)	1991–9	DR Congo	1999–present
Mozambique	1992–4	Ethiopia–Eritrea	2000–8
Somalia (2 operations)	1992–5	Côte d'Ivoire	2004–present
Liberia (2 operations)	1993–present	Burundi	2004–6
Uganda–Rwanda	1993–4	Sudan	2005–present
Rwanda	1993–6	Central African Republic–Chad	2007–present
Libya–Chad	1994	Darfur (Sudan)	2007–present
Sierra Leone (2 operations)	1998–present		

Table 4.1 UN military operations mandated for Africa since 1990

in many parts of Africa. A residual prop to the state was thus being gradually removed. Finally, in Africa as elsewhere, the end of the cold war brought to an end superpower interest in maintaining favoured states in their respective spheres of interest. The western powers freed themselves from their often uncomfortable supportive relationships with the regimes in Somalia and Zaire, for example, while Soviet support was no longer available to such regimes as those in Ethiopia and the Afro-Marxist states of Portuguese-speaking Africa. The final result of all of these forces of change was something of a 'perfect storm' leaving humanitarian crisis in its wake. Only the United Nations was apparently willing and able to intervene to deal with it.

The range and number of interventions in Africa by the United Nations during this period would make any attempt at a mission-by-mission examination unhelpfully superficial. It is more useful to focus on three operations which have attracted particular discussion and reveal broader truths about UN interventionism in general.

The first of these in chronological terms was the fraught involvement in Somalia between 1992 and 1995. The Somalia debacle, for that in any view is what it was, points up a number of issues which resonate with the larger discussion of humanitarian intervention. The involvement in Somalia, as already seen, was affected by the so-called CNN effect as a determinant of policy. Somalia also presented special problems for the United Nations in its relationship with the United States in what developed into an impossibly complex and uncomfortable joint undertaking between Washington and the organisation. The intervention also brought home, just as the Congo had three decades earlier, the danger of slippage (or 'mission creep') from impartial humanitarian exercise to coercive enforcement.

In the wake of Somalia, before even the last international troops had slipped away from Mogadishu, the UN was faced with genocide in Rwanda. The larger issues here include the role of the UN in the implementation of agreements regarding which it has virtually no role in negotiating and which appear to have only limited prospects of success. The question of mission creep also became pressing in Rwanda, but in a rather different way from Somalia. While the shift towards enforcement in Somalia was largely determined by the interveners themselves, the sudden horrific alteration in the terms of the Rwanda conflict with the start of the genocide appeared to demand a new type of intervention which was not forthcoming. Here the issue of the balance of authority (and culpability) between the UN as an institution and its controlling state members comes into harsh relief.

The final intervention in focus is that in Darfur. Here the pressing issues are ones of multi-agency intervention as in Somalia and the position of the individual members of the security council as in Rwanda, but cast in different terms. In Darfur the UN's partner in intervention is not a superpower as it was in Somalia, but a regional organisation – the African Union – which has lesser political and material resources than even the United Nations. In Darfur as in Rwanda the terms of the intervention are dependent on the politics of the security council. While in Rwanda the permanent members were more or less at one in their resistance to radical action, in Darfur the problem is one of establishing a fundamental unity among those five powers despite the countervailing pressures of their national foreign policies.

Somalia

The 1960s was the decade of African decolonisation. In 1960 alone fifteen new African states emerged. Two, which were to pose some of the greatest challenges to the UN's capacity for humanitarian intervention, became independent on the same day. On 1 July 1960 both the former Belgian Congo and Somalia entered the international system as sovereign states. While United Nations soldiers were deployed across the Congo within weeks, it would be another thirty-two years before blue-beret troops arrived in Somalia to confront a catastrophic humanitarian crisis.

Somalia had experienced a complex colonial history prior to 1960. The new state was composed of two former colonies: British Somaliland in the north and the larger Italian Somaliland in the south. Each part served a distinct role for its respective colonial power. Britain was primarily interested in Somaliland not as an 'African' territory *per se* but as part of possessions around the Arabian Gulf which had strategic importance to the sea route to India. For Italy, in contrast, Somaliland helped provide its credentials as an African imperial power, an important marker of prestige for a relative newcomer to European diplomacy. Following Italy's seizure of Abyssinia (Ethiopia) in 1935, the Fascist regime incorporated Somaliland in a new entity, Italian East Africa, which brought together Somalia, Abyssinia and Eritrea. Having ejected Britain from the northern territory during the second world war, Italy was then defeated in the war and the whole of what would become modern-day Somalia came under British control. After the war the former Italian part became a United Nations Trusteeship, but in a departure from the mandate process that had followed the first world war, Italy itself was appointed as the Trustee power. Throughout the 1950s London and Rome worked along with the UN Trusteeship Council to prepare for a unified independent Somalia.

Somalia's first years as an independent state were relatively success-ful. Although largely bereft of either agricultural or mineral resources, the country occupied (as its original British colonisers were very aware) an important strategic position in the Horn of Africa looking across the Arabian Gulf and the Indian Ocean. As such it had both military and commercial importance. It also had a relatively highly educated population in sub-Saharan African terms. By the end of the 1960s, however, tensions which had always been close to the surface began to challenge the political bases on which the unified state had been built. Following a period of political confusion, the military seized power in 1969 and General Muhammad Siad Barre declared himself president. Although Siad Barre's rule was to last for more than two decades, its longevity was not a product of its success or stability. The country remained fragmented along clan lines throughout his period in office. But Somalia's geostrategic position – and Siad Barre's skilful diplomatic manipulation of it – kept him in power. Initially reflecting the zeitgeist of the 1970s in African politics, he adopted radical socia-list rhetoric and leant diplomatically towards the Soviet Union. But after a disastrous war against Marxist-oriented Ethiopia in 1977, he switched allegiance to the west. Happy to win such a strategically important asset but suspicious of Siad Barre's history, the United States sustained him in power only for as long as his currency remained high. At the end of the cold war, of course, it became drastically devalued. Siad Barre was consequently cut adrift and factional chaos, which had been held at bay while Somalia remained important to the west, engulfed the country. At the beginning of 1991 Siad Barre was forced to flee the capital Mogadishu and a few months later went into exile abroad. Simultaneously, the northern part of the country which had originally formed British Somaliland seceded, declaring itself the Re-public of Somaliland.

The humanitarian impact of the conflict between clan factions was dreadful. Somalia's food security was precarious even at the best of times. But not only were the production and transportation of supplies now devastated by the fighting, the fighters themselves quickly adopted starvation as a tactic, controlling supplies and deliveries according to their own military calculations. The CNN effect now came into full play and international pressure mounted for 'something to be done'. The intervention that followed, which ended (or, more

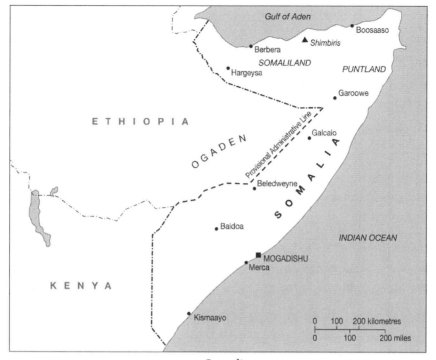

Somalia

accurately, petered out) in 1995, has come to be regarded as a major failure for humanitarian action and a particularly inglorious one for the UN even in a continent where the majority of its ventures have had at best limited success.

At the outset there is perhaps a fundamental question to be posed. That is, simply, could any intervention made on any terms by any agency have been anything other than a failure? Oddly, but probably understandably, this is a question which usually goes unasked in relation to humanitarian interventions. At risk of over-generalisation, humanitarian intervention is at root an optimistic project and those who advocate it are generally optimists. From this perspective all problems are generally assumed to have a solution. All conflicts can be resolved and all suffering ameliorated if only the correct approaches are proposed, adopted and pursued. The corollary of this, of course, is that failure is due to error, and blame is then usually assigned. There is, though, a less optimistic perspective which admits the possibility that some conflicts with massive humanitarian consequences are simply immune to successful intervention, however well-conceived and executed that intervention might be. Somalia in the early 1990s may well have fallen into this category. But having acknowledged this, it is possible to identify some key points of tension in the UN's engagement with Somalia. These are almost entirely to be found in relations either within the United Nations itself or between the United Nations and its partners in the intervention. The cumulative result of failures in these relationships was to contribute to the larger failure of intervention. This has had enduring consequences for Somalia, the region in which it is located and the wider international system.

The United Nations Operation in Somalia was agreed in principle by the security council in April 1992, though substantial forces did not arrive on the ground until mid-September.[7] The long periods between the unfolding of the humanitarian crisis in 1991 and the security council's consideration of a security force, and then between commitment and deployment, were indicative of a general wariness on the part of the council and potential contributor states. A major cause for concern was the absence of a host state which, according to the venerable rules of UN intervention, should consent to the undertaking. The traditional precept of the use of force only in self-defence was another important issue. While UN soldiers might not necessarily be called on to employ enforcement tactics, the threshold for self-defence looked as though it might be low in Somalia amidst the armed chaos of the factional conflict.

The genesis of the operation took place across the period in office of two secretaries-general: Javier Pérez de Cuéllar and Boutros Boutros-Ghali (who took over at the beginning of 1992). Pérez de Cuéllar had concentrated on the non-military possibilities of improving and rationalising food distribution but, intentionally or not, appeared to disregard the tactical uses of starvation by the armed factions. Boutros-Ghali for his part seemed to have a clearer understanding of the necessarily military nature of the problem but was faced with the caution of the security council. In his (admittedly self-serving) memoir of his period in office, he recalled trying to 'goad the security council into a sense of urgency. I contrasted their indifference to the horrors of the Horn of Africa with their preoccupation with the "rich man's war" in the former Yugoslavia'.[8] In the meantime he appointed the energetic Algerian diplomat Mohamad Sahnoun as his special representative. (This was the Sahnoun who was later co-chair of the Canadian initiative on 'responsibility to protect' discussed in the previous chapter.) Sahnoun immediately set about developing a plan for the rational distribution of food aid throughout the country under UN protection. Both these relationships of Boutros-Ghali – with the security council and with his own man Sahnoun – would eventually sour and in their different ways would point up some inherent difficulties in the management of humanitarian intervention.

The first phase of the intervention was not impressive. As feared, the factions were unwilling to surrender the weapon of hunger to the UN, and Sahnoun's carefully constructed plans for a nation-wide aid operation could not be implemented. Even in Mogadishu UNOSOM troops were harassed and humiliated by the two major rival factions: Ali Mahdi Mohammed's United Somali Congress (USC) and Mohamed Farah Aideed's breakaway group, the Somali National Alliance (SNA). It soon became unclear exactly what role the UN force was performing in the country.

Then, in October 1992 barely a month after the deployment of UNOSOM, Sahnoun resigned. He did so citing a lack of drive on the part of UN agencies on the ground and unrealistic expectations from New York. But at the root of his departure was a fundamental difference with Boutros-Ghali. This was over the extent to which a humanitarian intervention should seek accommodation with those generating the crisis in the first place. Sahnoun, understandably anxious to see practical results, was accused of becoming too close to the warlords themselves. In the secretary-general's view, although Sahnoun had managed to get food delivered, it was at too high a cost. According to Boutros-Ghali, the 'operation had fallen victim to a Somali protection racket'.[9] It is a dilemma that goes far beyond Somalia. Similar compromises have to be made in virtually all humanitarian interventions, and conflicts are inevitable over where the line of acceptability is to be drawn.

Sahnoun's resignation revealed another peculiar aspect of the management process of humanitarian intervention by the United Nations. Like other individuals appointed to very senior roles on a temporary and ad hoc basis within the UN system, he remained very much his own man. Men and women who take on these positions are usually public figures in their own right and only tenuously 'employees' of the UN. When their own, often strongly held, views conflict with those of the secretary-general or the security council they are much less likely to bite their tongues and continue than either their counterparts in national bureaucracies or permanent career members of the UN secretariat. This dispersal of UN authority has been a characteristic of other operations. Hammarskjöld's death in 1961 followed directly from controversial actions on the ground taken by his representative in Katanga, the Irish diplomat and public intellectual Conor Cruise O'Brien.[10] More recently, the political direction of the UN operation in Angola had been shaped, for better or worse, by the personal policies of Boutros-Ghali's special representative there, the former Malian foreign minister Alioune Blondin Beye.

Meanwhile in Somalia the CNN effect continued, if anything intensified by the apparent failure of UNOSOM. The UN proved unable to respond effectively to this glare of mostly bad publicity. Boutros-Ghali's proposal was for UN legitimisation of action by non-UN forces. The United States duly responded. The media impact contributed, though to what extent is contested, to the decision by the administration of President George H. W. Bush (which was then in its twilight months) to commit America to intervention. American motivations in this have been widely discussed. Some of the more conspiratorial explanations, such as the preparation of a deliberately poisoned chalice to be handed to the incoming Clinton administration, can probably be discounted. But there was certainly a range of elements in play. One factor was probably an instinctive assertion of America's status as the 'last superpower standing' along with a need to show that the US was ready to accept the global responsibilities implicit in this role. Another may well have been Bush's concern with his own political legacy. Having coined the expression 'new world order', he had gone on to demonstrate one aspect of it in Operation Desert Storm in the Gulf at the beginning of 1991. Somalia offered an opportunity for him to project his power in a kinder, more obviously humanitarian context in Operation Restore Hope, as it was to be called. Yet the CNN effect cannot be discounted. Lawrence Eagleburger, Bush's assistant Secretary of State at the time, later asserted that, 'quite frankly, television had a great deal to do with President Bush's decision to go in the first place; and I will tell you equally frankly, I was one of those two or three that was strongly recommending he do it and it was very much because of the television pictures of the starving kids, substantial pressures from the Congress . . . came from the same source . . .' Tellingly, Eagleburger went on speak of his 'honest belief that we could do this, do something good at not too great a cost. Certainly without any great danger of body bags coming home'.[11] Things were not to turn out that way.

Viewed post-September 2001, post-war on terror, post-Iraq invasion, the notion of an American military enforcement operation in a Muslim country would seem an unlikely venture to be authorised by the United Nations. In the early 1990s, however, there were few qualms either within the security council or UN bureaucracy. Rather there was a profound sense of relief that attention would now shift from the organisation's inability to make an effective humanitarian intervention on its own behalf. Accordingly, armed with authority under chapter VII of the charter to employ 'all necessary means' to ensure food distribution, the Unified Task Force (UNITAF) began Operation Restore Hope, on the seafront of Mogadishu at dawn on 9 December 1992.[12]

In its first phase Operation Restore Hope, which would eventually draw on a force of 37,000, had some real success. Aid distribution centres were established throughout the country protected by UNITAF personnel. Meanwhile, UNOSOM was not wholly supplanted by the US force and maintained a presence in Mogadishu. Encouraged by the extent of the American commitment, more states began to offer contributions when the time-limited UNITAF project ended and military responsibility passed back to the UN itself. There was, however, a basic flaw in the strategic basis of the UNITAF venture. In view of its apparent initial success, this was not fully comprehended at the time and would prove critical to the development of the situation. As with all such policy outcomes it is misleading to speak simply of the 'American decision' to take the lead role in Somalia. The final arrangement was arrived at only after some fierce bureaucratic politics had been played out within the US administration. The interventionist line was pursued most forcefully by the White House and the State Department. The Department of Defense, however, responsible for the military personnel who would pursue Operation Restore Hope, was much more wary of the commitment. Consequently, firm limits were placed on the degree to which UNITAF would actually engage the armed factions in pursuing the security council's 'all necessary means'.

Perhaps paradoxically, when it came to the use of force the US military was initially determined to conduct its intervention in the framework of traditional peacekeeping rather than as an enforcement operation. Force would be restricted to self-defence, narrowly defined. Most importantly, US forces would not seek to disarm and control the factions responsible for the crisis. In retrospect this may have been a catastrophic lost opportunity for Somalia. The strategy favoured by UNITAF's military planners in Washington could be described as a much diluted version of the 'shock and awe' which, a decade later, was supposed to ensure the occupation of Iraq without protracted fighting. Those in Somalia minded to oppose UNITAF would be dissuaded just by the knowledge of the overwhelming power at the disposal of the Americans. The dramatic – and tactically pointless – American 'invasion' of Mogadishu at the outset of Operation Restore Hope was partly an attempt to extract the best possible return from the CNN effect at home. But it was also designed to intimidate by demonstration. Fatally, though, it was based on a miscalculation of Somali circumstances. Initially, for sure, the visible force of the American presence had an effect. But the degree of determination underlying that presence was increasingly probed by the militia factions, particularly the most militarily formidable of these, Aideed's SNA.

One model for a productive relationship in humanitarian intervention between the United Nations and partners legitimised by it might be one in which the latter perform a surgical act of military enforcement to clear the way for a UN operation (or the resumption of one) which could engage with the underlying problem more effectively in a more secure environment. This may well have been the ambition of Boutros-Ghali for UNITAF, but it was not one shared by the Americans themselves. As a result, when the renewed UN effort got underway in the form of UNOSOM-II in May 1993, the environment had not been transformed and the central obstacles to the humanitarian intervention remained. Principal among these was the continued activity of heavily armed militias. Now it fell to the new UN force to attempt a dangerous but essential act of disarmament under the terms of a revised security council mandate agreed in March 1993, though with considerably fewer soldiers than UNITAF had deployed.[12]

The situation was complicated by the fact that the new phase of the intervention did not follow a clean break with the American-led operation. Instead there was an impossibly tangled set of inter-force relationships and lines of command. The United States provided a substantial proportion – some 4,000 soldiers – of the new UN force. Although led by a Turkish general, this had an American second in command. Moreover, the secretary-general's own representative (the post originally held by Mohamad Sahnoun) was now a retired US Navy admiral, Jonathon Howe. He had apparently been appointed by Boutros-Ghali at Washington's request. More concerning though for those who wished to see the humanitarian intervention returned to full UN control, a parallel American force remained which was not organically linked to UNOSOM-II. This was the 17,000-strong US Joint Task Force in Somalia.

This convoluted and opaque organisation would have made heavy weather of managing a complex humanitarian intervention even in a favourable security environment. Now, though, it was required to function amidst a rapidly deteriorating situation. Paradoxically but not untypically, this deterioration at the military level was partly driven by the promise of progress on the political plane. During March 1993, as UNOSOM-II was being prepared, talks in neighbouring Ethiopia between some fifteen Somali factions seemed to offer the prospect of a coalition government which might be capable of reconstituting the Somali state. Inevitably, this provoked attempts by the stronger factions to create facts on the ground ahead of any settlement. Prominent among those engaged in this tactic was Aideed's SNA. As one of the more powerful faction leaders, potentially he had more to lose than others in any agreed settlement. Individuals in this position are manoeuvred into the role of enemy of the intervention forces which have a responsibility to facilitate the political process underway. The basic principle of humanitarian intervention that 'enemies' should not exist can simply fall away in such circumstances.

This threatening situation, familiar later in a range of interventions from Liberia to Rwanda, was made worse by UNOSOM-II's initial attempts to fulfil its mandate to disarm the factions. At the beginning of June sporadic fighting began between UN troops and Aideed's militia around Mogadishu airport caused high losses on both sides. A particularly robust security council resolution was passed in the wake of this fighting permitting 'all necessary measures against those responsible'.[13] A military campaign against Aideed now began, and the conditions for the endgame of the Somali intervention were put in place. In this setting the humanitarian purposes of the intervention suffered badly. For one thing, Aideed's militia intensified its armed obstruction of food distribution. But perhaps more depressingly, humanitarianism was increasingly taking second place in the priorities of UNOSOM to the military defeat of the SNA and the capture of Aideed himself. A distinct mission creep had begun which was changing the objective of the entire Somalia project. While the disarming of the militias had probably always been a basic precondition for the success of the humanitarian intervention, it was not undertaken when it had a reasonable prospect of success at the outset of the UNITAF phase. Now a combination of political and military miscalculation in pursuing this aim was combining to bring the intervention to an end.

The final act came in October 1993 when an anti-Aideed action went dramatically wrong. The operation was not in fact undertaken by UN personnel but by US special forces operating directly on orders from their Florida headquarters. The encounter, fictionalised in Ridley Scott's 2001 film *Blackhawk Down*, began with a helicopter attack on the SNA's south Mogadishu heartland and ended with shocking images of American bodies being abused by enraged Somalis. These became the defining images of the conflict. The deaths of perhaps more than 1,000 mostly civilian Somalis in the action was little referred to in the west. The CNN effect giveth, and the CNN effect taketh away. The Clinton administration in Washington, which was already becoming anxious about the direction of the Somali venture, immediately announced that all American personnel would be out of the country by the following March. A UN presence stripped of its American core would have been meaningless in the prevailing conditions and any-way, the other main western contributors, Italy, France, and Belgium, quickly gave notice of their own intention to withdraw from the UN force. UNOSOM-II accordingly was drawn down completely in March 1995, a year after the American departure, though in truth its presence had become largely meaningless long before this.

The root causes of the Somalia debacle are easily enough listed. But the further they are unpacked, the less certain is the easy assignment of blame and the less confidence there can be that the lessons have been learned and there will be no repetition. The nature of the relation-ships among key players – both within the UN itself and between the UN and other powerful actors – were certainly far from perfect. Secretary-general Boutros-Ghali himself was clearly not the most emollient of individuals. Having a considerable sense of his own importance, highly developed even by the standards of his post, he would not easily defer to others. But no secretary-general could have managed the complex range of relations involved in Somalia with any ease. Boutros-Ghali was required to work constructively, for example, with an equally self-certain special representative in the person of Mohamad Sahnoun. Unconstrained by a fixed place in a professional hierarchy, Sahnoun had no reason to defer to higher powers. The secretary-general also had to work closely with two separate and very different American administrations with their own domestic and foreign policy agendas. Finally, the local protagonists on the ground in Somalia were by their number and nature extremely difficult interlocutors. Far from representing even the shadow of an established state, the militia leaders operated in a largely anarchic environment driven as much by the determination to deny political power to others as to acquire it for themselves.

There was perhaps one clear lesson to be learned in relation to the actors in the Somalia venture. During the cold war one of the defining characteristics of UN military intervention was the absence of contin-gents from big powers in the frontline. The classic peacekeeper was the so-called 'middle power'. This term had two distinct but complemen-tary connotations. One was ideological, and reflected an obvious concern in a polarised system. As far as possible the peacekeeping state should occupy the middle ground between the poles. The second was to do with capabilities. The presence of big powers, however well-intentioned, could be threatening to local protagonists. At the same time, very small powers might not be equipped to carry out the mandate of the intervention. The end of the cold war seemed to render at least the first of these prohibitions against big-power involvement irrelevant. The world was no longer polarised, so the idea of an ideological middle ground had no meaning. For this reason there appeared to be no essential political difference between American leadership of Operation Desert Storm in the Gulf in 1991 and its pursuit of Operation Restore Hope in Somalia in 1993. This was not so, however. While the overwhelming war-fighting capacity of the United States was essential to the success of the UN-authorised Gulf conflict, American power in Somalia could easily be presented as neo-colonialist bullying, whatever legitimacy the UN mandate may have bestowed on it. This became an important element of Aideed's propaganda against UNITAF and then UNOSOM-II. Big, powerful states remained, therefore, far from ideal participants in UN humanitarian interventions, cold war or no cold war. Subsequent interventions in which the United States took part – notably in Kosovo in 1999 – lay outside of the organisational framework of the United Nations.

The issue of operational objectives and the ambitions of the Somalia intervention is also a highly complex consideration. The apparent selection of Aideed and the SNA as the 'enemy' for UNITAF and UNOSOM-II has been adduced as a major cause of the failure of the operation. Humanitarian intervention, the argument runs, is not about the military defeat of enemies but about the amelioration of suffering. There are some important points to be considered here, however. It was clear to many from the outset that effective humanitarian action in Somalia, or anywhere else, could only be achieved in an appropriate security setting. Specifically, the factional militias – which were after all responsible for the humanitarian crisis – could not be allowed simply to continue with their violence. Whether their forcible disarmament was framed as a separate preliminary operation, or as the first phase of the humanitarian intervention itself, is really a matter of semantics: it should have been done. The failure in Somalia was firstly that this was not done at the appropriate time and secondly that it was later attempted at an inappropriate time. The early failure was largely due to American political considerations and tactical assumptions about what could be achieved by military demonstration rather than actual combat. When the UN did attempt to confront the armed factions militarily, the prospects of success had already dwindled. But as with so much else, retrospect clarifies everything here. The judgements made at the time were logically formulated within a spectrum of restraints, both national and international, which were relevant to the moment.

It is perhaps appropriate to return to the question posed at the outset of this discussion of what was by any measure a failure of humanitarian intervention: simply, was success actually possible, whatever the identity of those who intervened and whatever techniques they adopted? Given the complexity and virulence of the conflict dynamics in Somalia in the early 1990s, it is difficult to be confident that it was.

What was certain, however, was that the experience of Somalia would have an immediate effect on the future of humanitarian intervention by the United Nations. This became clear just weeks after the last American soldiers withdrew from Mogadishu when in another part of sub-Saharan Africa one of the most dreadful spasms of violence of the twentieth century took place.

Rwanda

Two days after the deaths of the eighteen American special forces troops in Somalia in the *Blackhawk Down* incident, the security council approved the creation of the United Nations Assistance Mission to Rwanda (UNAMIR). Not only did the gruesome public deaths of US soldiers in south Mogadishu in October 1993 signal the end of the Somali operation, but it would also have a profound, many would say fatal, effect on the UN's efforts, or lack of them, amidst the Rwandan genocide of the following year.

The background to the horror of 1994 in Rwanda – in which some 800,000 people died – was not an unfamiliar one in post-colonial Africa. It derived from long-standing and deeply embedded inter-ethnic relationships which predated the colonial incursion. The imperialist powers, however, sought to solidify and harness those divisions in their own interest and had created, at the point of independence, a set of social and political conditions which were simply unsustainable. The historical origins of the Hutu–Tutsi hostility which underlay the events of 1994 are somewhat opaque. It is likely that sometime around the fifteenth century Tutsi colonists moved into central Africa from the north-east, probably from the Horn of Africa. They established an ascendency over the Hutu, the indigenous Bantu population, across a large part of the Great Lakes region including present-day Rwanda, Burundi and parts of the east of the Democratic Republic of Congo. In the pre-colonial period the relationship between the cattle-owning

Tutsi and the agriculturalist Hutu appears to have been mainly peaceful and cooperative and involved a considerable degree of inter-marriage. This changed with the arrival of German colonisers during the late-nineteenth-century European scramble for Africa. The new colonial state co-opted the bi-ethnic social structure for their own administrative ends. In doing so they created a new power dynamic which consolidated and then exacerbated the unequal relationship between Tutsi and Hutu, who in Rwanda comprised about 15 and 85 per cent of the indigenous population respectively. It was in essence a politics of divide and rule by which Tutsis were groomed as a colonial middle class with favoured access to employment in the administration and those professions open to Africans. The Hutu became by default a second-class ethnicity.

After the first world war Rwanda and Burundi (or 'Ruanda-Urundi' as the imperial powers called them at the time) became League of Nations mandates, along with Germany's other territories in East, West and Southwest Africa. The mandatory power in the case of Rwanda (and Burundi) was Belgium, selected because of its imperial control over neighbouring Congo. The Belgians continued the practice established by the Germans of favouring the Tutsi over the Hutu as the most efficient means of imposing their authority. This was not an efficient means of preparing the country for independence, however. In Rwanda as elsewhere in Africa, decolonisation was seen, initially at any rate, as prefiguring a new state based on legislative democracy. For the Hutus, therefore, it appeared that their liberation, not just from European imperialism but also from domination by the Tutsi minority, had finally arrived. The run-up to independence saw widespread anti-Tutsi violence and the preparatory election held under Belgian super-vision in September 1961 confirmed the political dominance of Hutu-based parties.[14]

The decades following independence in 1962 were marked by periodic spasms of inter-ethnic violence. Much of the Tutsi political class had gone into exile in neighbouring Uganda as the Belgians withdrew. There they organized themselves into a more or less cohesive external opposition. The accident of Uganda's own location and colonial history grafted a further dimension onto Rwanda's conflict dynamic: the exiled Tutsis perforce became Anglophone, in contrast to the Hutu who now dominated their Francophone country of birth. This politico-linguistic division has had implications not just for Rwanda but across Africa.

The effectiveness of the Tutsi movement in Uganda grew over the coming years, particularly under the relatively stable presidency of Yoweri Musaveni who came to power there in 1986. Constituting

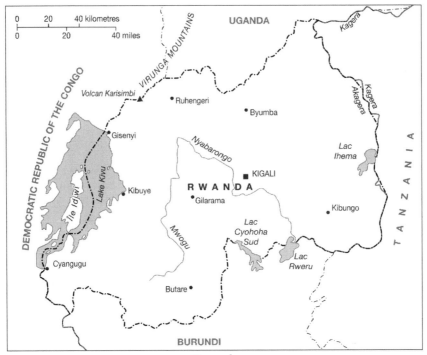

Rwanda

themselves into the Rwandan Patriotic Front (RPF), the Tutsis became a formidable political and military force. By 1990 the RPF was strong enough to challenge the Hutu regime and its forces crossed the border and engaged the Rwandan army in a civil war. So successful was the initial thrust of the RPF that the survival of the Hutu government of President Juvénal Habyarimana was only secured by the rapid supply of arms and equipment from France and Belgium. The RPF military campaign continued throughout 1992 and into 1993 at which point external political pressure on Habyarimana from the Organization of African Unity (the predecessor of the African Union) and in particular from Rwanda's neighbour Tanzania led to peace talks. These were held in the northern Tanzanian town of Arusha where an agreement was signed in August 1994.

Up to this point the United Nations, while urging on the peace process from the sidelines, had made no direct contribution to the details of the settlement. Nevertheless, the Arusha agreement, even in the absence of this input, was predicated on the UN assuming a major role in the implementation of the settlement. In retrospect, this should have set alarm bells ringing in New York. The previous year Angola had tumbled back into full-scale civil war when the Bicesse process collapsed. The Bicesse agreement of 1991 (named after the Portuguese town in which it was signed) had been overseen by the United States, the Soviet Union and Portugal. It committed the sides in the Angolan civil war – the MPLA government and the rebel UNITA movement – to a ceasefire, progressive demobilisation of forces and open elections. Although the process had been driven on by the triumvirate of external powers, the United Nations had played no direct role in the eventual agreement. This was soon exposed as ill-thought out and badly constructed. Nevertheless, the agreement simply took for granted that the UN would oversee and police the process. UNAVEM had just successfully supervised the withdrawal of Cuban forces from Angola as part of the linked agreement for Namibian independence. It is possible that there was an expectation among UN planners and security council members alike that the latest engagement would be similarly straightforward. There is perhaps a hint of this in the naming of the new operation as 'UNAVEM-II'. But it was not to be, and when UNITA, facing defeat in 1992 in the elections which were central to the Bicesse process, simply abandoned its undertakings and returned to war, the inadequately manned and mandated UN force was incapable of shaping developments in any significant way.[15] Now, only a short time later, the UN was faced with a similar situation in Rwanda. The danger of accepting responsibility for a military intervention according to a script which it had no role in writing should by now have been clear.

It would of course have been politically (and morally) difficult for the United Nations simply to have refused to participate in the *fait accompli* that the Rwandan factions presented to it in the form of the Arusha settlement. In this sense the UN was in a way a hostage to both Rwandan and international expectations. The settlement committed the United Nations to the provision of what was described originally as a Neutral International Force. This would assist local forces in maintaining order throughout the country and safeguard the distribution of humanitarian aid. These were both considerable 'asks' of the UN. The conditions of post-civil war society in Rwanda were as yet unclear and therefore so was the extent of the challenge in maintaining order. The difficulties – indeed impossibility – of guaranteeing aid delivery in an unstable and highly politicised environment had already been exposed in Somalia (and beyond Africa in Bosnia as well). But these were among the less onerous tasks previsioned for the force. It would also be responsible for disarming civilians, challenging armed groups, seeking out arms caches, and undertaking demining operations.

This would require, the Rwandan parties insouciantly suggested, a force of some 4,200. That would almost certainly have been inadequate for the tasks expected of it.[16]

Beyond these political and operational difficulties, practicalities determined that there was no possibility of the United Nations being able to provide the force that the Rwandan parties sought at this time anyway. The UN was already committed to an extensive – and expensive – series of military interventions elsewhere in Africa, the most burdensome being in Somalia, Angola and Mozambique. Further afield, huge undertakings were underway in the rapidly disintegrating Yugoslavia and in Cambodia. The cost of the military interventions at this time was draining about $US3 billion from the UN budget annually.

Boutros-Ghali therefore proposed to the security council a force of just over 2,500. But, with the trauma of Somalia still recent, even this relatively small presence would be deployed only gradually as the success of the Arusha process proved itself stage-by-stage.[17] This approach reflected a very understandable caution on the part of UN military and political planners. In a sense, however, it was counter-productive. One reading of situations such as that in Rwanda after the Arusha agreement is that any intervention should be as visible and assertive as possible in order to accelerate the momentum for change. The gradualism imposed by the UN on a commitment that would be sparse even when up to full numbers may actually have contributed to the unravelling of the peace process. Two points must be made here, however. Firstly, the weaknesses in the agreement itself and the lack of real enthusiasm for it on both sides probably ensured this unravelling anyway. Secondly, even had the UN wished to send a powerful early message in Rwanda, it would probably have been prevented from doing so by the general pressures on its resources in 1993.

Who, for example, was to provide the necessary contingents? Seventy United Nations members were already contributing some 70,000 military and police personnel to UN operations in 1993. In the event, and only after some effort, Boutros-Ghali managed to persuade Belgium, Ghana and Bangladesh to provide 1,400 troops between them. Belgium was prevailed on to participate on the obvious grounds of its historical relationship with Rwanda. This, though, complicated relations with the RPF, which regarded the former colonial master as compromised by its previous special relationship with the Hutu government. The Ghanaian and Bangladeshi contributions were problematic in another way. Ghana, as another sub-Saharan African state, was a suitable diplomatic choice. But along with that of Bangladesh its contingent was woefully under-equipped for the mission. This was and remains a general problem for United Nations interventions. Clearly, not all national forces are resourced, trained and experienced to the same level. The relatively modest but adequate and largely comparable military capacities of the traditional middle power peacekeepers of the cold war era was one of their strongest qualifications for the job. By the 1990s, however, there simply were not enough Swedens, Canadas and Irelands to go round.

From the beginning then, the configuration of UNAMIR gave serious cause for concern. The inadequacies of the force were reflected in its security council mandate. Far from the wide-ranging expectations of the Arusha signatories, its responsibilities were to be largely those of a traditional peacekeeping operation. It was not designed at the outset as a multi-functional humanitarian intervention (and could not have performed such a task even if it had been). It was to act as an interpositionary presence between government forces and the RPF and was to monitor their ceasefire. It would not disarm factions by force but would merely oversee 'weapons secure' areas declared as such by the parties themselves.[18] In this it followed the original approach of the intervention in Somalia – which had first of all permitted the continuation of violence and then, when abandoned by the Americans, precipitated the collapse of the entire mission. The abbreviated force in Rwanda began to pursue this restricted mandate in the final weeks of 1993. It was commanded by Brigadier-General Roméo Dallaire of Canada who was transferred from a small UN observer mission already deployed on the Ugandan side of the border. As a French Canadian, Dalaire was, importantly, bilingual in English and French.

The difficulties, ultimately insurmountable, in the implementation of the Arusha agreement were evident from the beginning of the mission. As in Angola, the peace agreement had come about more through external pressure than genuine commitment on the part of the antagonists. Such commitment would have been only the minimum prerequisite for its success, however. Although a considerable body of Hutu political opinion favoured accommodation with the RPF, President Habyarimana himself was only a reluctant participant in the process. Critically, there was a large movement of even less conciliatory 'Hutu power' extremists on his other flank who were utterly opposed to any concessions to the Tutsi whatsoever. This was the recruiting ground for the soon to be notorious *interahamwe* militias which, along with elements of the army and willing civilian helpers, would carry out the coming genocide.

The peculiarity of an agreed peace process to which the signatories were fundamentally hostile had an obvious impact on the position of UNAMIR. The basic condition of consent, central to the traditional notion of non-coercive intervention, was distorted. On one level UNAMIR was welcome as a central part of the agreed peace process. On a more realistic plane, however, it was resented for just that reason. The majority of Hutus involved in the political process, including the president himself, regarded the UN presence as a threat to their interests simply because it was a central part of the Arusha process. The end result of this, after all, was to be a radical curtailment of the hitherto dominant power of the Hutus. On the other side the RPF was sceptical of the capacity of the small and more or less toothless UN presence to deliver the agreed outcomes from Arusha. Having agreed to suspend its own military campaign against the Hutu state, the RPF had leased a great deal to the UN; it was doubtful from the outset of the wisdom of having done so. As far as the principle of consent was concerned, the UN force found itself in the middle of a complex fiction.

In the months leading up to the start of the genocide, during which UNAMIR maintained its limited presence in the capital Kigali, one possible opportunity to divert the march of events arose. The failure to act on this provides an example of the potentially dangerous space between those involved in humanitarian intervention on the ground and their 'managers' in New York. Early attempts by General Dallaire to establish approved rules of engagement which would have permitted his troops to protect civilians under threat were apparently disregarded by the Department of Peacekeeping Operations (DPKO) at UN headquarters. More specifically, in January 1994 one of Dallaire's network of informants within the regime warned him of a plan to assassinate leading Tutsi and moderate Hutu politicians in the ruling Broad Based Transitional Government which had been established by the Arusha agreement in anticipation of a permanent political settlement. The plan also involved the manufacture of an international crisis through attacks on the Belgian UNAMIR contingent.

To pre-empt the conspiracy Dallaire sought permission from the DPKO to lock down the weapons secure area in Kigali. This, however, would have stretched the interpretation of the force's mandate (which was simply to 'supervise' these areas). The decision on this apparently lay with the under-secretary-general in charge of peacekeeping, who was then Kofi Annan. Questions about Annan's action – or inaction – at this time would follow him into the post of secretary-general when he succeeded Boutros-Ghali at the beginning of 1997. Dallaire was instructed simply to make it known as widely as possible that he was aware the conspiracy existed. These difficulties inherent in relations between the field and the centre in UN interventions have already been touched on in respect of Somalia, barely a year previously. Similar problems also had consequences long before, just across the border in the Congo when conflicting New York–field views led to the death of Dag Hammarskjöld. In each of these cases, however, the conflicting views were between independently minded local civilian representatives and UN headquarters (Sahnoun in Somalia and Conor Cruise O'Brien in the Congo). Dallaire was a professional soldier and more inclined to accept orders without demur.[19] The failure of UNAMIR to have any real impact on events, whether for reasons of resources or mandate, simply accelerated its loss of credibility on all sides of the Rwandan conflict. As a result, when the genocide began, the force found itself more easily abused and marginalised than might otherwise have been the case.

The trigger for the convulsion came on 6 April 1994 when an aircraft carrying both President Habyarimana and his Burundian counterpart was shot down as it approached Kigali from Tanzania where the two heads of state had been at a follow-up meeting on the Arusha agreement. Although never conclusively established, the attack was almost certainly the work of Hutu extremists engaged on a larger conspiracy to destroy the peace process. While the RPF has also been accused (most volubly by France as part of a long and bitter dispute with the post-genocide government in Rwanda), it is difficult to see what it could have gained from the attack. In the immediate aftermath, first the army and then the broader Hutu population turned on not only the Tutsis, but also any fellow Hutus considered to be less than absolute in their commitment to radical Hutu power. The fundamental inadequacy of UNAMIR was now cruelly displayed as its meagre numbers and resources were overwhelmed by the violence.

As in Somalia, it was not the 'background' deaths of thousands of local people that had the greatest immediate impact and shaped reactions outside of Africa, but the killing of peacekeepers – in this case ten Belgian soldiers in the first hours of the genocide. The ensuing debate about the UN's responsibilities to Rwanda and its capacity to meet them took place primarily with reference to the national interests of western states rather than the imperatives of humanitarian intervention. Two hard truths were thus highlighted. Firstly, when national interests are clearly at stake, *real politik* will usually trump humanitarian responsibility. Secondly, to speak of 'UN' peacekeeping or 'UN' humanitarian intervention is fundamentally misleading. In times of severe pressure the United Nations is revealed as an inter-governmental organisation rather than an autonomous actor; it quickly disaggregates into the collection of sovereign states that, essentially, it always has been.

In response to the killing of its soldiers, the Belgian government announced the immediate withdrawal of its contingent. More worryingly for those in the UN committed to a meaningful role for UNAMIR, the Belgians, perhaps mindful of the CNN effect on public opinion at home, also called for the abandonment of the UN intervention in its entirety. Publicly, this position was simply an acknowledgement of the total failure of the mission. Politically, though, it was more likely to be a means by which Belgium could spread the opprobrium of having abandoned its commitments when the going got tough. The parallels with the American reaction to the death of its soldiers in Somalia the previous October were plain. So were the larger implications for multilateral interventions. These were certainly not lost on the secretary-general who later dismissed Belgium as having been 'afflicted with the "American syndrome"'.[20]

The memoir in which this taunt was made was part of Boutros-Ghali's payback for what he perceived as Washington's sabotage of the UN's agenda for humanitarian intervention in the mid-1990s or, perhaps more truthfully, just the sabotage of his own prospects for a second term in office. In reality, blame for the security council's reluctance to confront the UN's shortcomings in Rwanda and to act robustly to redeem the situation cannot be laid at the American door alone. The permanent members of the council collectively turned away from Rwanda. Their response provided a depressing but perhaps necessary corrective to those who saw the post-cold war years as a *tabula rasa* on which the UN could prepare a new project for humanitarian intervention. The truth was that, from the perspective of distant governments subject to a range of domestic and diplomatic pressures, mass killings in Central Africa did not have a high policy priority. It has to be acknowledged that in realist terms this was a rational response by the security council members. It was a mode of state behaviour in evidence six decades previously in the response (or lack of one) of the League of Nations to the fate of Manchuria and Abyssinia. What were the national interests of the United States, Russia, China and Britain in Rwanda? They were scant. Only France could be said to have a special relationship with the region, having supported the Hutu government during the early phase of the conflict in pursuit of its policy of influence-building in Francophone Africa. The brutal truth was that Rwanda had minimal diplomatic or, perhaps more importantly, economic significance. Its internal convulsions were shocking and horrifying, but could they justify the national commitments of blood and treasure clearly necessary for any intervention which would have even a prospect of success? This calculation might have been different had the longer-term effects of the crisis on the larger Central African region been clear in the northern spring of 1994. But they were not. The consequence of the spread of the conflict to the Congo, where its impact would eventually prove catastrophic, could not be fully grasped at the time.

The judgments involved were not just narrowly political. Policy was shaped by an interwoven assessment of what was actually possible in military terms. What, practically, could be achieved by a stronger military intervention? There was a common (perhaps racially rather questionable) assumption on the part of those advocating 'decisive' intervention that the arrival of a relatively small force of 'western' troops could quickly put an end to the killings. The *génocidaires* would slink away when confronted with a disciplined and determined foreign military presence and stability would soon be established. This was, of course, the American game plan for Operation Restore Hope in Somalia, and it had signally failed there. But the situation in Rwanda was if anything less promising for such a scenario. The killings were both highly organised and widely dispersed. The genocide was orchestrated by the mass media and took place virtually throughout the small but topographically complex country. The *génocidaires* were well equipped (at least in part by one of the permanent members of the security council, France) and had shown themselves from the beginning ready, willing and able to kill highly trained European troops. The political costs of large-scale intervention in Rwanda, therefore, might have been greatly increased by the failure of that intervention. The UN's inability to act decisively in Rwanda was a major driver behind the 'responsibility to protect' commission seven years later, discussed in the previous chapter. In light of this it is ironic that Rwanda may well have failed the 'prospect of success' precautionary principle set out in its report. It had been no easy task, it will be recalled, for Boutros-Ghali to assemble a viable force when UNAMIR was first established to carry out a largely monitoring role. How much more difficult would it have been to persuade UN member states knowingly to commit their national forces to what would almost certainly be a bloody conflict?

This emerging new realism which was edging aside the rhetoric of a new post-cold war world order was on display at the beginning of May when the Clinton administration adopted Presidential Decision Directive No. 25 (PDD25). Although principally a response to events in Somalia, it had clear implications for UN humanitarian intervention in Rwanda and elsewhere. PDD25 set out a restricted set of criteria for future American support for (and not just participation in) United Nations military operations. If American troops were to be involved, identifiable American interests had to be at stake and there must be a UN command structure acceptable to the United States. More broadly, operations would only be supported if clear and achievable objectives were set out in mandates. Proper financial provision must be in place and a clear end point to the intervention had to be fixed. None of this boded at all well for the formulation of any new radical approach to the intervention in Rwanda.[21]

By the end of April the United Nations found itself in an irresolvable dilemma. The departure of the Belgians (along with their transport and heavy equipment which had served the force as a whole) left a vulnerable rump of UN troops concentrated in Kigali powerless to make any impact on events. On a number of grounds total withdrawal would now have been the logical step to take. Not only was UNAMIR merely a silent witness to genocide, but also its original mandate – oversight of the implementation of the Arusha agreement – was no longer relevant. The peace process was far beyond revival now and the RPF was once more at war with government forces. But the national political calculations which had ruled out any forceful intervention against the genocide also prevented the withdrawal of the hapless remains of the UN presence. Here too a variation on the CNN effect operated. Irrationally, public opinion in western states which forbade the deployment of national contingents to combat the genocide would at the same time have balked at a positive act of withdrawal while the killing continued.

Faced with complex considerations and the impossibility of either expansion or withdrawal, UN planners cast around for a meaningful role for the reduced UNAMIR. In the third week of the killings the security council adopted a proposal to drastically reduce the remaining force to a strength of less than 300. This unit, effectively UNAMIR-II, would be given a new mandate to pursue mediation between the Rwandan army and the RPF, now engaged in a conventional military campaign against the background of the genocide.[22] Against American opposition the secretary-general later won security council agreement in principle to a more robust force which could be mandated with a 'responsibility to protect'. But not surprisingly, despite concentrated effort by Boutros-Ghali and Kofi Annan, contingents were not forthcoming from member states.[23]

In mid-June one permanent security council member did offer to become militarily involved in Rwanda, though on its own terms. In a project reminiscent of the American Unified Task Force in Somalia, France offered to lead a 'Francophone' operation which would be legitimised by the council but which would not be a UN force as such. The flaws and dangers in such a venture should have been obvious. France was not universally regarded as disinterested in Rwanda: it had a history of support for the Hutu regime in Kigali and was viewed with deep suspicion by the (Anglophone) RPF. More generally, France had an established record of military intervention in French-speaking Africa in pursuit of its own political and economic interests. It was not easy to square this history with the impartial humanitarian intervention proposed by Paris. Perhaps it was a measure of the moral discomfort which pervaded the security council over its inaction in the face of genocide that it was ready to accept the French proposition. Only China and some of the non-permanent members demurred, and then only by abstention. The council accordingly agreed to authorise France's Operation Turquoise, perhaps with added enthusiasm as France undertook to meet the costs of the venture as well as provide the personnel. And provide the personnel it effectively did. Despite the operation's supposedly multinational character, its strength of 2,500 was overwhelmingly French in composition. One, admittedly strongly hostile, writer described it as a French 'military expedition . . . with some rented Senegalese troops along for the ride to create an aura of multilateralism'.[24]

Operation Turquoise proved largely irrelevant to the outcome of events. The genocide was already subsiding as the RPF advance across the country rolled up government forces and their *interahamwe* supporters. Later, though, the RPF was to accuse Operation Turquoise, which established a so-called 'humanitarian protection zone' in the southwest of the country, of facilitating and covering the flight of leading *génocidaires* out of the country. On the ground, opposition to the French force was not restricted to the RPF. General Dallaire was also strongly against the intervention which in his later account of the Rwanda disaster he referred to as the Turquoise Invasion. Instinctively suspicious of French intentions, he foresaw a raft of problems in the venture. He questioned France's objectives on the grounds that it could simply have reinforced UNAMIR if their motives had been genuinely humanitarian. The remains of UNAMIR would inevitably be overshadowed by the much larger French presence and its credibility further undermined. His relations with his French military counterparts were certainly uncomfortable. Although not a 'UN force' in the narrow sense, Operation Turquoise existed with security council authorisation. The hostility of the RPF towards it would deepen its resentment over the UN's response to the genocide in general and this would inevitably pollute RPF–UNAMIR relations.[25] Operation Turquoise, taken along with France's broader history in Rwanda, did indeed prove to be a point of bitterness between Paris and the shortly to be installed RPF government in Kigali.

Even if the French mission had little concrete impact on the general situation, it was still capable of distorting perceptions of the humanitarian intervention. It also highlighted some of the general problems associated with interventions by coalitions of the willing, with or without United Nations legitimisation. There was, firstly, the political baggage carried into the conflict by France, which immediately undermined two of the three traditional criteria for successful third-party intervention. France's neutrality in the conflict was compromised from the outset by its past history and, presumably, present interests. Secondly, it could hardly claim to have the clear consent of the parties, being regarded with undisguised hostility by the RPF. Only the impending victory of the RPF, by the stage of the French intervention just a matter of time, and the limited geographical scope of the French presence, permitted Operation Turquoise to take place without a physical challenge. Other interventions by actors with special interests in other conflicts would follow – Australia in East Timor and Britain in Sierra Leone are obvious examples – but they would not be encumbered with the same political complexities as that of France in Rwanda. A closer parallel might be with the interventions of the Russian-dominated Commonwealth of Independent States (CIS) in areas of the former Soviet Union. Then there is the difficulty of inter-operational relations where, as in Rwanda, a formal UN mission is also in place. Where there is no clear precedence among the agencies involved, the result, as Dallaire anticipated, is likely to be at best one of unproductive duplication and at worst rivalry and competition. The UN was encountering this problem in Liberia at the very time of the Rwanda crisis. Its observer mission in Liberia (UNOMIL) had a poor relationship with the larger forces of the Economic Community of West African States which it was mandated to supervise.[26] However, searching for a way out of the moral morass of Rwanda, these were lessons in which the security council had no interest.

In the event, Operation Turquoise proved short-lived, being withdrawn long before the expiry of its two-month mandate. By the end of June the RPF had effective control of Rwanda. This created the conditions for the meaningful deployment, finally, of UNAMIR-II. With the end of the fighting, and despite a less than enthusiastic level of consent from the new RPF government which was keenly aware of 'United Nations' shortcomings during the genocide, member states were now willing to provide the necessary contingents. UNAMIR-II, which grew to a strength of more than 5,000, operated across the country in a range of reconstructive functions. Uppermost among these was the security and resettlement of returning refugees, both Tutsi and Hutu. The UN operation, now truly a 'humanitarian' one, played an important if undramatic role in the critical first phase of Rwanda's reconstruction. Given the performance of its predecessor, however, UNAMIR-II could not do much to redeem the United Nations in the view of the new rulers of Rwanda and the survivors of the genocide.

The official United Nations post-mortem on the Rwanda intervention appeared in December 1999. This was the report of the Independent Enquiry into the Actions of the United Nations during the 1994 Genocide in Rwanda which was set up by Kofi Annan, now secretary-general of the UN.[27] The report criticised a number of low-level procedural shortcomings on the part of the UN mission in early 1994. More substantially, it also made some pertinent points about the responsibility of states providing contingents to UN forces not to interfere in the military command structure. Here the finger here was pointed at Belgium, which had started issuing instructions to its own forces as the slaughter got underway. It was not, of course, a new problem for interventions. The complex chain of command in Somalia in 1993 was a major impediment to the efficient operation of UNOSOM-II as we have seen. The fundamental problem according to the Rwanda enquiry report, however, was the basic configuration of the force. While adequate to supervise the implementation of a peace process to which the parties were properly committed, it was adrift when the situation deteriorated and the killings began. The findings of the Enquiry then seemed to go off in a peculiar direction: '. . . the onslaught of the genocide', it pronounced, 'should have led decision-makers in the United Nations . . . to realise that the original mandate . . . was no longer adequate, and required a different, more assertive response, combined with the means necessary to take such action.' The plain fact was that UN decision-makers very quickly realised that the original configuration of the mission was no longer adequate. The member states were wholly unwilling to provide the means necessary to reconfigure the intervention.

British journalist William Shawcross in his book on the interventionism of the 1990s, *Deliver Us from Evil*, recalls accompanying secretary-general Kofi Annan on a visit to Rwanda in 1998. Annan was shaken by the hostile reception from politicians and officials in Kigali who were angered by the failures of the United Nations four years earlier. This treatment was compared with that extended to President Bill Clinton who had made a very brief visit two months before. Clinton, after presenting a disingenuous apology – 'seared with hypocrisy' – for the shortcomings of 1994, was warmly embraced by his audience.[28] For Shawcross this illustrated two contrasting personal styles: Annan the thoughtful international civil servant and Clinton the ever-slick political operator. But the contrast in the treatment of the two men in Kigali points up the central paradox of 'UN intervention'. In Rwanda as elsewhere the failure to act forcefully in the face of the slaughter was only a 'UN' failure to the extent that it was a failure on the part of the organisation's member states. And the greatest culpability here was on the part of the United States, then sunk in its post-Somalia introversion. To adapt an aphorism: success in humanitarian intervention has many fathers, while failure is an orphan – left on the doorstep of the United Nations.

Darfur

The UN's military presence in Rwanda ended in 1996 with the withdrawal of UNAMIR-II. Despite the universal perception of failure there, interventions by United Nations forces remained a feature of the many conflicts throughout the continent into the new century. Operations already established at the time of the Rwanda crisis continued in Western Sahara and Angola where successful outcomes still eluded the peace-makers as the 1990s drew to a close.

In the meantime, many more new missions were created, including the massively scaled operation in the Democratic Republic of Congo to which the UN returned in 1999, thirty-five years after the end of its first, troublesome engagement there. This operation, the United Nations Mission in Congo ('MONUC' – which like its predecessor took its name from the acronym of its French title, *Mission de la Organisation des Nations Unies au Congo*), was in many ways a consequence of the Rwanda crisis of 1994. Following the end of the genocide there was a huge movement of Hutu refugees, including leading *génocidaires*, across the border from Rwanda ahead of RPF forces (which now formed the basis of the Rwandan national army). The regional instability which this generated helped to tip the vast, chronically unstable and perpetually misgoverned Congo into a multidimensional civil war which drew intervention from states across the region. Burundi too became the subject of a UN operation in 2004 which for the following two years sought with uncertain results to help manage that country's ethnic divisions. Major UN commitments were also made in West Africa to the management of complex internal regional conflicts in Liberia, Sierra Leone and Côte d'Ivoire. These crises, hugely destructive within their own borders, were worsened by cross-infection between them. Also in place was the classic Hammarskjoldian peacekeeping operation when UN troops were interposed on the Eritrea–Ethiopia border between 2000 and 2008 following the 'old-fashioned' – and for Africa highly unusual – territorial war between the two countries.

Much more typical of humanitarian intervention in Africa – and representative of some of the particular problems that have attended it – is the UN intervention in the Darfur region of Sudan. The United Nations–African Union Mission in Darfur (UNAMID) (or the AU–UN Hybrid Operation in Darfur as it is more commonly called) was formally established by the security council in July 2007. It was designed at that time to replace a purely African operation, the African Union Mission in Sudan (AMIS) which since its deployment in 2004 had proved unable to control the violence or advance the peace process in the territory.

Many of the issues and problems facing UNAMID and its political managers have broader resonances for multilateral military intervention in Africa. The Darfur crisis is rooted in ethnic and regionalist conflicts over access to very scarce but basic resources. The conflict, like that in Rwanda in the mid-1990s, has spread, with refugee movements across land borders to afflicted neighbours, in the case of Darfur, Chad and the Central African Republic. This spill-over has itself necessitated a separate UN humanitarian intervention, in the form of the Mission in Central African Republic and Chad (MINURCAT – *Mission des Nations Unies en République Centrafricaine et au Tchad*), established in September 2007. Darfur confronts the UN not with a 'clean' armed conflict but with a complex humanitarian emergency, in some ways similar to that in Somalia, in which the war takes place amidst famine and displacement on a massive scale. The issues, practical and ethical, of the 'responsibility to protect' are unavoidable for the UN in Darfur. There has been a major problem around consent; for example the Sudanese government, which legally holds sovereignty over the region, has adopted changing and inconsistent positions on its acceptance of intervention. A recurring rhetorical trope of the Khartoum regime has been to denounce UN intervention as inherently neo-colonial. Finally, at the level of high diplomacy, consensus among the permanent members of the security council has been difficult to achieve. The United States has calculatedly deployed the word 'genocide' with all that implies for states' obligations under the 1948 Genocide Convention (see Chapter 1). This was a term the Clinton administration had been at great pains not to use in the case of Rwanda in 1994. In view of the nature of the conflict in Darfur, this has brought accusations from the Arab world of anti-Islamic prejudice. Meanwhile, China has been a reluctant participant in the politics of intervention in Darfur and this has in turn brought the charge that Beijing has placed its economic and diplomatic interests in Sudan above its humanitarian responsibilities. This is an accusation heard increasingly frequently in the west in relation to Chinese policy across sub-Saharan Africa. Packaged up in the Darfur situation, therefore, is an entire collection of issues typical of the practical difficulties of humanitarian intervention by the UN in Africa.

Darfur occupies almost 500,000 square kilometres of western Sudan, bordering both Chad and the Central African Republic. The political and social archaeology of the conflict dates back at least to the Anglo-Sudanese war at the end of the nineteenth century. Britain's eventual defeat of the Sudanese army in 1899 brought the country as a whole under Anglo-Egyptian control. The remote and economically unproductive Darfur region was left largely under local rule, however. Only during the first world war, when a larger regional threat from Ottoman power was feared, was Darfur fully incorporated in the Sudan under British control. Henceforward, and particularly after Sudan's formal independence in 1956, Darfur became merely an outlying region of a large and ethnically fractious country. The main fracture line in Sudan in the unstable decades following its independence did not directly involve Darfur, however. From the early 1960s until 2002 Sudan was afflicted by a civil war with only intermittent intervals of peace between the Muslim north, represented by successive regimes in the capital Khartoum, and the non-Muslim 'black African' south. Its eventual resolution with the help of Libyan and Egyptian mediation came with a peace agreement which a large UN force – the UN Mission in Sudan (UNMIS) – was established in 2005 to help implement.

As if determined by baleful fates, the end of fighting in the war between north and south coincided with the outbreak of violence in the west. The Sudanese army was now sent to confront an uprising in Darfur. Eventually another civil war was underway between the Justice

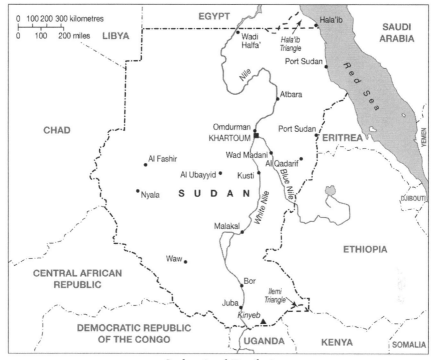

Sudan (and Darfur)

and Equality Movement and the Sudanese Liberation Movement on one side and the Khartoum government on the other. It was not only the national armed forces which were deployed by the state, however. So-called Janjaweed militias composed of 'Arab' Africans recruited from the northern regions of Sudan were also unleashed against the rebels and, indiscriminately, against local villagers as well (a situation which inevitably draws comparison with the *interahamwe* in Rwanda). Between the outbreak of violence in Darfur and the eventual approval of a UN intervention, an estimated 300,000 people, the vast majority civilian, died as a result of the fighting and perhaps as many as three million had become refugees either internally within Sudan or across its borders in Chad and the Central African Republic.

Early attempts by the UN to engage with the problem met with mixed results. Strong security council pressure had ensured that a reluctant Sudanese government accepted the presence of the African Union mission in 2004.[29] A peace agreement of sorts was signed by the Sudanese government and the Sudanese Liberation Movement in May 2006, but it was fragile, particularly as it was rejected by the other main rebel grouping, the Justice and Equality Movement. It did little to ease the security situation on the ground and it was now clear that AMIS, the African Union intervention, was inadequate to manage the military and humanitarian crisis. Although steadily increasing in numbers from a first deployment of only 150 to about 7,000 at the beginning of 2006, the African Union force made little impact on the violence while itself suffering a stream of casualties. By that point the war in Darfur as a whole had cost about 300,000 lives and created 2.5 million refugees. In short, that particular attempt to impose African solutions on African problems had failed. Anxious to maintain momentum following the partial agreement, secretary-general Annan put forward a plan in August 2006, approved by the security council, for the expansion of UNMIS (the existing UN operation in Sudan) into Darfur.[30] The mission would then have been responsible for humanitarian intervention in two separate civil conflicts in the country. This was rejected by the government in Khartoum on the grounds that as a non-African force it would impinge unacceptably on Sudanese sovereignty. Two months later relations between the Sudanese regime and the UN deteriorated further when the UN's senior representative in the country was expelled. Successive 'final' extensions to the mandate of AMIS followed, but the crisis in Darfur itself deepened while the effectiveness and morale of the force declined. Finally, in mid-2007, both the African Union and the individual contributing states made it clear that the operation was on the point of collapse and would have to be drawn down. In July of that year, the security council finally agreed the establishment of the UN mission in Darfur and UNAMID came into being at least formally.[31] At the end of the year AMIS was absorbed by the new operation under UN command.

The first two years of UNAMID's deployment provided a virtual checklist of the difficulties inherent in large-scale humanitarian intervention in Africa. Still playing the neo-colonial card, the Sudanese government systematically obstructed the effective deployment of the operation. It was, if not actively encouraged, certainly not deterred in this by the larger politics of the security council. China, although finally formally associated with UNAMID's mandate, remained ambivalent in its support of the intervention.

By the end of 2009 some 20,000 international military and police personnel had been deployed. This was slow to build however, as contributors, conscious of the risks of the operation and the casualty levels previously experienced by AMIS, dragged their feet. It was one thing to bend before the CNN effect of the humanitarian crisis on public opinion at home; it was another to subject national forces to the sorts of risk which would see that same CNN effect going into reverse as bodies returned for burial. This might be called the 'Mogadishu effect', after the impact on American policy of the descent of the Somalia intervention into chaos in 1993 which subsequently shaped the security council's approach to Rwanda the following year. And while the number of international boots on the ground might have appeared to be large, spread across the vast and difficult territory of Darfur, those 20,000 troops and police looked much less adequate.

The necessity of meeting Khartoum's demands for a large African component in the force – together with the political requirement in the UN itself to foreground the hybrid nature of the operation – meant that of the thirty-nine countries contributing to UNAMID at the end of 2009, twenty-one were from sub-Saharan Africa and the force as a whole had a Rwandan military commander and a South African police commissioner. However politically appropriate or expedient this may have been, it was not the most effective or rational way to structure and organise a large-scale international intervention.

In the end it was unclear to what extent the presence of UNAMID was materially affecting the realities of the conflict. Much of the mission's energies appeared to be spent on the interior demands of its composition and structure rather than on its contribution across the territory. Certainly the level of violence in Darfur appeared to decline in the second half of the decade. But the extent to which this was due to the limited impact of the 2006 peace agreement, to a new awareness on the part of the Khartoum government of the potential international consequences of its policies in Darfur, or just to war weariness, is impossible to assess. Probably all of these factors had a role, but none of them, and certainly not the presence of UNAMID, appeared to play the critical one.

African solutions to African problems?

The experience of UNAMID in Darfur – and AMIS before it – throws into question the viability of the much heralded but only sporadically realised idea of 'African solutions to African problems'. The UN position on the regionalisation of intervention, so far as one can be discerned, has been ambivalent. In 1992, as both financial and manpower pressures mounted on the UN's capacity for intervention, secretary-general Boutros-Ghali appeared to see regionalisation (not necessarily in Africa or in Africa alone) as one way forward. Regional arrangements, he wrote, 'in many cases possess a potential that should be utilised.' The security council would always maintain primary responsibility 'but regional action . . . could not only lighten the burden of the council but also contribute to a deeper sense of participation, consensus and democratisation in international affairs'.[32] In this view, regional responsibility would be symbiotic. It would ease the burden on the centre while enhancing the self-identity of the region. Later, in 2000, the Brahimi Report was less enthusiastic. Brahimi appeared to give short shrift to the idea of the regionalisation of military intervention. Although he accepted the potential role of co-operation between the UN and regional organisations in conflict preventions and post-conflict peace-building, he seemed wary about the deployment of regional forces. Military resources and capability, his report noted, 'are unevenly distributed around the world, and troops in the most crisis-prone areas are often less prepared for the demands of modern peacekeeping than is the case elsewhere'. Much better, he suggested, that the capacity of states be improved by training and the supply of equipment by more experienced 'mentor' states to enable them to contribute to United Nations operations.[33] The contrasting views of Boutros-Ghali and Brahimi would seem to reflect the shifting reality of the Darfur intervention. AMIS, run and manned by the African Union, seemed to be the appropriate approach at the outset of the crisis in 2004. But over the ensuing period Brahimi's depiction of such undertakings as impaired by the 'uneven distribution' of resources and capabilities seemed to be vindicated.

In truth, the limitations of regional intervention had already been in evidence in Africa in the 1990s when the Economic Community of West African States (ECOWAS) deployed troops to both Liberia and Sierra Leone. But the activities of this ECOWAS Military Observation Group (ECOMOG) had been neither mere observation as the title suggested nor humanitarian intervention. ECOMOG was involved in fighting wars to deny Charles Taylor the presidency of Liberia and to shore up the weak central government of Sierra Leone against the challenge of the rebel Revolutionary United Front. While the West African forces achieved results that the UN seemed incapable of, they did so with a very high degree of violence, and frequent criminality.[34] Moreover, the interventions in both countries were dominated by Nigerian troops. This gave rise to regional concerns that the operations were more about the pursuit of national foreign policy objectives by the local hegemon than genuine humanitarianism or peacekeeping interventions. A similar accusation was laid against ECOWAS elsewhere in West Africa at the end of the 1990s when it intervened in the civil war in the Portuguese-speaking territory of Guinea-Bissau.[35] Here the national interests were allegedly those of neighbouring Francophone Guinea Conakry and Senegal rather than Anglophone Nigeria. This highlights two further problems associated with regional interventions to be added to Brahimi's concerns about resources. Firstly, regional forces are not necessarily in tune with the UN's culture of military intervention or sympathetic to its traditional methods. (This had already been an issue with the United States' efforts in Somalia in the early 1990s.) Secondly, regional interventions may be subject to 'co-option' and diversion to serve the interests of powerful local states

The wider based the regional organisation, the less pressing these threats tend to be. There was no suggestion of systematic misbehaviour by the African Union in Darfur, nor that any special interests were pursued by AMIS forces there. Moreover, the AU intervention in Somalia established at the beginning of 2007 explicitly excluded neighbouring states from participating. But the potential for the interests of dominant powers to come into play in local conflicts remains. Within the AU there are two rivals for an Africa-wide leadership role: South Africa and Nigeria. Each represents different geographical ends of the continent; each has very different foreign policy interests. They are already competing claimants to the proposed African permanent seat in the UN security council. The danger this nascent regional bipolarity represents for the success of humanitarian interventions in Africa is real.

Against these impediments, there are four principal arguments in support of African solutions to the demands of intervention. These range from the functional to the philosophical. Local forces can be expected to have a clearer understanding of the underlying dynamics of African conflicts and therefore should be in a better position to apply more effective means of resolving them. Arguably, the robustness of the ECOMOG interventions in Liberia and Sierra Leone should be seen less as a departure from the 'rules' of proper humanitarian intervention than as the result of a realistic appreciation of what was required in these circumstances. Secondly, as well as a precise and focused understanding of African conflicts and the best means of resolving them, local forces would have a more immediate self-interest in seeing them resolved. Spill-over and 'infection' are obviously going to concentrate the minds of African states on the fate of their neighbours much more than they would Canada or Sweden. Next, this special regional interest might be seen to serve a larger integrative purpose. The sense of regional responsibility involved in interventions contributes to an emerging norm of collective responsibility. It extends the possibilities of co-operation across the spectrum of problems facing contemporary Africa and not just armed conflict. Finally, there is a non-African benefit to African interventionism which returns to Boutros-Ghali's thinking in the early 1990s: local responsibility eases the burden on the United Nations at the centre.

Attempts to lay out a balance sheet for African solutions to African problems are ultimately rather theoretical and academic, however. Any practical discussion must start with what is possible rather than what is in principle desirable. The capacity and resources for effective intervention have to be there in the first place. The experience of the African Union in Darfur is salutary here. AMIS, even with extensive UN support in the background, was simply not capable of fulfilling a meaningful mandate for humanitarian intervention. Even Nigeria, a big and relatively wealthy country with a large and experienced army, could not sustain its intervention in either Sierra Leone or Liberia and in both cases UN forces with strong mandates were required to relieve ECOMOG.[36]

There is one circumstance though in which 'regional' involvement might make a significant contribution to humanitarian intervention in Africa – but not in the sense of local African solutions. The European Union has for some time been developing intervention capacity, in the context of its evolving European Security and Defence Policy (ESDP). EU troops have already been active alongside the UN's MONUC forces in the Democratic Republic of Congo and in the Central African Republic and Chad. Ironically, British and French forces seem to have less trouble co-operating within a multinational command in Africa than their Anglophone and Francophone former colonies – which is a curious comment on post-imperial attitudes. With this in mind it may be that the approach advocated in the Brahimi Report – external support to bring national forces up to a standard that would permit them to operate across the range of the UN's interventions – might be a better way forward than attempts to map regional forces to regional crises. This type of responsibility might equally be borne by organisations like the EU as well as the UN itself.

For all this, there are some grounds for optimism that the African problems to which solutions from whatever source are required may in fact be easing. Analysis of the number and intensity of conflicts in Africa over the decades appear to indicate a peak in the first half of the 1990s which has been followed by a remarkably sharp and reasonably consistent decline.[37] It is possible then that the demands for armed humanitarian intervention in Africa, which threatened to overwhelm both the resources and the political resolve of the United Nations in the 1990s, may not be a long-term feature.

In the meantime, a balance sheet of the UN's performance is not easy to prepare. Certainly, it is easy to point to the apparently catastrophic failures of intervention in Somalia, Rwanda and Angola. These dwarf in both numbers and consequences the more clear-cut successes in Namibia and Mozambique, for example. But, of course, the idea of 'failure' in these instances is open to examination. For one thing, as far as Somalia and Rwanda at least are concerned, the outcomes were really determined by the states of the security council rather than by the UN as an institution. More fundamentally, there is another difficult truth which has already been touched on: 'failure' is only a meaningful descriptor when 'success' is a feasible alternative. In Africa perhaps more than elsewhere the hard truth has been that some problems simply have no ready solutions, African or otherwise.

Notes

1. As might be expected, humanitarian intervention in Africa has been the subject of extensive analysis. Most of this has been concerned with individual crises and operations, however, there are relatively few studies covering Africa as a whole. Among these are Norrie MacQueen, *United Nations Peacekeeping in Africa since 1960* (London: Longman, 2002); E. G. Berman and K. E. Sams, *Peacekeeping in Africa: Capabilities and Culpabilities* (Geneva: United Nations Institute for Disarmament Research, 2000); and Oliver Furley and Ron May (eds), *Peacekeeping in Africa* (Aldershot: Ashgate, 1998).

2. The security council mandated UNTAG in its final form by S/RES/629 (1989), 16 January 1989. UNAVEM had been authorised three weeks earlier by S/RES/626(1998), 20 December 1988.

3. On the political background to the settlement in Namibia see G. R. Berridge, 'Diplomacy and the Angola–Namibia accords', *International Affairs*, 65(3) 1989, pp. 463–79.

4. Each operation is analysed separately by Virginia Page Fortna in William Durch (ed.), *The Evolution of UN Peacekeeping: Case Studies and Comparative Analysis* (New York: St. Martin's Press, 1993): 'United Nations Transition Assistance Group', pp. 353–75; 'The United Nations Angola Verification Mission I', pp. 376–405.

5. For accessible overviews of dependency and world systems theories see Andre Gunder Frank and Barry Gills, *The World System: Five Hundred Years or Five Thousand* (London: Taylor and Francis, 1993) and *The Essential Wallerstein* (New York: New Press, 2001).

6. An early systematic exposition on neo-patrimonial theory was provided by Shmuel Eisenstadt in *Traditional Patrimonialism and Modern Neo-patrimonialism* (Beverly Hills: Sage, 1973). Later discussions can be found in Jean-François Bayart, *The State in Africa: The Politics of the Belly* (London: Longman, 1993) and Michael Bratton and Nicholas van de Walle, *Democratic Experiments in Africa* (Cambridge: Cambridge University Press, 1997).

7. The initial intervention, authorised by security council resolution S/RES/751 (1992), 24 April 1992, involved only military observers. The larger intervention was approved by resolution S/RES/775(1992) on 28 August.

8. Boutros Boutros-Ghali, *Unvanquished: A US–UN Saga* (New York: Random House, 1999), pp. 54–5.

9. Ibid., pp. 56–7.

10. On the O'Brien affair see the protagonist's own account, Conor Cruise O'Brien, *To Katanga and Back* (London: Hutchinson, 1962) and for a view reflecting that of Hammarskjöld himself, Brian Urquhart, *Hammarskjöld* (London: Bodley Head, 1973), pp. 545–89.

11. Quoted in transcript of Brookings/Harvard Forum, 'The CNN effect': How 24-Hour News Coverage Affects Government Decisions and Public Opinion, 23 January 2002. Found at http://www.brookings.edu/events/2002/0123media_journalism.aspx

12. The American intervention was authorised by security council resolution S/RES/794(1992), 3 December 1992.

12. UNOSOM-II was established by security council resolution S/RES/814 (1993), 27 March 1993.

13. The new mandate called for the 'arrest and detention for prosecution, trial and punishment' of those responsible for the attacks on UNOSOM-II personnel and 'those responsible for publically inciting such attacks'. Security council resolution S/RES/837(1993), 5 June 1993.

14. An excellent account of the historical setting of the Rwanda crisis and the politics of the pre-independence years is provided by Gerard Prunier in *The Rwanda Crisis: History of a Genocide* (London: Hurst, 2002), pp. 1–54.

15. On Bicesse and its aftermath see Norrie MacQueen, 'Elusive Settlement: Angola's "Peace processes", 1975–2002', in Oliver Furley and Roy May (eds), *Ending Africa's Wars: Progressing to Peace* (Aldershot: Ashgate, 2006), pp. 137–54. The UN special representative in Angola at the time of the collapse of the process, Dame Margaret Anstee, has written a comprehensive account of events from the inside, *Orphan of the Cold War: The Inside Story of the Collapse of the Angolan Peace Process, 1992–93* (London: Macmillan, 1996).

16. The Arusha agreement is analysed in Prunier, *The Rwanda Crisis*, pp.159–64. See also Christopher Clapham, 'Rwanda: The Perils of Peacemaking', *Journal of Peace* Research, 35(2), 1998, pp. 84–6.

17. Secretary-general's letter to the security council, security council document S/26488, 24 September 1993.
18. This mandate was approved by the security council in resolution S/RES/872(1993), 5 October 1993.
19. The force commander later wrote his own detailed and somewhat tortured account of the Rwanda crisis: Roméo Dallaire, *Shake Hands with the Devil: The Failure of Humanity in Rwanda* (London: Arrow, 2004). The incident over the arms secure area and Annan's role in it are dealt with in pp. 133–67.
20. Boutros-Ghali, *Unvanquished*, p. 132.
21. On the political and diplomatic framework from which PDD25 emerged see Michael G. MacKinnon, *The Evolution of US Peacekeeping Policy Under Clinton: A Fairweather Friend?* (London: Cass, 1999).
22. This new configuration was authorised by security council resolution S/RES/918(1994), 17 May 1994.
23. The new mandate was mooted in security council resolution S/RES/924(1994), 8 June 1994.
24. Philip Gourevitch, *We Wish to Inform You That Tomorrow We Will be Killed With Our Families* (London: Picador, 1999), p. 155.
25. Dallaire, *Shake Hands with the Devil*, pp. 421–60.
26. See MacQueen, *United Nations Peacekeeping in Africa*, pp. 173–80.
27. Report of the Independent Enquiry into the Actions of the United Nations during the 1994 Genocide in Rwanda (1999). Security council document S/1999/1257, 16 December 1999. Found at http://www.un.org/Docs/journal/asp/ws.asp?m=S/1999/1257
28. William Shawcross, *Deliver Us From Evil: Warlords and Peacekeepers in a World of Endless Conflict* (London: Bloomsbury, 2000), pp. 258–63.
29. Security council resolution S/RES/1564(2004), 18 September 2004, threatened the application of sanctions against Sudan's oil exports under the enforcement powers of the charter (article 41) if it did not accept the deployment of AMIS.
30. The proposed mandate for the expanded UNMIS was set out in security council resolution S/RES/1706(2006), 31 August 2006.
31. UNAMID was created by security council resolution S/RES/1769(2007), 31 July 2007.
32. *An Agenda for Peace: Preventive Diplomacy, Peacemaking and Peacekeeping* (United Nations document A/47/277-S/24111,17 June 1992), paragraphs 64–5. Found at http://www.un.org/Docs/SG/agpeace.html
33. Report of the Panel on United Nations Peace Operations, issued as United Nations documents A/55/305 (general assembly); S/2000/809 (security council), 21 August 2000, paragraph 54. Found at http://www.un.org/peace/reports/peace_operations
34. See Christopher Tuck, '"Every Car or Moving Object Gone": The ECO-MOG Intervention in Liberia', *African Studies Quarterly*, 4(1), February 2000. Found at http://www.africa.ufl.edu/asq/v4/v4i1a1.htm

35. See Norrie MacQueen, 'A Community of Illusions? Portugal, the CPLP and Peacemaking in Guinea-Bissau', *International Peacekeeping*, 10(2), 2003, pp. 10–15.
36. The UN Mission in Sierra Leone (UNAMSIL) was created in 1999 after the ECOMOG intervention and was in place until 2005. The UN Mission in Liberia was established in 2003 and directly replaced ECOMOG forces.
37. For example, Monty G. Marshall, *Conflict Trends in Africa, 1946–2004: A Macro-Comparative Perspective* (Washington DC: Africa Center for Strategic Studies, 2005). Found at http://africacenter.org/wp-content/uploads/2005/07/Conflict-Trends-in-Africa-1946-2004.pdf

Chapter 5

Humanitarian intervention and coercive action: the Balkans

The end of the cold war re-shaped international relations, subverting what had been assumed to be the fixed norms of late-twentieth century world politics. It did so moreover at a speed and to an extent that defied prediction or planning. In Europe the end of the bipolar world order first engendered then accelerated a wave of ethnic nationalism which unravelled the territorial disposition put in place after the first world war. Following on quickly from the breaching of the Berlin Wall in 1989 and German reunification, the Baltic territories of Estonia, Latvia and Lithuania broke from the Soviet Union, establishing a trio of new sovereign states in north-central Europe. Further east, Ukraine and Belorussia also moved from their status as component Soviet republics to full statehood.

Two European 'multinational' states whose creation had been the result of the pressures for national self-determination after 1918 paradoxically succumbed at the other end of the century to the same, now re-emergent, pressures. January 1993 saw the creation of the Czech Republic and Slovakia from the now defunct Czechoslovakia. The parting of the ways was ill-tempered but largely peaceful. The contrast between this so-called 'velvet divorce' and the parallel disintegration of Yugoslavia, another post-1918 construct, could hardly have been greater. The violence and chaos of this process in the form of war, massacre, rape and ethnic cleansing forced Europe in the early 1990s to confront the fragility of the moral advance supposedly made since the defeat of Nazi Germany in 1945.

The end of a twentieth-century experiment

Yugoslavia – the land of the 'South Slavs' – was constructed from the wreckage of two of the defeated empires in 1918: Austria-Hungary and Turkey. After a war fought under the banner of national self-determination – waved pragmatically by the European allies and flown as high principle by Woodrow Wilson's United States – the creation of new states was inevitable. The problem lay in the delineation of their frontiers and the construction of their ethnic identities These states had to be viable as sovereign independent members of the international system. For this reason the creation of a scatter of mono-ethnic microstates was not an option. The problem was particularly acute in the Balkans – whose fractious politics had, after all, been a contributing fact to the outbreak of the war. The response of the allied powers was therefore to create a new entity built around the existing state of Serbia (which had itself been on the winning side in the war). This new entity would extend from Slovenia on the frontier of Italy in the north-west to Macedonia in the south bordering Greece, Albania and Bulgaria. Originally established as the 'Kingdom of Serbs, Croats and Slovenes' in 1918, Yugoslavia began as a constitutional monarchy under the Serbian royal family. In 1929 it adopted the less wordy title of 'Kingdom of Yugoslavia'.

Given its historical and geographic foundations (the product of remnants of two culturally opposed empires and an assertive nation state at the junction between industrialised western Europe and a still economically backward east), the new state encompassed a range of diverse societies. In terms of religion it was Catholic in the north and west, Orthodox in the east and Muslim in the centre and south. Although inter-ethnic tensions were present in the new state from the beginning, particularly between Serbia and Croatia, the novelty of independent nationhood carried the state forward in the 1920s and 1930s. It was the experience of the next decade, however, that consolidated Yugoslav identity. Invasion and resistance during the second world war shaped the country and its politics for the rest of its existence. The Communist leader Josip Broz – or Tito – led a fierce partisan war against the Germans and eventually became the unquestioned leader of the post-war state. Appropriately perhaps (and politically usefully), Tito's own family background crossed the country's ethnic divide, his father being a Croat and his mother from Slovenia. The post-1945 state – sometimes called the 'second Yugoslavia' to distinguish it from the original construct after the first world war – was described as a Federal People's Republic. The federal units – or 'autonomous republics' – making up Yugoslavia were effectively the component regions of the state at its foundation.

Internationally, Yugoslavia's position in the emerging cold war balance was ambiguous. Those who assumed that it would follow the other communist-dominated states of central and eastern Europe into the orbit of the Soviet Union were proved wrong. Tito was not of a temperament which would accept a satellite role for Yugoslavia (or personal subordination to Joseph Stalin for that matter). Throughout the post-war decades Yugoslavia maintained a unique form of national communism which, in the 1960s, found external expression through leadership within the emerging post-colonial non-aligned movement.

The close identification of the 'idea' of Yugoslavia with the personality of Tito himself which grew in the post-1945 decades, while a point of strength in the fraught cold war years of the 1950s and 1960s, proved to be a hostage to fortune. His death in 1980 exposed persisting tensions between the state's component parts and this eventually grew into a complex pattern of competing micro-nationalisms. At the centre lay the federal government in Belgrade – the capital not just of Yugoslavia but also of its historically dominant element, Serbia. Following the death of Tito the extent of the series of 'national questions' facing Yugoslavia and the delicate situations they created was acknowledged in the formation of a collective presidency among the heads of the separate federal units. This was designed to allay nationalist suspicions and hold the Yugoslav state together. Instead it accelerated the process of disintegration by removing an important constitutional symbol of national unity. Crucially, in 1989 the Serbian presidency passed to Slobodan Milošević who, while nominally the leader of a unified socialist state, was in essence a Serb nationalist. Milošević's accession to power and the suspicion in the component republics that his image of Yugoslavia was essentially one of a 'greater Serbia' rather than a truly federal state further unsettled the situation. These centrifugal pressures on the Yugoslav entity were then intensified in the late 1980s by exposure to the pan-European wave of nationalism which had been bottled up since the end of the second world war by the external pressures of cold war polarisation.[1]

The first positive moves towards disintegration came in mid-1991 when both Slovenia and Croatia separately announced their secession from Yugoslavia. In the case of Slovenia the separation was consolidated after a short-lived and limited attempt by the central government in Belgrade to hold it by force. The Yugoslav National Army – the JNA – was ordered to suppress the secession but was deployed into a novel situation in Slovenia where it faced a relatively well-prepared local force. This unfavourable military balance had to be considered alongside the special situation of Slovenia within the federation. Located on Yugoslavia's western borders and largely mono-ethnic in its population, Slovenia represented one extreme of Yugoslavia's economic and cultural spectrum. The magnetic pull of western Europe was strong – as was the moral support of the countries of that region.

The situation of Croatia in geographical, political and ethnic terms was entirely different – and much more threatening in the perceptions of Belgrade. In 1990 Croatia had elected the conservative nationalist politician Franjo Tudjman as its president within the Yugoslav federation. With two irreconcilable nationalist in power – Milošević in Belgrade and Tudjman in Zagreb – the omens for a peaceful resolution of difficulties were discouraging to say the least. In contrast to Slovenia, Croatia was typical of the other Yugoslav republics in its complex ethnic composition. Crucially, about 12 per cent of the Croatian population was ethnic Serb and neither they nor Milošević (already suffering a loss of face after the successful secession of Slovenia) were willing to countenance the assertion of Croatian independence. There was also a national strategic dimension to Croatia's secession because of its long Adriatic–north Mediterranean coastline. Without this the rump of Yugoslavia would be dependent for its outlet to the sea on the much less developed Montenegro further to the south.

Consequently the JNA was sent into Croatia to suppress the breakaway. By the end of 1991 a third of Croatian territory was under the control of the Belgrade government. Initial peacekeeping and peacemaking efforts undertaken by the European Community and the Organization for Security and Cooperation in Europe (OSCE) proved unavailing. These organisations lacked institutional experience in such interventions. Beyond this, the situation was complicated for European regional bodies by disagreements among their members about the most desirable outcome. These differences reflected the long and divisive narrative of the impact of Balkans politics on European diplomatic relations. Germany, with a history of at least a century of hostility to Serbia and parallel sympathy towards rival Croatia, had encouraged the secession. France, in contrast, had traditionally been warmer towards Serbia. Britain, maintaining its own long-standing conservative – and Conservative – foreign policy tradition, sought to minimise any international engagement.[2] In this way one of the recognised obstacles to intervention by regional organisations was displayed – the pollution of humanitarian action by the local interests of the interveners. On display too, of course, was the enduring capacity of long-dormant affinities to rise from the grave and confound the management of contemporary conflicts.

Partly as a result of the failure of regional intervention, in the autumn of 1991 the Croatian problem passed to the United Nations. The security council was left to grapple with a deepening crisis embracing large-scale humanitarian challenges (including the mass expulsion of populations, an activity which now for the first time acquired the ominous description of 'ethnic cleansing'). Preliminary attempts to negotiate a settlement were unsuccessful and at the beginning of 1992 the newly appointed secretary-general Boutros Boutros-Ghali convinced the security council that there was no alternative but to mount a large-scale armed humanitarian intervention. He did so in the face of the reluctance of both Serbia and Croatia, each of which saw UN involvement as potentially damaging to its respective objectives. The obvious complexities of 'host state' consent in a conflict where the identity of the state itself was at the forefront were overcome, however, and a force which would eventually reached 14,000 in strength was deployed.[3] This UN Protection Force (UNPROFOR) had some success in establishing Protected Areas for the victims and potential victims of ethnic cleansing and in restraining the outbreak of full-scale fighting. The intervention worked reasonably effectively from its inception until late 1994 when large-scale inter-ethnic fighting erupted. The situation was not finally resolved by the UN presence, but it did reduce the ferocity of the conflict on the ground. In essence, 'resolution' came with the military victory of Croatia, which was consolidated in 1995. The cost of this was about 10,000 deaths with some three-quarters-of-a-million people being displaced either internally or beyond Croatia itself. In this way Croatia provided a timely lesson in the limited reach of humanitarian intervention in conflicts where negotiated compromise is simply unavailable. It was a lesson which should, of course, have been obvious and quickly taken to heart, but in the euphoria of the post-cold war 'new world order' it had only limited impact.

Bosnia: the hard school of intervention

While UN officials watched with alarm the outbreak of fighting in Croatia, those with the most sensitive political antennae and a grasp of the historical dimension to the larger Yugoslav predicament were most concerned about the likely next stage of national disintegration: Bosnia. The conflict in Croatia was driven in large part by the presence of the Serb minority; in Bosnia (or Bosnia-Herzegovina to give it its full historical name) the mix was even more complex and explosive.

The ethnic Bosnian (or Bosniak) population formed just 43 per cent of a population of around 4 million. Reflecting the long history of Ottoman Turkish domination, this community was predominantly Muslim, but with a strongly secular tradition. The capital of Bosnia, Sarajevo, was recognised as one of the most liberal and free-spirited

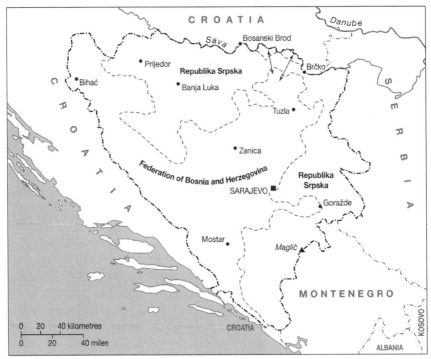

Bosnia

centres of Yugoslavia. About 31 per cent of the population was Serb, many of whose communities were concentrated in the small towns and villages in the hills of eastern Bosnia. Like their counterparts in Croatia, these Serbs felt threatened by the prospect of secession from Yugoslavia, though probably with less justification in Bosnia where historic inter-ethnic hostilities were less marked. Many Serbians in both Croatia and Bosnia had, however, been infected by the resurgent Serbian nationalism (or 'imperialism' depending on perspective) so skilfully generated and exploited by Slobodan Milošević from Belgrade.

Where the Bosnian situation differed most fundamentally from that in Croatia, however, was in the presence of a third ethnic dimension: some 17 per cent of the population was composed of ethnic Croats. If a certain Bosnian Serb 'colonial' mentality tainted inter-ethnic relations with the Muslims, the attitude of the Bosniaks towards Croatia was partly shaped by the experience of Bosnian subjugation to a pro-Nazi Croat regime during the second world war. Although the largest single population group, the Bosnian Muslims were the only one without the support of a geographically contiguous ethnic 'motherland'.

146

Consequently, they were forced to rely instead on the larger 'international community' beyond the old Yugoslav borders.

Three wholly incompatible political aspirations were now pursued by the main micro-nationalist groups: the Bosnians sought sovereign independence; the Bosnian-Serbs were determined to maintain Bosnia in the (Serbian-dominated) rump of the Yugoslav state; and Bosnian Croats nurtured the dream of Bosnia's annexation by the new state of Croatia. It was clear to those familiar with the complex architecture of Bosnia's religious and ethnic situation, therefore, that any attempt at secession could trigger a level of violence unthinkable in Slovenia and unseen even in Croatia. Amidst the general collapse of Yugoslavia, however, such a secession was virtually inevitable and came in April 1992. It did so only after a carefully organised and internationally supervised referendum held the previous month which returned a 99.4 per cent vote in favour of independence. This was declared, with only reluctant external support, under a government formed by the (initially) moderate nationalist president, Alija Izetbegović. The Bosnian Serbs, fully aware of the inevitable outcome, had sought to undermine the legitimacy of the result by boycotting the entire process.

As predicted, violence erupted immediately, with Bosnian Serbs rounding on the new Muslim-dominated national government in Sarajevo and with the deployment of the JNA against the nascent Bosnian national army. Although the UN had imposed a general arms embargo on the area of the former Yugoslavia as a whole in 1991 in anticipation of generalised violence, Serbia and its clients were effective beneficiaries of this as they monopolised the control of the national weapons stockpile. The well-equipped Serbian forces soon dominated about 70 per cent of the territory of Bosnia and presided over the establishment of a so-called Republika Srpska (Serb Republic), essentially a puppet of Milošević's regime in Belgrade, with ethnic cleansing rife within it. Soon after this the government in Sarajevo was forced to fight on a second front, against the Bosnian Croats of the Herzegovina region, who sought to attach their territory to the new state of Croatia.

The immediate pressure for intervention in Bosnia could not have been unexpected, but for UN planners in New York it was hardly a welcome development. The first pressures of post-cold war resource-stretch were already being felt. Aside from the major operation in neighbouring Croatia, in 1992 the UN was engaged in twelve interventions elsewhere in the world. Five of these were long-standing commitments from the cold war years but the majority were 'new world order' ventures including the large-scale and expensive interventions in Cambodia, Angola, Mozambique and Somalia. Initially Boutros-Ghali sought to limit involvement in Bosnia to the deployment of military observers against the hope of a negotiated settlement. Even more so than in Croatia, however, the prospect of such an outcome was vanishingly remote. Moreover, the supposed impact of even a token UN presence (on which the classic Hammarskjöldian model of peacekeeping relied) was simply non-existent in the no-man's-land between intra- and inter-state conflict which the Bosnian war occupied. The symbolic presence of UN observers in the historic Bosnian town of Mostar, for example, which was populated by all three ethnic groups, ended ingloriously when it became clear that of itself the blue flag of the United Nations exerted no influence.

In August 1992 the security council attempted to shift the burden of intervention to regional organisations (or perhaps to shame them into accepting their responsibilities). A resolution called on UN members acting alone 'or through regional agencies or arrangements' to take 'all measures necessary' to deal with the humanitarian crisis which the war had created in Bosnia.[4] The European powers best equipped to respond (including two permanent members of the security council, Britain and France, who themselves had made the appeal) declined to respond, however. Europe's institutional failure to take up the challenge in Bosnia cast a less than encouraging light on one of Boutros-Ghali's favoured projects: the regionalisation of intervention under UN authorisation. The assumption underlying his advocacy of this (outlined in *An Agenda for Peace*) was that regional organisations were poised to undertake such interventions, even enthusiastic, but were constrained mainly by the absence of legitimisation and support. Europe's studied evasion of direct intervention in Bosnia at this time – after some ineffectual efforts elsewhere in the Yugoslav space – suggested otherwise. Very reluctantly therefore, the following month, with the approach of the fierce Bosnian winter, the security council agreed to the creation of a new Bosnian wing of UNPROFOR.[5] This was to have a primarily humanitarian role, its principal function being the oversight of essential aid supplies to remote communities on much the same pattern as UNOSOM in Somalia which had been established the previous April.

In Bosnia as in Somalia the mandate proved impossible to implement effectively. Dogged and determined efforts were made by UNPROFOR to ensure the delivery of aid and manage at least the worst consequences of ethnic cleansing, but the operation was hobbled from the outset by its configuration as a traditional peacekeeping mission. The combatants, and in particular the Bosnian Serbs, quickly realised that whatever the potential firepower of the UN contingents, it would never be unleashed against them. The 'rules' of peacekeeping here coincided neatly with the caution and reluctance of the contributing states. Among the largest of these were core western members of the European Union (and the UN security council) including Britain, France, Denmark and Holland, none of whose governments had any enthusiasm for the robust levels of engagement which could have controlled the behaviour of the antagonists. Instead, inadequate and pusillanimous responses by UNPROFOR to aggressive challenges simply emboldened those presenting the challenges and alienated their victims from the international intervention.

One of the most depressing illustrations of this failure on the part of the UN to match its reach with its grasp was the issue of the so-called no-fly zone (NFZ) imposed by the security council in an attempt to prevent the Yugoslav air force from supporting the Republika Srpska army in operations against the Bosnian government.[6] Initially UN member states were resistant to the idea of enforcing such an arrangement. But with the deepening humiliation of UNPROFOR over the winter of 1992–3 as Serb-aligned forces became increasingly contemptuous of the UN's evident impotence, the organisational basis of the Bosnian intervention changed in March 1993. Responding to ever more forlorn security council calls for 'regional agencies or arrangements' to engage with the conflict, NATO undertook to enforce the NFZ.[7] This, of course, was a 'regional' intervention only in name. The range of the Atlantic alliance was, by this stage in post-cold war developments, already global. NATO's involvement was, moreover, largely determined by United States foreign policy. The successive administrations of the first President Bush and then of Bill Clinton resolutely opposed committing American ground troops to the UN effort despite signs that US public opinion would have been more favourable than the White House assumed.[8] Bosnia had generated a particularly powerful CNN effect, especially after the footage of Serb-run concentration camps, frighteningly reminiscent of the Nazi era, appeared on television. Meanwhile the harrowing daily coverage of the brutal Serb siege of Sarajevo provided a constant backdrop to these shocking images. But the official response in Washington appeared to be to criticise the inadequacy of the United Nations intervention rather than to strengthen it with an American presence on the ground. The commitment of NATO air power served to demonstrate to both the domestic and the global audience America's commitment to dealing with the crisis while keeping US personnel out of harm's way. Britain, France and Turkey (by virtue of both its geographical proximity and perhaps its natural sympathies with the Bosnian Muslims) committed elements of airpower along with those of the United States.

Although initially NATO involvement had little impact on the day-to-day performance of the international force, it would lead ultimately to the denouement of the conflict when UN humanitarian intervention gave way to military enforcement. The narrative leading to that denouement casts an important light on the nature of inter-agency relationships in humanitarian interventions and the potential for collisions of culture between the traditions of peacekeeping and the realities of enforcement. More broadly, it reveals the limitless possibilities for tension among member states of organisations engaged in interventions when their own immediate interests collide over the direction of operations.

Although Bill Clinton maintained his predecessor's general opposition to the use of American ground troops when he took office at the beginning of 1993, he arrived at the White House having raised public expectations of a more muscular American stance. To this end he floated a proposal for a new approach which would have involved the end of the UN arms embargo on Bosnia and the use of aggressive NATO airpower against Serb forces in the territory (going far beyond the mere policing of the NFZ). This came to be described as the 'lift and strike' strategy. From the American perspective it seemed to provide an ideal form of intervention. The Bosnians would be empowered in their own defensive operations (with Serbia's hitherto automatic advantage in weaponry neutralised). This resulting increase in operational effectiveness on the part of the Bosnians would then be complemented by air resources far in advance of anything the Serbians could deploy – or, crucially, effectively counter. And all this would be achieved without a single American boot on Bosnian soil. The plan immediately drove a wedge between the United States and its fellow security council members and NATO partners, Britain and France. Both had already committed large contingents to UNPROFOR and were prominent in its command structure. Both, too, were resentful of America's persistent criticism of the operation and its parallel refusal to become properly involved in it. The Anglo-French position was that UNPROFOR was, however imperfectly, a peacekeeping operation and that 'lift and strike' was calculated to extinguish any last possibility of reaching a peace because it would reconfigure the intervention as an enforcement action. This would expose British and French UNPROFOR forces to vastly increased dangers and would most probably lead to their withdrawal and the consequent collapse of the UN intervention as a whole. In view of this allied dissent and the implied threat of even greater pressure for American ground involvement in a post-peacekeeping crisis, Clinton had little option but to withdraw his proposal.[2]

Against the background of an ever-deteriorating humanitarian situation, particularly in Sarajevo which remained at the mercy of Serb artillery and snipers in the hills surrounding it and threatened with famine with the onset of the 1993–4 winter, there was no let-up in domestic pressure in the United States for some effective action. Clinton now proposed a diluted version of 'lift and strike' to his European allies which would involve the use of narrowly targeted NATO airpower alone. The objective would be threefold: reduce the capacity of the Serbs to maintain their siege of Sarajevo and open the airport to relief supplies; ensure the capacity of the UN to maintain 'safe areas' established for the victims of ethnic cleansing; and, on the political plane, persuade the Serbs into negotiation by exposing their military vulnerability which had hitherto been unchallenged, at least by UNPROFOR. Again, Britain and France were reluctant to accept the American proposal on the basis of the risks it posed to their forces on the ground. The price they demanded was a so-called 'dual-key' arrangement whereby the UN locally in Bosnia would have to agree to any specific NATO proposal for airstrikes. In short, the fundamentally different perspectives on either side of the Atlantic between a risk-averse United States determined nevertheless to take some action, and the British and French who would incur the 'transferred risks' of this action, produced a weak compromise. It was one which would shape an increasingly difficult relationship between the intervening agencies, the UN and NATO, and lead ineluctably to a decisive end-game. This would only be reached, however, at a cost of thousands of innocent lives and a major crisis for the entire interventionist role of the United Nations.

The problems raised by the involvement of NATO were not only internal to the alliance itself. The legal basis of the original United Nations intervention was reasonably clear. It had been approved by a resolution of the security council whose standing in the matter was unquestioned as a result of the precedence of the UN charter in international law. The role of NATO, however, was questionable. Chapter VIII of the charter, as we have seen, empowers the security council to work through regional agencies on issues of international security (see Chapter 2). But while NATO just about qualified as a 'regional agency' in the Balkans in a broad geographical sense, it was not one in a political sense. Neither Yugoslavia nor its successor states were members. It was unclear whether this 'out-of-area' action could be covered by chapter VIII. Moreover, the charter made it quite clear that if regional organisations were to be involved in security operations, it would be under the control of the security council. Precedence among the intervening agencies, in other words, was clearly set. But this hierarchy of authority did not correspond with realities in Bosnia where there was at best a dual key on NATO's actions imposed on behalf of the UN and accepted by the United States only reluctantly. This was potentially problematic. Russia, another permanent member of the security council, was at this time suspicious of NATO's general intentions in post-cold war central and eastern Europe. More immediately, it was clear that NATO power was to be directed primarily against the Serbs – with whom Russia had a historical affinity based on pan-Slav sentiment and their shared Orthodox Christianity. Consequently, NATO could only act in Bosnia on the basis of what has been described as 'a framework within which a group of states happened to be joined', rather than a regional agency within the meaning of chapter VIII of the charter.[10] The absence of a clear legal status for NATO and the implication of the dual key meant above all that there was no clear hierarchy of control of the intervention, a situation that did not conduce to effective performance.

It may be, of course, that any such defined line of command was neither possible nor even desirable. A certain creative ambiguity may have been the price of the continuation of the arrangement. The absence of any reference to chapter VIII of the UN charter in security council mandates may have been the preference of either one or both of the dual key-holders. From the UN perspective, to invoke chapter VIII would have risked raising expectations of coercive enforcement as that was the original context of that part of the charter. More fundamentally, as we have suggested, NATO's status as a regional agency in the context of Yugoslavia was highly questionable. On its side, to have acknowledged the relevance of chapter VIII in its intervention would have been to accept a subordinate status to the UN. The security council's supremacy in relation to chapter VIII is absolute. Tellingly, perhaps, in 1994 the Belgian NATO secretary-general Willy Claes had rejected any such notion. NATO was not, he made clear, 'a subcontractor of the United Nations'.[11]

Yet it would be wrong to characterise the Bosnian intervention from 1993 until the decisive events of 1995 simply in terms of a timid UN frustrating the more determined instincts of NATO. Within NATO itself there were very different national positions on the degree of offensive air power that should be used. Britain and France did not suddenly abandon their concerns over the threat to their UNPROFOR contingents posed by the use of airpower against the Serbs. But a fundamental clash of interventionist cultures was exposed between the peacekeeping traditions of the United Nations and the war-fighting assumptions of NATO, which was, after all, a military alliance. Boutros-Ghali's representative in Bosnia was the Japanese diplomat Yasushi Akashi, who exercised (or, in the view of his critics, failed to exercise) considerable powers. He had in effect overall control of the UN-PROFOR operation (which grew in strength during 1994 to a formidable force of 34,000). Akashi however showed a persistent reluctance to use the NATO airpower which in principle was at his disposal for use either in support of UNPROFOR operations or as a punitive weapon against Serb provocations. While the NATO position, shaped by a membership with their own national concerns over the crisis, might not itself have been especially robust, it was not put to the test as the UN fingers on the dual key consistently refused to turn it. Inevitably, the Bosnian Serb forces did not acknowledge the humanitarian instincts which underlay Akashi's approach, instead taking it as proof of the UN's weakness and as an invitation to further probing of the limits of the international intervention.

In mid-1995 these provocations led to a curious diversion in the international effort in Bosnia. Angered by news film of French UN-PROFOR troops shackled to Serbian artillery as human shields against air strikes (following some limited NATO action against Serb positions bombarding a defenceless Sarajevo), President Chirac negotiated the creation of a Rapid Reaction Force of 10,000 French, British and Dutch troops. This would be empowered to use much more aggressive tactics than UNPROFOR. But significantly it was designed to provide only 'force protection'. That is to say, it would safeguard UNPROFOR units themselves (and prevent further national humiliation for the contributing states); it was not to be a new, more direct means of confronting Serb aggression.[12] This apparent concern with *amour propre* over the more direct needs of the Bosnian Muslims could be interpreted in different ways. It might be seen as an affirmation of the classical peacekeeping model in Bosnia by which neutrality was safeguarded but the self-defence capacity of the peacekeepers enhanced. Or alternatively it could equally be seen as a confirmation of the political confusion which afflicted the entire Bosnian intervention and as an attempt simply to reassure domestic audiences about the safety of their personnel while maintaining a distance from the political and moral questions surrounding the Bosnian conflict. Either interpretation pointed to a central dilemma in the paradigm shift underway in the early and mid-1990s from Hammarskjöldian peacekeeping to more deeply engaged forms of military humanitarian intervention.

The United States for its part still refused to contemplate committing American ground troops either as part of UNPROFOR or in any other configuration. The US air force continued to operate protected airdrops of humanitarian supplies, though often at an altitude which while protecting aircraft from surface-to-air attack compromised the effectiveness of the operations.

This situation would change decisively in July 1995. At the beginning of that month Bosnian Serb forces marched into the supposedly UN protected area of Srebrenica in eastern Bosnia close to the Serbian frontier. The Dutch UNPROFOR contingent charged with maintaining the safe area made no attempt at resistance and after some equivocation air power was not deployed against the Serb forces. A massacre then followed of some 8,000 Muslim men and boys who had sought refuge with their families from ethnic cleansing elsewhere in eastern Bosnia. Srebrenica and the Rwandan genocide of the previous year were the two defining events of UN intervention in the 1990s which drove the search for the new doctrine of 'responsibility to protect'.[13] More immediately, the horrors of Srebrenica ended finally the fallacy that traditional United Nations peacekeeping could make any significant contribution to the resolution of the Bosnian conflict.

After Srebrenica: humanitarian intervention as enforcement

In the underlying conflict between the competing interventionist cultures of peacekeeping and enforcement, the latter now took the upper hand. The initiative here came from the United States but, significantly, not by virtue of its position in the security council. Washington now acted via its leadership of the western alliance. The Clinton administration, it seemed, now had no fundamental objection to intervention; the problem for Washington lay in the nature of that intervention and the agency through which it took place. In the contest between the UN and NATO it was clear that the American preference was for the latter. During the later summer of 1995, NATO aircraft and artillery made short work of the Bosnian Serb military machine that had hitherto ranged across eastern Bosnia unopposed by international forces. NATO's 'Operation Deliberate Force' was pursued without any reference to 'dual keys' or inter-agency co-operation. The pressure driving the Bosnian Serbs to negotiations was not solely international, however. During the summer of 1995 their army had begun to suffer significant defeats on the ground in north-east Bosnia at the hands of the forces of the Sarajevo government acting in coordination with those of the Bosnian Croats after both anti-Serb forces managed to submerge their own differences the better to confront the larger common enemy. It was evident, though, that the mix of external and internal forces that had changed the terms of the conflict in this fundamental way did not include the UN force in the territory. In effect, the United Nations and UNPROFOR had been elbowed aside.

In November 1995, the warring factions in Bosnia were simply compelled into negotiations. Appropriately perhaps, given where the international initiative now lay, these were held in the United States (in Dayton, Ohio), organised by the Clinton administration. The final agreement, which was signed in Paris, created two statelets within what was already the microstate of Bosnia-Herzegovina: a unified Muslim-Croat one occupying the west and centre of the old Yugoslav federal state, and a formalised Republika Srpska in the north and the east. A High Representative for Bosnia and Herzegovina with wide-ranging powers and effectively appointed by NATO oversaw the entire territory. The agreement was enforced by a NATO Implementation Force (IFOR), whose mandate and functions were very far from the terms of the UN's humanitarian intervention. The role of the UN in the arrangements amounted to little more than formal acquiescence. Immediately following the Dayton settlement a security council resolution transferred UNPROFOR's residual mandated powers to IFOR, which remained under NATO command.[14] An enduring irony of the Bosnian intervention after 1995 was that NATO, having changed the fundamental dynamics of the conflict, could henceforward deploy IFOR as what was in essence a classical peacekeeping mission. UNPROFOR, by cleaving to the peacekeeping model in circumstances which were wholly inappropriate to it, merely invited its own demise.

Lessons learned? Kosovo

A simplified account of the international intervention in Bosnia would portray an inadequate and inappropriate UN mission based on a classical peacekeeping model ultimately being pushed aside by a non-UN enforcement operation. By these terms, the Kosovo narrative reversed the process. Here a NATO military operation enforced a particular outcome after which the United Nations was invited to secure the post-conflict environment largely on the basis of traditional peace-keeping. This reversal of sequence reveals much about the Bosnian experience and how it was processed by international institutions and their state members.

Unlike Bosnia (and the other successor states of the former Yugoslavia), Kosovo was not one of the federal republic's constituent 'nations'; it was an autonomous area within Serbia. Kosovo had an almost mystical significance for Serbian nationalists, having been the site of a famous fourteenth-century battle against the Turks. (This, paradoxically but not unusually for such national myths, ended in the defeat of those who would ultimately celebrate it.) Kosovo's importance to Serbia's national story was not reflected in the territory's ethnic composition, however. By 1998 approximately 90 per cent of Kosovo's population of about 2.2 million was ethnic Albanian (or Kosovar). They were predominantly Muslim, not Orthodox, and far from content to remain part of 'greater Serbia'. Only about 7 per cent of Kosovo's people was ethnic Serbian. By the 1990s the proportion of Albanians to Serbs had steadily increased over the recent decades, largely as a result of differential birth rates.[15]

While Kosovo had enjoyed a considerable degree of autonomy even within Serbia during the later years of Tito's Yugoslavia, its status became a potent element in Milošević's aggressive centralising nationalism in the early 1990s. But even before the rise of Milošević, Kosovo had been touched by the centrifugal forces that affected Yugoslavia as a whole following Tito's death in 1980. Initially this was expressed through pressure for full federal republic status within Yugoslavia, but as the multinational state disintegrated in the early 1990s, agitation for total independence grew. Simultaneously, the autonomy that Kosovo had enjoyed within Serbia was systematically reduced by Milošević during 1989 and 1990 as he attempted to exploit Serbian nationalism to concentrate Yugoslav power in Serbian Belgrade. Accordingly, as the wars of succession elsewhere in the former Yugoslav territories began to subside in the mid-1990s, two utterly irreconcilable forces of nationalism were accelerating towards a decisive conflict in Kosovo. Different strands of Kosovar nationalism emerged as the Yugoslav state began to fall apart in the early 1990s. One was a separatist movement, the League for a Democratic Kosovo (LDK), committed to political rather than military methods and led by the intellectual Ibrahim Rugova. But as the LDK's brand of non-violent nationalism failed to prevail in any significant way against an uncompromising Milošević, a guerrilla

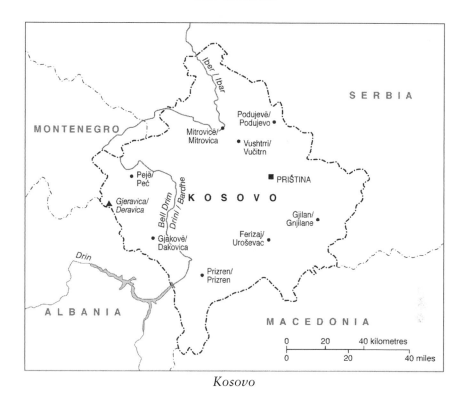

Kosovo

movement, the Kosovo Liberation Army (KLA), which confronted
Serbian military and paramilitary forces directly, grew in strength. The
KLA campaign, which involved the attempted ethnic cleansing of the
Serb minority from some parts of the province, unsurprisingly provoked
a brutal response from Belgrade. This in turn created refugee flows into
the Albanian 'homeland' and to the new state of Macedonia which had
asserted its own independence from the Yugoslav federation (largely
uncontested by Belgrade) in 1992.

Although the critical events leading to multilateral military action
against Serbia and the eventual administration of the territory by the
United Nations took place in 1998–9, international involvement had
already been considerable. Alex Bellamy provides a useful seven-part
'periodisation' of this intensifying intervention across the post-Tito
decade.[16] The first phase was one of 'non-engagement', between
January 1991 and August 1992 during which, while international
attention was given to Kosovo, it was seen as essentially a Serbian issue.
There followed a period of 'limited engagement' which lasted until
June 1993 – in other words during the first phase of the wars elsewhere

in Yugoslavia. At this time states and organisations, notably the United States and the Conference on Security and Cooperation in Europe (CSCE), began to signal to Serbia that it would be held accountable for any extension of violence to Kosovo. The third phase then covered the extended period between mid-1993 and the spring of 1998 which Bellamy characterises as one of 'malign non-engagement'. This was the high-water mark of Milošević's power in Serbia, during which he was able to thwart foreign involvement in the deteriorating situation in Kosovo because of his perceived importance to international attempts to broker peace in Croatia and Bosnia. In 1998 two linked phases were seen, which Bellamy describes as 'debating intervention' and 'unarmed intervention'. Serbia had exploited international caution during the preceding period to intensify its actions against the KLA and this led to mounting losses among ethnic Albanian civilians. A number of initiatives on the part of both western states and Russia failed to impress Belgrade. This brought an increasingly credible threat of NATO air-strikes against Serbian forces in Kosovo. Milošević, now since 1997 president of the rump state of Yugoslavia, backed down to the extent of accepting the presence of an Organization for Security and Cooperation in Europe (OSCE) Verification Mission mandated to observe the behaviour of his security forces in the territory.[17]

The decisive 1999 intervention in Kosovo occupies Bellamy's final two phases. 'Coercive diplomacy' which began at the beginning of the year gave way to 'limited war' in March which finished in the defeat of Serbia, the effective end of its control of Kosovo and the transfer of government functions to the United Nations. The actual trigger for the shift to military action was a massacre of Kosovar villagers by Serbian forces in pursuit of KLA elements. Ironically, these killings – of about forty-five civilians in the village of Račak – were far from the worst atrocity committed by the Serbs in retaliation for separatist violence. But Račak was investigated and reported on by the OSCE mission with high-profile results. Last-chance talks were hastily convened by a largely NATO group at Rambouillet in France where an ultimatum was delivered to the Serbian delegation (see below). It was rejected by Milošević who perhaps believed after a decade of brinkmanship in the face of international pressure that he could once again exploit international differences and the lack of appetite for military engagement. If so, he misread the situation disastrously. In truth, after the Srebrenica massacre five years earlier a germ of shame and guilt among states and organisations had developed to a point where the old obfuscations and temporisations would simply no longer be tolerated.

Significantly too, recent political changes among leading NATO states had changed government positions.

Tony Blair's Chicago speech and the 'doctrine of international community'

In particular, the Labour government which took office in Britain in 1997 brought a decisive shift from the 'realist' caution and traditional suspicion of moral rhetoric which had marked the Balkans policy of its Conservative predecessor. A major impetus for decisive military intervention was now provided by Tony Blair, the Labour prime minister. Blair gave a flavour of the moral imperative underlying his championing of armed intervention in April 1999, four weeks after the launch of NATO's air war against Serbia, in a widely reported speech in Chicago. In this he set out the political imperative of interventionism:

> No one in the West who has seen what is happening in Kosovo can doubt that NATO's military action is justified . . . This is a just war, based not on any territorial ambitions but on values. We cannot let the evil of ethnic cleansing stand. We must not rest until it is reversed. We have learned twice before in this century that appeasement does not work. If we let an evil dictator range unchallenged, we will have to spill infinitely more blood and treasure to stop him later.[18]

Blair then laid out the objectives of the intervention which included both the withdrawal of Serb forces from the territory and 'the deployment of an international military force'. These objectives were non-negotiable. Sovereignty, it was clear, would not impede them: 'Milosevic must accept them'.

But his concerns were not localised in the Balkans. Blair was setting out nothing less than a 'doctrine of international community' which appeared to embrace the idea of a right and responsibility for humanitarian intervention regardless of traditional notions of Westphalian sovereignty. This, in his perspective, was a natural concomitant to a post-cold war, globalised world. A new, systematic approach to such intervention had to be developed. Global policy could not be left to follow the random dictates of the CNN effect.

> As yet . . . our approach tends towards being ad hoc . . . We are continually fending off the danger of letting wherever CNN roves be the cattle prod to take a global conflict seriously. We need to focus in a serious and sustained way on the principles of the doctrine of international community and on the institutions that deliver them.

These institutions, in Blair's view, were primarily the United Nations and NATO. There should be 'reconsideration of the role, workings and decision-making process of the UN, and in particular the UN security council' while 'for NATO, once Kosovo is successfully concluded, a critical examination of the lessons to be learnt, and the changes we need to make in organisation and structure' must take place. In language in some ways markedly similar to that of the Responsibility to Protect Commission but which also placed national interests in the frame, Blair used Kosovo as the starting point for a new approach to interventionism. The Commission, when it reported nearly three years later, was to set out four 'precautionary principles'. These, it will be recalled, were: right intention; last resort; proportionality; and reasonable prospect of success (see Chapter 3). For his part, Blair proposed that five considerations should precede humanitarian intervention. Firstly, the moral case for intervention must be clear before force, an 'imperfect instrument for righting humanitarian distress', is unleashed. This approximately mapped the Commission's principle of 'right intention'. Secondly, before armed intervention takes place all possible diplomatic means of conflict resolution must be exhausted (as, he insisted, they had been over Kosovo). In other words, armed intervention was a 'last resort'. Thirdly, in practical terms 'are there military operations we can sensibly and prudently undertake?' This would be expressed by the Commission report in terms of 'proportionality' and 'prospects of success'.

Blair's final two considerations, however, were rather more 'realist' and state-centric in that they focused on questions of the national possibilities and interests of those countries undertaking intervention. There must be a commitment to seeing the task through: 'In the past we talked too much of exit strategies'. Finally, Blair openly appealed to the national interests of potential intervening states. In doing so he might be seen to transgress the precautionary principle of 'right intention'. His position, however, was that it was right and proper that extended national interests in the settlement of a humanitarian crisis should be engaged. In the specific case of Kosovo the transnational nature of refugee flows 'in such a combustible part of Europe' was a clear concern to the states of the larger region. This point could be seen as a rationalisation, conscious or otherwise, of the fact that the initial (and decisive) intervention in Kosovo was by NATO and not the United Nations. The circumstances around this fact were politically and diplomatically complicated and went to the heart of some of the historical dilemmas of armed intervention by the UN.

Resonances of the Chicago speech were to be heard in the subsequent

Responsibility to Protect Commission report as we have suggested. As a blueprint for future international behaviour, or even British foreign and security policy, its impact was less than clear, however. The year after the NATO intervention in Kosovo, British forces were sent to Sierra Leone where the UN mission (UNAMSIL) seemed powerless in the face of a brutal insurgency threatening the capital. The intervention of elite and special forces units was instrumental in turning the situation in favour of the weak though democratically legitimate government. The background to this humanitarian intervention remains opaque, however. The initial deployment was ostensibly a familiar type of post-colonial operation with the objective of evacuating British nationals from the country. Initially the British government was emphatic that this was the limit of the mission's objectives and seemed anxious that it should not be interpreted by the British public as anything more. The subsequent mission creep which saw British forces, independent of the UN operation, engage in offensive operations in the bush and then undertake long-term training duties for the national army has never been fully explained. It is unclear whether this was a planned assertion of the 'doctrine of international community' as articulated in Chicago or an ad hoc and opportunistic expansion of the original narrowly focused, conventional rescue mission.[19]

Whatever the background to the Sierra Leone intervention, the entire basis of the Chicago doctrine was to be undermined, along with the project of humanitarian intervention, as a whole three years later with the invasion of Iraq. The tendency of those opposed to the Iraq war has been to interpret the British government's involvement as a craven attempt to retain a supposedly favourable position with the administration of George W. Bush. In other words, Blair was branded as 'Bush's poodle'. Interestingly, however, the Chicago speech itself may point in another direction. Blair specifically identified 'two dangerous and ruthless men . . . prepared to wage vicious campaigns against sections of their own community'. Milošević was of course one of these men, in a speech primarily concentred to justify the Kosovo intervention in ethical terms. The other was Saddam Hussein, who presided over an Iraq 'reduced to poverty, with political life stultified through fear'. On this reading it is possible to see Blair's enthusiasm for the invasion of Iraq not, or not merely, in terms of a determination to travel on the political coat-tails of a right-wing American president, but as the natural continuation of the 'doctrine of international community'. If so, it was a catastrophic miscalculation for someone set on a widening of the liberal interventionist project. It brought the ever-present dilemma of humanitarian intervention being seen as the bedfellow of western dominance into the sharpest of relief. Certainly it profoundly dismayed a majority of those across the world who had previously been most committed to humanitarian interventionism as a principle and who had already had this commitment tested over the exercise of military might in Kosovo.

NATO leads: the United Nations marginalised?

The decisive air war against Serbia which created the conditions for the establishment of the United Nations Mission in Kosovo (UNMIK) was fought by NATO. This is not to say that the UN was not active in the crisis. But the politics and structure of the organisation simply ruled out any possibility of its providing a lead in Kosovo. The requirement here was for the sort of coercive enforcement action that would reverse a decade of international equivocation and retreat which had convinced Milošević of his invulnerability to decisive external intervention. A sequence of security council resolutions – none vetoed but none adopted unanimously – provided way-markers to NATO airstrikes. In March 1998, as the conflict between Serb-dominated Yugoslav forces and the KLA intensified, the Blair government enlisted the support of the Americans to press for a resolution clearly condemning Milošević's actions. To secure its passage, however, it had to be rigorously even-handed in its terms.[20] While Belgrade was pressed to reach a viable political solution based on an extensive degree of autonomy for Kosovo, the ethnic Albanian leadership was required to condemn the 'terrorist' actions of the KLA. Even this was not enough to ensure the support of the five permanent members. China abstained on the point of perhaps self-interested principle that the UN should have no role in what were essentially the internal ethnic difficulties of Yugoslavia. Behind this lay article 2 of the charter with its prohibition on United Nations intervention 'in matters which are essentially within the domestic jurisdiction of any state'. Russia, though it ultimately supported the resolution, had doubts about UN involvement based in part on its traditional affinity with its fellow Slavs in Serbia. On the other side of the argument over charter interpretations was the over-spill case – that instability within states in an inherently unstable international region was by its nature a 'threat to the peace' in the terms of chapter VII of the charter. It was this view that prevailed in the security council vote but the broader context within the council indicated the difficulties likely to be encountered in engineering a UN military intervention capable of shaping 'facts on the ground' in Kosovo.

This was underlined when the council returned to the Kosovo issue in September 1998. The outcome of this was a further resolution. But it was one which, despite the hopes of the British and American delegations and the fact that it referred to the enforcement chapter (VII) of the charter, still did not raise the possibility of military action to enforce the will of the security council. This was quite simply the price for the passage of the resolution (on which China again abstained).[21] The primary demand of the resolution was a ceasefire and the facilitation of the work of external observers. Again there was sharp condemnation of the 'terrorism' of the KLA and its supporters. Over the following months the fundamental division in the security council between Britain and the United States on one side and Russia and China on the other was consolidated. The ever-present possibility of a veto guaranteed that the western aspiration for a stronger position which would explicitly threaten the use of force against Milošević would not be achievable. A further resolution passed at the end of October brought no advance for the western position.[22] This endorsed the OSCE's Verification Mission and repeated its calls for negotiations, but while maintaining the reference to chapter VII of the previous resolutions, it made no reference to UN military intervention. Nevertheless, Russia now joined China in abstaining and stated clearly that despite references to chapter VII in the various Kosovo resolutions, it did not consider any of them to justify the use of force.[23] The widening differences of view also affected the role of the long-standing, semi-formal Balkans Contact Group which had operated in close co-operation with but slightly apart from the security council. Of the six members of this group, five – Britain, the US, France, Germany and Italy – were NATO members. The sixth, Russia, emphatically was not.

In the meantime, parallel institutional politics were being played out in NATO. The alliance was not wholly united behind the Anglo-American position on the use of force. Germany in particular was concerned about any role it might be expected to play in military action against Yugoslavia. It was not just that any such action would strictly speaking be 'out of area' for NATO; for Germany especially, military action against Yugoslavia would have dark resonances from an early phase in Europe's twentieth-century history.[24] Germany's apprehensions deepened as the extent of the Anglo-American strategy emerged. In an approach that would famously be repeated four years later concerning Iraq, the proposition was advanced by Britain and the US that a new security council resolution explicitly legitimising the use of force – or 'all necessary means' – was not in fact necessary. The references in prior resolutions to chapter VII, where the UN's original processes for coercive collective security are set out, implicitly opened the way for enforcement in the event of non-compliance, it was claimed. Milošević had failed to fully meet the demands of these resolutions, particularly in their requirement for a cessation of fighting. Serbia could therefore in principle be subject to enforcement action. In 2003 this position, adopted when it became clear that France and probably Russia would veto the crucial 'second resolution' authorising force against Iraq, violently divided opinion both internationally and within the countries that advanced it, Britain and the United States. The Anglo-American case was pored over by legions of international lawyers, the majority dismissing it. At the beginning of 1998, however, it did not elicit the same reaction. For one thing Kosovo was not Iraq. Given the balance of forces (NATO airpower against the JNA), any war was almost certain to be limited and short-lived. Beyond this, the motivations of those urging the use of force were viewed with more respect in relation to Kosovo, even among those opposed to the intervention. Tony Blair, who was evidently taking the lead, was not in alliance with George W. Bush but with the 'liberal' Bill Clinton and his vision of an effective international community as set out in his Chicago speech, while contestable, was widely viewed as genuinely held.

In Kosovo meanwhile, inter-ethnic fighting intensified as 1998 gave way to 1999 while NATO demanded that Serbia de-escalate its offensives against the KLA and its supporters. An emboldened KLA intensified its attacks against Yugoslav military and police and the inevitable reprisals increased Kosovar refugee flows into Macedonia and Albania. A series of contradictory Serb responses to western demands, which veered between defiance and co-operation, was interpreted abroad as just more of Milošević's well-tried games designed to out-manoeuvre external intervention. In reality, the inconsistencies in Belgrade's reactions may well have reflected a simple lack of policy direction as the uniqueness of the situation and its gravity for Serbia finally began to impress itself on the leadership.

It was against this confused background that in mid-January 1999 the OSCE Verification Mission reported the killings at Račak, triggering a sharp escalation in the movement towards war. Serbian rejection of the subsequent Rambouillet declaration virtually ensured that this would follow. The settlement on offer at Rambouillet involved internationally supervised elections in Kosovo and the presence of an international military presence in the territory. At the outset, however, it was accepted as a given by the Contact group that that Yugoslav sovereignty over Kosovo would continue.[25] After some protracted equivocation, Milošević rejected this last escape route on 15 March, at which point Yugoslav forces and Serbian irregulars launched an intensive campaign of ethnic cleansing against the Kosovar population. Accordingly, on 24 March, NATO airstrikes first authorised in principle by the alliance's supreme body the North Atlantic Council at the end of January were launched against targets in Kosovo and Serbia.

The initial effect of the air war – or Operation Allied Force as NATO planners styled it – was to further accelerate the ethnic cleansing. Refugee flows reached tidal-wave proportions with some 20,000 Kosovars moving across Kosovo's international borders daily for a time. The final outcome was in little doubt, however. After seventy-eight days of intensive airstrikes Milošević agreed to withdraw his forces from the territory and accept the presence of an international military presence. Accordingly, NATO secretary-general Javier Solana ordered a cessation of the offensive on 10 June.

How does this NATO phase of the Kosovo intervention measure against the 'precautionary principles' of the subsequent Responsibility to Protect Commission report (or indeed the criteria for action by the 'international community' set out in Tony Blair's Chicago speech which sought to justify it at the time)? The Commission was equivocal in its judgement, merely posing some of the more trenchant questions around the issue:

> The operation raised major questions about the legitimacy of military intervention in a sovereign state. Was the cause just: were the human rights abuses committed or threatened by the Belgrade authorities sufficiently serious to warrant outside involvement? Did those seeking secession manipulate external intervention to advance their political purposes? Were all peaceful means of resolving the conflict fully explored? Did the intervention receive appropriate authority? How could the bypassing and marginalization of the UN system, by 'a coalition of the willing' acting without Security Council approval, possibly be justified? Did the way in which the intervention was carried out in fact worsen the very human rights situation it was trying to rectify? Or – against all this – was it the case that had (NATO) not intervened, Kosovo would have been at best the site of an ongoing, bloody and destabilizing civil war, and at worst the occasion for genocidal slaughter like that which occurred in Bosnia four years earlier?[26]

The principle of 'just cause' based on the apprehension of genocide or 'large-scale' ethnic cleansing was probably applicable. The history of Serbian behaviour in other multi-ethnic parts of the former Yugoslavia would have to be considered. So too would the evidence of forced refugee movements prior to NATO action. And, as we have suggested, the 'right intention' was probably present if Blair's claims in the Chicago speech are accepted as genuine. Beyond a concern with regional stability (which Blair himself emphasised), the motivations of the leading actors appear to have been genuinely humanitarian (even if driven in part by a CNN effect on and from public opinion). Given the gradual diplomatic build to war and Milošević's continual defiance of international opinion displayed not just in his reaction to NATO, but to the United Nations security council and the Contact Group at Rambouillet as well, it is not difficult to portray the use of force as the 'last resort'. The massive military power which NATO had at its disposal clearly guaranteed 'reasonable prospects' of the success of intervention. But this power and the manner in which it was used raises questions about the last of the Commission's precautionary principles: proportionality. The NATO coalition's aversion to risk helped dictate the decision to launch an air war rather than a land invasion. The United States, it will be recalled, had been markedly reluctant to commit its own ground troops to Bosnia until a political settlement had been forced by air power and long-range artillery in Operation Deliberate Force. This reluctance was now shared by its NATO partners in Kosovo, who were willing to deploy ground forces only after the surrender of Belgrade. The price of this was a high casualty rate, both civilian by way of unintended consequences of aerial bombing and among Yugoslav forces who might otherwise have been contained by superior forces on the ground. On balance, therefore, Kosovo could not be said to be a model of successful humanitarian intervention.

More broadly, the action dramatically widened the cleavage between the permanent membership of the security council. Here in particular the vexed question of proportionality was prominent. The inevitable 'collateral damage' of a war fought from aircraft thousands of feet in the air and from missile launching pads hundreds of miles away had deepened the resentment of Russia and China towards what they saw as NATO's unilateral action and disdain for the security council itself. In particular, at the beginning of May a NATO attack on Belgrade struck the Chinese embassy, killing three of its staff. This provoked Russia to join China in condemning the bombing as 'an act of aggression'. Then, as the air war ended and ground troops moved into Kosovo, Russia sent a force of its own which occupied the principal airport in the capital Pristina, triggering a tense stand-off with western forces.[27] The omens for the reappearance of the United Nations were therefore not wholly encouraging.

The potentially fraught presence of both NATO and Russian troops in Kosovo in the aftermath of the Yugoslav surrender was in fact a consequence of UN re-engagement. On 10 June, alongside the cessation of NATO's military operations, a security council resolution called for the establishment of an international civil and security presence in Kosovo to coincide with Belgrade's 'withdrawal from Kosovo of all military, police and paramilitary forces according to a rapid timetable'.[28] Crucially though, this international security presence was not to be a United Nations one as such, but constituted 'under the auspices of the United Nations'. The result was KFOR (Kosovo Force), an acronym which inevitably recalled IFOR, the non-UN military presence deployed in Bosnia after NATO's Operation Deliberate Force. KFOR was not, however, to be a NATO force – as the appearance of Russian troops in Kosovo testified.

International administration: United Nations Mission in Kosovo

In the event, neither Moscow on one side nor Washington and London on the other were prepared to see their bilateral relations entirely degraded by the Kosovo crisis. They were helped to avoid this by the dominance of the UN – under a security council mandate – in the post-conflict administration of the territory. This role fell into the general category of UN 'government' as exercised in the past from West New Guinea to Cambodia. The United Nations Mission in Kosovo (UNMIK) was the 'international civil presence' established by the 10 June security council resolution. It was charged with the establishment of a 'transitional administration' to operate within the supposedly secure environment guaranteed by KFOR.

Over the following decade UNMIK struggled to square an impossible circle. As the 'successor regime' to Milošević's Serbia, installed after a successful war fought on behalf of the ethnic Albanian majority, local expectations that it would in turn give way to independent statehood were high. This was, after all, the project being pursued simultaneously by the UN administration in East Timor, where Indonesian rule had been overthrown by popular resistance and eventually an electoral process (see the next chapter). Yet the security council's mandate for Kosovo required UNMIK to operate on the basis of the continuation of the pre-war sovereignty of Yugoslavia. It did not represent any dramatic advance for Kosovar aspirations on the Rambouillet declaration which Serbia had rejected on the eve of the war. The council's key resolution had in fact been based on a blueprint drawn up by the G-8 grouping at the beginning of May in anticipation of NATO's victory. This called for 'substantial self-government for Kosovo, taking full account of . . . the principles of sovereignty and territorial integrity of the Federal Republic of Yugoslavia'.[29] Even without the presence of Russia in both the G-8 and the security council, it is unlikely that the world's leading states would have taken such a radical step as to demand independence at this stage. NATO had been involved in a humanitarian intervention, after all, and even that had been viewed warily by some of its members. It had certainly not been a war to re-draw the national frontiers of south-central Europe. Despite this, the ethnic Albanian view was that NATO had 'intervened in a civil war and defeated one side, but embraced the position of the party it had defeated on the issue over which the war was fought'.[30]

The reaction of significant elements of the Albanian majority to this frustrated ambition was to switch status from victim to aggressor. The Serb population declined sharply as it in turn fell victim to *de facto* ethnic cleansing, with many seeking refuge in Serbia proper or in Serb-dominated enclaves in Kosovo, particularly the town of Mitrovica which became the scene of violent ethnic clashes in 2004. Writing in 2003, four years after the establishment of UNMIK, the Canadian commentator Michael Ignatieff described the situation and its broader resonances for humanitarian intervention with characteristic elegance. UNMIK had achieved much in this 'the most ambitious project the UN [had] undertaken'. Schools had been reopened, returning refugees sheltered and the economy stabilised. But UNMIK's 'signal failure':

> has been to get Kosovars to live with the remaining Serbs. This is a significant embarrassment: the NATO intervention was defended as a human rights operation, to put a stop to Slobodan Milosevic's ethnic cleansing. It stopped Milosevic, but it has not stopped the Kosovars attempting to drive out the remaining Serbs. A cloud of disillusion has descended over the Kosovo operation, and by extension to all such exercises in humanitarian intervention. What is the point of assisting people to be free if they use their freedom to persecute their former persecutors? The moral script that justifies humanitarian intervention demands noble victims and the Kosovars are not playing by the script.[31]

In Kosovo as in other parts of the world where a decisive intervention has changed the balance of social and political forces on the ground, the fallacy of the automatic moral superiority of the victim was sharply exposed.

In this environment the UN's interim administration inevitably became the focus of complaint. This went beyond the actors, local and diplomatic, who were directly involved. As in the case of the contemporaneous administration in East Timor, it has been criticised by academics and commentators for being out of touch with realities on the ground, for being unaccountable and lacking vision. One recurring complaint was that it had 'consolidated' ethnic politics in the structures it established and in its means of relating to the local populations. This, some have argued, has entrenched ethnicity in the political culture rather than challenged it.[32] Yet here as in each of the other significant interventions it has undertaken, the possibilities of the United Nations have been determined largely by forces on the ground and by the international politics surrounding the conflict. A temporary administration, ultimately, is just that: time-limited and aware of its own political separateness from national processes. UNMIK had to work with the political realities which it encountered in 1999, and no amount of wishful thinking or academic abstraction could change the fact that foremost among these realities was the almost absolute socio-political division of Kosovo along ethnic lines. This ethnic basis to Kosovo's politics was set by Kosovo's people. To have pretended that this was not the case and to have disregarded it in the pursuit of the limited 'nation-building' possibilities available to an administration uncertain of its own longevity would have been, it can be argued, wilfully counterproductive.[33] In November 2001, elections to a Kosovo Assembly, which were supervised by the OSCE rather than the UN, were boycotted by almost all of the remaining Serbs quite simply because the ethnic arithmetic made the outcome inevitable.[34] In fact, the results were not as radically disastrous for the Serb minority as they might have been, as the moderate Ibrahim Rugova became president (though he died in office in 2006). In the circumstances, it is unclear what UNMIK in Kosovo or the security council in New York could have done to engineer a less ethnically based outcome.

Beyond the territory itself, the international politics of Kosovo, its geopolitical position and the external historical affinities involved confounded for almost a decade the UN's search for a solution to the 'final status' problem. The numbers were stark and relentless, however. More than 90 per cent of Kosovo's population aspired to independence and once the territory had been detached from Serbia by the UN it simply could not be reattached with any democratic legitimacy. While the intervention may not have been designed to change the formal international order, that inevitably was the result. Appeals to the juridical niceties of Westphalian sovereignty had little effect in Kosovo itself, whatever the instincts of the major powers in the security council. Kosovo's UN-bestowed special status meant that the basic principles of self-deter-mination would ultimately prevail. The UN grasped the nettle of Kosovo's final status in 2006 when the former Finnish president and veteran UN trouble-shooter Martti Ahtisaari began a round of inter-national negotiations. It soon became clear that the long-standing international fault-lines remained. Ahtisaari's proposal for 'supervised independence' for the territory – an interim stage between UN administration and statehood – was not acceptable either to Serbia or, more importantly, Russia. The Russian position was that any final status must be accepted by both ethnic Albanians and Serbs, regard-less of the wishes of the Kosovan majority. That position was main-tained by Moscow despite repeated revisions to the details of the plan. This effectively handed a veto to the (dwindling) Serb minority.

The deadlock was broken following elections at the end of 2007 which brought the former KLA commander and head of the Albanian Rambouillet delegation, Hashim Thaçi, to power. Leader of the radical Democratic Party of Kosovo, Thaçi had promised to declare the independence of Kosovo unilaterally if elected, which he duly did in February 2008. The results, local and international, were predictable but unavoidable. The Serb minority immediately set up its own rival 'government' in Mitrovica, confirming its long-standing rejection of the post-1999 political process. Serbia and Russia denounced Thaçi's declaration as illegal, while most of the leading west European powers and the United States recognised the new independent republic. At the level of the United Nations, while the security council was rendered paralysed on the issue, the general assembly referred the question to the International Court of Justice for an advisory opinion on the legality of independence. In the circumstances, however, such an opinion was unlikely to shift significantly the positions already taken on the issue by the principal interests involved.

UNMIK remained in Kosovo following the disputed independence, though it gradually ceded functions to the European Union as the principal regional agency. The EU Rule of Law Mission (EULEX) was established shortly after the declaration of statehood in 2008, although its status under international law remained opaque. It could not super-sede UNMIK without a security council resolution and this would not be possible as long as Russia refused recognition. Even within the European Union doubts remained about the legality of Kosovo's independence, the diplomatic desirability of recognising it, and the danger of EU involvement being interpreted as formal recognition (the main dissenting voice was Spain, supported by Cyprus, Greece and Romania).

Nevertheless, policing functions were gradually transferred from UNMIK (which had maintained a UN Civilian Police Force, UN-CIVPOL) to EULEX. Ironically, the EULEX presence is also viewed with suspicion – and met with occasional violence – by the Albanian majority because of its necessary operational relationship with Serbia. UNMIK remained, and though its operational future was uncertain, its presence looked to be long-term, or at least for as long as security council consensus remained out of reach. The self-declared independence of Kosovo, sixteen years to the month after the blue helmets were first deployed in the former Yugoslavia, clearly did not mark the end of United Nations intervention.

The UN and the end of Yugoslavia: A spectrum of intervention

Even a year or two before the United Nations first intervened militarily in the Balkans, the prospect would have appeared outlandish. Intervention by UN forces was simply not a 'European' thing. Continental Europe was off-limits to intervention because intervention was neither politically feasible not likely to be required as long as Europe remained subject to the politics of bipolarity and the tenuous domestic stability that this tended to bring. The case of Cyprus was in this regard a special one in the European context, in which a post-colonial conflict between ethnic groups affected two alliance partners. Yet predictions of the end of the cold war and the dramatic changes this would bring to European politics would have seemed equally outlandish even in the latter part of the 1980s.

When UN military intervention came to the Yugoslav space as the state that once occupied it disintegrated, it drew widely across the repertoire of the established military and political techniques, and indeed expanded them. Traditional interpositionary peacekeeping of a type readily recognisable in the 1950s was first attempted by UNPROFOR in Croatia. This then evolved with the creation of UN-protected areas. When UNPROFOR's mandate was extended to Bosnia, a crucial addition involved the protection and delivery of emergency aid, a responsibility more reminiscent of recent operations in Somalia than of the Hammarskjöldian tradition. In Kosovo the UN's intervention followed a period of coercive military action by a non-UN agency, NATO, and took the form of the provision of an interim administration.

This was another venerable form of multilateral intervention which even pre-dated the UN, going back to the League of Nations governing commission in the Saar in the 1920s and 30s.

Wholly new approaches to intervention were also developed by the UN in the Balkans. In Macedonia, which seceded relatively amicably from the Yugoslav federation, the first ever UN force with a specifically preventive mandate was deployed, between 1995 and 1999. The Preventive Deployment Force (UNPREDEP) monitored Macedonia's northern borders with Serbia to discourage any spill-over of the developing conflict in Kosovo. As this conflict intensified Macedonia became a major recipient of Kosovar refugees, but no major violence occurred in its territory.

The Macedonia intervention was, however, the only one in which the UN could claim a clear success in the Balkans. All of its other engagements in the region were at the least mixed in their outcomes. In Bosnia the peacekeeping model of humanitarian intervention simply proved inapt given the nature of the conflict. This problem was not to be solved by establishing a relationship between the UN and NATO and the provision of a dual key for robust action to both of them. On the contrary, problems of inter-agency relations if anything undermined the intervention and aided the campaigns of the Bosnian Serbs who proved adept at exploiting international divisions. Ultimately enforcement by a single – and single-minded – organisation seemed to be the only route to ending the war and the beginning of conflict resolution. Consequently the UN found itself effectively marginalised while NATO forces applied 'Deliberate Force'.

By the time of the Kosovo intervention the suggestion that the United Nations could mount a successful enforcement action was not even considered by the leading powers in the Contact Group and beyond. UN action had been rendered impossible at a more fundamental political level. Even if, and precedent for this was not encouraging, the UN could have gathered the physical resources for such an operation from among is members, there was simply no possibility of the necessary political consensus in the security council given the position of both Russia and China. Although involving great political risk, the lead had to be taken by NATO. It was the only organisation with sufficient consensus among its membership (and even this was far from complete) and sufficient material resources to mount an effective enforcement action. Importantly, however, the next – post-war – phase of the Kosovo intervention required the United Nations to take the major responsibility. The NATO air war and even its subsequent domination of KFOR was not sufficient to provoke a fatal reaction from Moscow. But any attempt by a 'western' organisation – whether NATO or the European Union – to impose an interim government on Kosovo and to guide it towards a 'final status' would almost certainly have done so. The continuing presence of UNMIK after the *de facto* independence of Kosovo at the beginning 2008 was itself a means of maintaining a reasonable level of diplomatic stability.

The experience of intervention in the Balkans highlights two essential truths for the UN, both of which have been present across the range of its military experience. Firstly, at the operational level, humanitarian intervention is rarely compatible with military enforcement. Even if the security council can be persuaded to back enforcement (which was not the case in the Balkans), the UN tradition of intervention and the problems inherent in joint command in the United Nations militate strongly against success. And this is perhaps more a strength than a weakness for the organisation. Enforcement by regional agencies or ad hoc coalitions of the willing will usually be available, leaving the UN itself innocent of direct involvement in offensive military action with all the physical and political hazards that go with it. The second truth intersects with this first one at various points and stands constant reiteration. The 'agency' of the United Nations in all matters, but especially issues of military intervention, is in reality very small. It is the security council that determines UN intervention or non-intervention and it does so according to calculations of interest, national and international, by each individual member. This was as true in the Balkans as it was in Rwanda. The five most powerful of these members have an individual veto at their disposal. All of this was in evidence during the years of UN intervention in the former Yugoslavia and most prominently in Bosnia and Kosovo. The limited but tangible achievements of the United Nations there, when these huge constraints are considered along with the nature of the conflicts taking place, were far from negligible.

Notes

1. The protracted disintegration of Yugoslavia during the 1990s and its historical background have been the subject of a huge volume of published analysis and comment, some of it rather tendentious. The journalist Misha Glenny's *The Fall of Yugoslavia* (3rd ed., Harmondsworth: Penguin, 1999) is very accessible and carefully and convincingly argued. Among other recent works are John R. Lampe, *Yugoslavia as History* (2nd ed., Cambridge: Cambridge University Press, 2000); Leslie Benson, *Yugoslavia:*

A *Concise History* (London: Macmillan, 2001); Richard West, *Tito and the Rise and Fall of Yugoslavia* (London: Faber, 2009). Sabrina Petra Ramet's, *Thinking About Yugoslavia* (Cambridge: Cambridge University Press, 2005) discusses the ideological and historiographical complexities surrounding the topic.

2. On the position of British prime minister John Major at this time see Nicholas Wheeler, *Saving Strangers: Humanitarian Intervention in International Society* (Oxford: Oxford University Press, 2000), pp. 246–7.

3. UNPROFOR was established by security council resolution S/RES/743 (1992), 21 February 1992.

4. Security council resolution S/RES/770(1992), 13 August 1992.

5. Security council resolution S/RES/776(1992), 14 September 1992.

6. The flight ban was imposed by security council resolution S/RES/781 (1992), 9 October 1992.

7. The critical plea here came in security council resolution S/RES/816 (1993), 31 March 1993.

8. See Richard Sobel, *The Impact of Public Opinion on US Foreign Policy* (Oxford: Oxford University Press, 2001), p. 184.

9. Dick Morris, *Behind the Oval Office: Getting Reelected Against All Odds* (New York: Random House, 1997), pp. 247–8.

10. Spiros Economides and Paul Taylor, 'Former Yugoslavia', in *The New Interventionism 1991–1994: United Nations Experience in Cambodia, Former Yugoslavia and Somalia* (Cambridge: Cambridge University Press, 1996), p. 80.

11. Quoted in Sashi Tharoor, 'United Nations Peacekeeping in Europe', *Survival*, 37(2) (1995), p. 125.

12. Ivo H. Daalder, *Getting to Dayton: America's Bosnia Policy* (Washington DC: Brookings Institution, 2000), pp. 44–9.

13. Secretary-general Kofi Annan produced a formal report on the massacre at the request of the general assembly four months after it had taken place. He largely absolved the Dutch contingent on the grounds that requested air power had not been deployed and insisted that the responsibility lay with those who had carried out the killings. 'The cardinal lesson of Srebrenica', he concluded, was 'that a deliberate and systematic attempt to terrorise, expel or murder an entire people must be met decisively with all necessary means, and with the political will to carry the policy through to its logical conclusion'. Report of the Secretary-General on the Fall of Srebrenica, general assembly document A/54/549, 15 November 1999.

14. UN member states were authorised 'acting through or in cooperation with [NATO] to establish a multinational force under unified command in order to fulfil . . . the Peace Agreement'. Security council resolution S/RES/1031(1995), 15 December 1995. A small police operation, the Mission in Bosnia and Herzegovina (UNMIBH), remained under UN control but its functions were restricted to support and training of local police forces.

15. These are estimated figures. The last full census of Kosovo had been in 1991 when a total population of just under two million was recorded. At that time the respective proportions were 82.2 per cent Albanian and 9.9 per cent Serb. The remainder came from a range of minorities, including Roma and non-Albanian Muslims. See Tim Juddah, *Kosovo: War and Revenge* (2nd ed., London: Yale University Press, 2002), p. 313.

16. Alex Bellamy, *Kosovo and International Society* (London: Palgrave, 2002), pp. 12–15.

17. The OSCE was created in 1995 as the successor institution to the CSCE – the Conference on Security and Cooperation in Europe. The CSCE began in 1973 as part of the new security architecture in Europe created by the superpower détente of the time. Its importance – and longevity – lay in its composition, which included both sides of the cold war divide. After the end of the cold war it was restructured and renamed to meet the new international realities within which east and west European states now co-existed.

18. Text of the speech can be found on the US Public Broadcasting Service website at www.pbs.org/.../bb/.../blair_doctrine4-23.html

19. For a view of the Sierra Leone intervention which relates it firmly to the Chicago doctrine see Andrew Dorman, *Blair's Successful War* (Aldershot: Ashgate, 2009).

20. Security council resolution S/RES/1160(1998), 31 March 1998.

21. Security council resolution S/RES/1199(1998), 23 September 1998. See Wheeler, *Saving Strangers*, pp. 261–2.

22. Security council resolution S/RES/1203(1998), 24 October 1998.

23. See Patrick T. Egan, 'The Kosovo Intervention and Collective Self-Defence', *International Peacekeeping*, 8(3) (2001), p. 44.

24. Wheeler, *Saving Strangers*, pp. 261–2.

25. The full text of the interim agreement can be found (from the US State Department site) at http://www.state.gov/www/regions/eur/ksvo_rambouillet_text.html

26. Report of the International Commission on Intervention and State Sovereignty, paragraph 1.2. Found at http://www.iciss.ca/report-en.asp

27. The incident also exposed differences in approach between the NATO forces on the ground. Ordered by the force commander General Wesley Clark of the US to deploy his paratroops to cut off the Russian advance, the British general, Michael Jackson, famously refused, telling Clark that he was 'not going to start the Third World War for you'. *The Guardian*, 2 August 1999.

28. Security council resolution S/RES/1224(1999), 10 June 1999.

29. Statement by the Chairman on the conclusion of the meeting of the G-8 Foreign Ministers, 6 May 1999, issued as annex 1 to security council resolution S/RES/1224(1999), 10 June 1999. At this time the G-8 consisted of the original Group of 7 formed in 1976 (Britain, Canada, France, Germany, Italy, Japan and the United States) along with Russia.

30. Michael Mandelbaum, 'A Perfect Failure: NATO's War Against Yugoslavia', *International Affairs*, 78(5) (1999), p. 125.
31. Michael Ignatieff, *Empire Lite: Nation-Building in Bosnia, Kosovo and Afghanistan* (London: Vintage, 2003), pp. 51–2.
32. See for example Isa Blumi, 'Ethnic Borders to a Democratic Society in Kosova: The UN's Identity Card', in Florian Bieber and Zidas Daskalovska (eds), *Understanding the War in Kosovo* (London: Cass, 2003), pp. 311–56 and Aidan Hehir, 'Autonomous Province Building: Identification Theory and the Failure of UNMIK', *International Peacekeeping*, 13(2) (2006), pp. 200–13.
33. In 2000 the Independent International Commission on Kosovo – a grouping of the liberal great and good chaired by Richard Goldstone who had been chief prosecutor at the UN International Tribunals for both Rwanda and the former Yugoslavia – characterised the process as 'nation-building for a non-nation'. *The Kosovo Report: The Independent Commission on Kosovo* (Oxford: Oxford University Press, 2000), p. 106.
34. UNMIK's responsibilities were based on four 'pillars'. Police and justice and civil administration were the responsibility of the UN itself. The OSCE was responsible for democratisation and nation-building while the EU oversaw reconstruction and economic development.

Chapter 6

A model intervention? The birth of Timor Leste

The multinational involvement in East Timor (now officially known in its Portuguese form as Timor Leste) began after the violence surrounding the independence referendum in 1999. At various points in the unfolding of the situation, the international presence in Timor seemed to represent the best efforts of humanitarian intervention. This external involvement took a number of familiar forms. There was, successively, intervention by a coalition of the willing legitimised by the United Nations, a UN force, and a United Nations transitional administration in the territory. The conflict that brought about this complex intervention was both inter-state and intra-state in character. The referendum that acted as the trigger for the conflict in East Timor was held to determine whether it should become an independent state, freed from annexation by Indonesia imposed in 1975. But the immediate conflict on the ground was primarily between local factions acting in part as proxies for Indonesia and others fighting for separation. The eventual declaration of East Timor's independence in May 2002 and its admission to the United Nations as a new sovereign state was regarded at the time as a powerful vindication of the entire interventionist project after the high-profile failures of the 1990s from Rwanda to Bosnia. Yet both the course and conduct of the involvement and its post-independence aftermath raise important questions about the broader possibilities of humanitarian intervention. Timor therefore merits particular attention in any general account of the interventionist role of the United Nations.

The background to the intervention

In 1975, at the time of its annexation by Indonesia, East Timor was one of the more peculiar of the manifold peculiarities of European imperialism. The Portuguese had first occupied the whole island of Timor (which lies towards the eastern end of the vast Indonesian archipelago) in 1520 as part of their 'first' – Asian – empire (the 'second' being Brazil and the 'third' Africa). At the beginning of the seventeenth century

Portugal was displaced from the western part of the island by the new imperial power on the scene, the Netherlands. This began a half-hearted wrangle for control which lasted for the best part of the next three centuries and which eventually ended with the formal allocation of East Timor to the Portuguese and West Timor to the Dutch. With the transition of the Dutch East Indies into the independent state of Indonesia after the second world war, East Timor was left as a back-water of the Portuguese empire. Despite the fact that it was neither a feasible colony of settlement nor a viable colony of economic exploi-tation, East Timor was held close by the authoritarian regime in Lisbon which affected to regard its colonies as sacred, indivisible extensions of metropolitan Portugal.

The situation changed dramatically after the military coup in Portugal in 1974 which led to a rapid and chaotic process of decolon-isation. Amidst this, the attention of the new government in Lisbon – and of the world as a whole – was understandably focused on Africa. There, the large geostrategically important territories of Angola and Mozambique had become independent under avowedly Marxist regimes and this had huge implications for both regional and global politics (see Chapter 4). East Timor therefore went unregarded by the outside world. Unquestionably, though, the spirit of the times guar-anteed that East Timor was destined for independence. The principal nationalist grouping in the territory, again reflecting the zeitgeist of the 1970s, styled itself as a Marxist revolutionary movement.

An independent East Timor under the Revolutionary Front of In-dependent East Timor (Fretilin – *Frente Revolucionária do Timor Leste Independente*) would present a major challenge to western interests in southeast Asia at a particularly sensitive time immediately following the withdrawal of the United States from Vietnam. Although this was the period of superpower détente, there were limits to how far either one was willing to see any significant shift in their relative spheres of regional influence. In Indonesia the prospect of a new Marxist micro-state nested at the heart of the 'national' archipelago was anathema to the long-standing authoritarian and anti-communist regime of General Suharto. Unsurprisingly, therefore, Indonesia took a close interest in the sequence of events in East Timor after Portugal's intention to divest itself of its colonies became obvious. In August 1975 violence erupted between three distinct interests: a vocal anti-independence movement (the UDT); a pro-Indonesian integrationist party (APODETI); and Fretilin. From the outset Indonesian forces, which were infiltrated across the border from West Timor, operated in a barely covert way in support

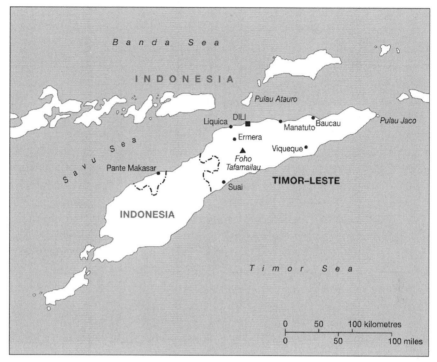

East Timor/Timor Leste

of APODETI. Then, in December, following a brief visit from US secretary of state Henry Kissinger which may or may not have been significant, Indonesian forces annexed the territory by force, declaring it in the following July to be Indonesia's twenty-seventh province.[1]

The armed wing of Fretilin, the Armed Forces for the National Liberation of East Timor (Falintil – *Forças Armadas da Libertação Nacional de Timor Leste*), now took to the mountainous interior from where it conducted a long, bitter and at times successful guerrilla campaign against the invaders. The repression with which the Indonesian occupiers responded to this, along with an associated protracted famine, cost the lives of some 200,000 Timorese, about a quarter of the entire population, during the period of Indonesian occupation.

The United Nations had been involved in the situation from the outset following the Indonesian invasion in 1975. Immediately after the annexation the security council unanimously reaffirmed the territory's right to self-determination under the UN charter and called for the immediate withdrawal of Indonesian forces. The resolution stopped short, however, of framing its condemnation in terms of chapter VII of the charter which would have raised the possibility of enforcement action and signalled to Indonesia that its behaviour was considered with real gravity.[2] In the years that followed, general assembly resolutions were passed affirming East Timor's right to self-determination as it remained formally a 'non-self-governing' territory under the terms of the charter, never having been formally decolonised by Portugal.[3]

In 1982 the assembly instructed the secretary-general to exercise his good offices in pursuit of a political solution.[4] Although annual reports were subsequently presented to the assembly by successive secretaries-general, no substantive advances were made against Indonesian intransigence and the matter was not regarded as sufficiently serious to be turned over to the security council as a threat to international peace. Even if it had been, western support for 'friendly' Indonesia would almost certainly have prevented any effective pressure on Jakarta as long as the cold war continued. But just as global and regional politics had combined to bring about East Timor's enforced annexation by Indonesia in the 1970s, the transformation in both international and Indonesian politics in the 1990s radically altered the situation. The end of the cold war removed the strategic and ideological grounds for Indonesia's suppression of Timorese aspirations for independence and the west's acquiescence to this.

In 1991 a massacre of more than 180 local protesters at the Santa Cruz cemetery in East Timor's capital, Dili, during an anti-Indonesian demonstration refocused international attention on the territory, including that of the UN Human Rights Commission. A wave of criticism of Indonesia worldwide resulted, to a degree that would have been unlikely when cold war calculations and loyalties still prevailed. Pressure on Indonesia was maintained when the 1996 Nobel Peace prize was awarded jointly to the exiled Fretilin leader José Ramos-Horta and the Roman Catholic Bishop of Dili, Carlos Belo, who had used the limited protection of his position to make outspoken criticisms of Indonesian behaviour in the territory. The crucial development, however, came two years later when a democratising wave in Indonesia itself swept away the Suharto regime amidst the region-wide economic meltdown of the time in southeast Asia. Some of the nationalist obduracy of the old dictatorship was now taken out of the equation. In 1998 the new Indonesian president, B. J. Habibie, proposed greater autonomy for East Timor within Indonesia. But this partial concession was quickly engulfed by a renewed push for full independence which Jakarta was now ill-equipped to resist, and in January 1999 Habibie conceded for the first time that such independence could be an option.

In May 1999 Indonesia and Portugal (still regarded by the United Nations as having legal sovereign authority as decolonisation had never formally taken place) agreed with the encouragement of secretary-general Kofi Annan to a referendum – or 'popular consultation' – on the future of the territory.[5] Following this the UN established a major support presence in the territory in the form of the United Nations Mission in East Timor (UNAMET) which was mandated by a security council resolution to organise and then oversee the referendum.[6] This, at Indonesia's insistence, was to be held within a very short time-scale of just a few months (the original date was at the beginning of August 1999), a task that stretched UNAMET's relatively scant resources to the limit. The situation was made more difficult because UNAMET was not given any direct security functions or resources. Law and order remained the responsibility of Indonesia. The UN mission's mandate included the provision of police advisers and military liaison officers but these were to work strictly on planning issues with local counterparts. That civil order remained the responsibility of Indonesia was strongly emphasised by the security council in its mandate. The problem now was that, as street violence worsened in the run-up to the vote, Indonesian police and troops proved unable (and, in the view of most observers, unwilling) to impose order. The referendum campaign was scarred by the violence of anti-independence 'militia' groups – in reality undisciplined armed gangs. These were actively supported by elements of the Indonesian army which was, of course, by the terms of the Indonesia–Portugal agreement in May, supposed to be responsible for the security of the campaign and the vote. The extent of government complicity in this behaviour was unclear but it is likely that President Habibie's administration would have been largely powerless to control the military in East Timor even if it had wished to do so. His decision to permit an independence option in the referendum had surprised and angered many in the army and amidst the uncertain politico-military relationship of the immediate post-Suharto period in Indonesia this was a test of wills that the civilian-led government would have wished to avoid

It seems likely in fact that the Indonesian government, in a state of collective self-delusion, believed that the vote would be in favour of limited autonomy within Indonesia (its own strongly preferred option) and not independence. But this view was not shared by other observers. As widely expected, the poll, held on 30 August, produced an overwhelming vote for full separation. Five days later UNAMET announced that on a turnout of 98 per cent of the 446,953 East Timorese registered,

78 per cent had voted to break away from Indonesia. Fretilin leader José Ramos-Horta had in the meantime returned from exile in the United States and Xanana (José Alexandro) Gusmão, the commander of Falintil who had been in prison in Indonesia since 1992, had been released.

By now, though, East Timor had descended into chaos. The Indonesian-backed militias responded to the pro-independence vote with a dramatic intensification of the violence they had deployed during the campaign. Figures remain uncertain but about 1,000 people were killed, the physical infrastructure of the territory was largely destroyed and more than 70 per cent of the population was displaced, with a large proportion fleeing across the border to the relative security of Indonesian West Timor. The small rump of UNAMET personnel who had not been evacuated from the territory amidst the deepening violence of the referendum campaign was now concentrated within the limited protection of the UN's compounds.

Immediately following the announcement of the result, Kofi Annan had called on the Indonesian government either to impose order on the territory or, if unable to do so, accept the intervention of an international force. A security council delegation visited the territory and held discussions with the Indonesian leadership in Jakarta. With evident reluctance and little grace, the government there bowed to the inevitability of external intervention. The realities on the ground in the territory were inescapable. There had been an overwhelming statement of popular will for independence expressed through a UN-organised referendum which had been closely followed across the world. It was simply impossible to row back from this under the cover of local violence (especially as official Indonesian complicity in this violence was widely recognised). Moreover, the United States, Indonesia's global ally both before and after the fall of the Suharto regime, made its position clear: it expected Jakarta's acquiescence to East Timor's independence.[7] In a particularly strong statement on 9 September, President Clinton, after suspending all military co-operation with Indonesia, indicated that if unable to end the violence itself, the Jakarta government 'must invite – it must invite – the international community to assist in restoring security'.[8] Simultaneously, the Bretton Woods institutions – the International Monetary Fund and the World Bank – further turned up the pressure by suggesting that their massive support package to Indonesia in response to its current economic crisis (the very crisis whose political fallout had opened the way for East Timor's independence) would be jeopardised unless the violence ended.[9] In this way the traditional peacekeeping requirement of 'host state consent' was achieved – though 'consent' might have been a questionable term to use in such a coercive diplomatic and economic climate.

Whatever the basis of Indonesia's acquiescence, however, the necessary conditions emerged for the first multinational military intervention. This would not take the form of a specifically mandated 'UN' force but would be a security council-legitimised and Australian-led coalition of the willing. The original UN planning assumption had been for a transitional process of three stages. The referendum itself would be the first of these, the responsibility of 'UNAMET-I'. If this resulted in a vote for independence there would then be an interim (and potentially dangerous) period during which the Indonesian government and legislature would formulate their response. In the meantime 'UNAMET-II' would begin preparations for the transfer of power. Finally, 'UNAMET-III' would manage this transfer as a fully constituted transitional administration. A United Nations blue beret force would be assembled and then deployed following the disciplined and phased withdrawal of Indonesian forces. In a curious reversal of roles, this process would have been similar to the one by which Indonesia acquired West New Guinea in 1962–3 when the Dutch handed the territory over to the UN Temporary Executive Authority pending its transfer of sovereignty (see Chapter 1). The chaos in East Timor following the referendum, however, made such a plan, based as it was on optimum political and security circumstances, wholly unrealistic.

INTERFET: coalition of the willing

In different senses Australia was both the most and the least likely regional state to offer leadership in what would become the International Force in East Timor (INTERFET). Australia's stance and motivations resonate with broader issues surrounding the regionalisation of interventions and the role of dominant regional powers within them. For one thing, East Timor lay only 800 kilometres from Darwin, the capital of Australia's Northern Territory. It was therefore a close neighbour, at least in the particular context of the Pacific and its distances. And Australia was beyond doubt one of the best equipped military powers in the Asia-Pacific region. Its forces were very well experienced in multinational operations. Since the 1950s Australia had been a major contributor to both UN and non-UN international interventions.[10] Despite these evident qualifications to lead an intervention, however, a number of complex political and diplomatic issues had to be considered. The very fact of Australia's dominant presence in the region would inevitably raise questions about its motivations and the bases for its actions. Was it merely exploiting an opportunity to assert its hegemonic position? Would Australian national preferences shape the outcome of the crisis and subsequent regional relationships with the new, putative state of East Timor?

These questions were complicated enough in a region not distinguished by a history of inter-governmental trust and confidence, but there was of course another dimension: Australia was regarded by its neighbours as an essentially 'European' state in a post-imperial Asian setting. In this sense it might be thought that the obvious regional agency to have led and coordinated any intervention should have been the Association of Southeast Asian Nations (ASEAN). Indonesia was a leading actor in this. Its membership included the major powers of the region: Malaysia, Singapore, Thailand and the Philippines among them. But ASEAN's institutional culture was strongly non-interventionist. Its relative success in bringing together a disparate collection of states, which had from time to time harboured deep suspicions of each other, was largely based on its minimal involvement in collective political and security matters.[11] No ASEAN member or group of members was likely to offer a lead in any controversial humanitarian intervention within its own region. Yet this refusal among Indonesia's partners to take any initiative still did not free Australia from accusations of neo-colonial calculation.

There were also particular historical difficulties in the relationship between Australia and Indonesia. At the level of formal foreign policy, successive Australian governments, both Labor and Liberal (conservative), had pursued a careful and usually sensitive approach to Indonesia. Australia was in fact one of the first of the few countries to formally recognise Indonesia's sovereignty over East Timor after the 1975 invasion (this put it at odds with Portugal which still asserted its *de jure* authority over the territory). But this delicate diplomacy was frequently undermined by the pronouncements of both individual politicians and pressure groups. An undercurrent of hostility to Indonesia existed across the political spectrum in Australia, uniting right and left. On what might be described as the nationalist right there was a suspicion of Indonesia's perceived tendency for expansionism. Jakarta's acquisition of West New Guinea in the early 1960s contributed to this wariness. Indonesia's subsequent difficult border relationship with neighbouring Papua New Guinea, a former Australian trust territory, continued to feed it. There was, no doubt, a racist element present in this Australian suspicion as well. But at the same time, more liberal and left-wing Australians were often equally suspicious of Indonesia's behaviour on the grounds of its repressive authoritarianism. Here too there was hostility to Jakarta's supposed expansionism – provoked not least by the original annexation of East Timor in 1975. In response, Indonesia had tended to be relatively cool in its diplomacy towards Australia. It was unlikely then to regard Australia as a neutral mediator, even despite Canberra's readiness, against the current of international opinion, to recognise Indonesian rule in East Timor in the 1970s.

Despite these significant obstacles, Australia offered its services as coalition leader. One factor in the government's decision-making was probably the CNN effect. Continuous and graphic reports of the horrific (and one-sided) violence in the territory were broadcast worldwide in August and September 1999 and these had a more immediate effect on Australian audiences than other more distant ones. As one writer put it, 'public support and demand for Australian intervention in East Timor were such that . . . any government could only have ignored them at its own peril'.[12] While the suggestion of serious electoral consequences might be overstated, there seemed certainly to be a powerful popular momentum in Australia for intervention (strengthened no doubt by the breadth of support across traditional left–right divisions). Certainly the offer was received with great gratitude and relief by secretary-general Kofi Annan, although it confronted him with a delicate diplomatic task in persuading Indonesia to accept Australian leadership of the intervention. The inescapable fact, however, was that if an effective force were to be deployed it would be one dominated by the Australian contingent and Australia could not be expected to place this contingent under non-Australian command in what was an informal alliance and not a United Nations operation.

While the longer-term plan was to have a formal UN force in place, there was clearly no prospect that the necessary institutional procedures for this could meet the immediate and urgently pressing problems of East Timor at the beginning of September 1999. This of course revealed an essential truth about the limitations of the UN's own organisational capacity for rapid response. The normal process of procurement of an appropriate range of contributors followed by negotiations over costs and resources would have ruled out any significant intervention within less than several weeks. INTERFET began deploying in East Timor on 20 September – just five days after UN authorisation.

The question of consent was clearly an important consideration at this stage. There was no likelihood of Australian command of an intervention without at least the acquiescence of Indonesia, and certainly not in the face of its active opposition. Yet legally speaking there was no specific requirement for the traditional peacekeeping precondition of host state consent to be met by Indonesia. In the institutional view of the United Nations, Indonesia was not, after all, the 'host state'. If consent had been required of any country it would, legally speaking, have been that of Portugal which remained theoretically the state with responsibility for what was a non-self-governing territory in the terms of the United Nations charter. But *de facto* power unquestionably lay with Indonesia, whose army remained the dominant force in the territory. After the exercise of considerable pressure which culminated in what effectively was an ultimatum from secretary-general Kofi Annan, Jakarta gave way.[13]

The authorisation for INTERFET came in a security council resolution based on chapter VII of the charter. This legal reference point immediately underlined the potential enforcement role envisaged for the intervention. A 'multinational force under a unified command structure' was authorised 'to restore peace and security in East Timor, to protect and support UNAMET in carrying out its tasks and . . . to facilitate humanitarian assistance operations'.[14] Crucially, the force was 'to take all necessary measures' in pursuit of these tasks – the standard security council formulation authorising the use of force which dates back to the Congo operation of the early 1960s. With a glance to the then considerable pressures on the UN's resources, the resolution 'stressed' that the costs of the operation would be borne by those participating in it, though other member states were invited to contribute. In the financial sense too, it was not to be a formal UN operation.

The force was indeed widely multinational as the security council resolution suggested. There was no sense in which it was an Australian venture with a few token 'foreigners' included to confer some multilateral respectability. In other words, this was no Operation Turquoise in Rwanda. There too a UN member state, France, had been authorised by the security council to do something where the United Nations itself was unable or unwilling to act. But that had been in essence a 'French' intervention with some Francophone African involvement (see Chapter 4). The force, which eventually reached a strength of about 11,000, was not only multinational, but also multi-continental. Contingents came from more than twenty countries including Bangladesh, France, Ireland, Kenya and South Korea. Two Portuguese-speaking countries, Portugal itself and Brazil, also made an important contribution. Both

Britain and the United States provided essential transport and logistical support.[15] Most importantly from a regional political perspective, however, was the presence of four members of ASEAN: Malaysia, Singapore, Philippines and Thailand, the last of which provided the deputy force commander. These countries had offered to participate largely at Indonesia's behest when, as international pressures to agree to a multilateral intervention became irresistible, Jakarta sought to secure some degree of influence over its composition.[16]

The ASEAN presence proved to be of great importance in confirming the legitimacy of INTERFET – and at no cost to the effectiveness of the operation. In one respect the security council's mandate was misleading and might have created significant difficulties for INTERFET. The legitimising resolution authorised 'the establishment of a multinational force under a unified command'.[17] Although undoubtedly multinational, the force did not operate under a 'unified command'. From the outset Australia, as well as providing the majority of troops, took firm overall operational control of the mission. In reality it is unlikely that the security council had any strong position on the nature of the command structure and the reference to a unified command was most likely just a form of words. But the strategic and tactical effect of single-country authority was positive. The danger of political differences affecting operational control was avoided by this clear lead-contributor approach. And it was a danger that had to be taken very seriously. While the strong ASEAN presence in INTERFET was political extremely significant, its value would have been rapidly squandered had the differing underlying views on the crisis among force participants been expressed in a joint command.[18] The potential for significant conflict between Australia and New Zealand (which also had a strong presence in the force) on one side, and the ASEAN contingents on the other, was considerable.

This situation contrasted well with other recent humanitarian intervention where command structures had been more complex. The ambiguous relationship between United States generals and UN-appointed commanders during the UNOSOM-II phase in Somalia was one obvious example of the damage a confused command structure could inflict on the pursuit of a force mandate. Similarly, the supposed dual key system which had operated in the latter phase of the UN-PROFOR mission in Bosnia in which UN and NATO commanders were required to act as one in pursuit of strategic ends seemed to serve only to push these ends further from reach.

In one sense INTERFET did follow the pattern of the initial American intervention in Somalia, though with much greater success. The quick arrival and rapid build-up of a large and potentially robust external force had an immediate impact on the violence in East Timor. The militia groups, now facing an irresistible military challenge (rather than the benevolent ambivalence of the Indonesian army) quickly disintegrated, with most fleeing for the safety of Indonesian West Timor. Admittedly, the challenge posed by the armed groups in East Timor was small in contrast to the determined and relatively heavily armed clan militias in Mogadishu. While the numerical strength of the militias in East Timor was around 10,000, not far short of that of INTERFET itself, their capacities and resources were small. But it was the failure of the United States to pursue its advantage in Somalia by decisively reducing the assets of factions that, as we have seen, was to prove a major source of the trouble which would later afflict and ultimately curtail the intervention. In the weeks following the arrival of INTERFET the focus of conflict shifted from Dili and other population centres to the West Timor border itself. Infiltration and spasmodic cross-border provocation became the major operational problem for the force. But this proved manageable, and violence never approached the intensity of the period before the intervention.

Transfer to the UN: the transitional administration in East Timor

The resolution authorising the deployment of INTERFET had explicitly indicated that the force was a temporary measure pending the deployment of a formal UN operation.[19] Consequently, after a five-month deployment during which the situation in the territory was effectively stabilised, the coalition of the willing gave way to a fully constituted United Nations operation. The rapid improvement in the security situation following the arrival of INTERFET meant that the original UN mission, UNAMET, was able to re-establish itself at the end of September 1999. It now began to pursue its original mandate, prefigured in the May 1999 agreement between Portugal and Indonesia, to facilitate the implementation of whatever outcome had been produced by the referendum. This now involved aiding a transition to independent statehood. A month after the re-establishment of UNAMET, and on the eve of the withdrawal of the last Indonesian troops from East Timor, the security council authorised one of the UN's most ambitious ventures. On 25 October 1999 the United Nations Transitional Administration in East Timor (UNTAET) was established.[20] This was to be a multi-functional undertaking which, on the security front, would supplant INTERFET with a formal UN peacekeeping and policing operation of a similar range. The UNTAET military force would be the equivalent size to INTERFET (which had grown to 11,500) and there was to be a civilian police component of about 1,600 international officers. But more than this, UNTAET would provide the other principal services of a state. It would form the public administration of the territory, provide social services and oversee the economy. It was to do this, moreover, amidst a major humanitarian aid operation aimed at the rehabilitation of the territory after the violence of the previous months and a contested occupation of a quarter of a century. Additionally, UNTAET would have the parallel responsibility of institution-creation and the training of personnel capable of assuming control of a new independent sovereign state. All of this had to be achieved within an extremely short time-frame. To preside over this Kofi Annan appointed as his special representative, the highly experienced Brazilian UN official Sérgio Vieira de Melo.

Vieira de Melo's powers and responsibilities were unprecedented for a UN official. UNTAET faced the formidable task of not just state-building, but also of 'nation-building' in a very particular sense. The United Nations had of course intervened to provide transitional administrations in the past. The Temporary Executive Authority (UNTEA) in West New Guinea in the early 1960s was one such intervention, as was the Transitional Authority in Cambodia (UNTAC) thirty years later. The mission in Kosovo had been formed just before UNTAET. But UNTEA had been was responsible for the transition of West New Guinea from Dutch colony to province of a well-established state; however some may have regretted the fact, West New Guinea was not destined to become a new sovereign country. In Cambodia the UNTAC's role was – though perhaps more dangerous and politically delicate – even less fundamental in that the UN was required to provide a temporary administration within the frontiers of an already established state. In Kosovo UNMIK's day-to-day functions were broadly similar to those of UNTAET (and Vieira de Melo had been a leading figure there at the outset too). But in Kosovo the UN maintained at least the outward form of operating within the continuing context of Serbian autonomy: the 'final status' problem was for the future. In East Timor Vieira de Melo on behalf of the UN not only exercised the full range of legislative and policy authority, but also had the power of international treaty-making.[21] He exercised these powers in the name of a country that did not yet exist and for the creation of which he was ultimately responsible.

Control of UNTAET was the subject of some fierce internal UN politics with the Department of Peacekeeping Operations (DPKO) competing, ultimately successfully, with the Political Affairs department. While Political Affairs had been responsible for UNAMET and therefore the political process between the May 1999 agreement and the referendum in August, the security situation had subsequently become a dominant consideration and control was therefore assigned to the bureaucratic agency best equipped to manage it.[22] The DPKO's most immediate recent experience had been in Kosovo and this may have contributed to, as it has been described, a 'tension between the "logic of peacekeeping" and the "logic of development" [which] remained a persistent predicament throughout UNTAET's existence'.[23] This circumstance may go some way to explaining the mixed performance of the Transitional Administration.

UNTAET took over formally in the military sphere from INTERFET in February 2000 under the command of a Philippines general and its force was successful in maintaining broad security. The peacekeeping model which dominated its operations may, however, have had a more profound impact on UNTAET's performance. In one view, which was widely held among the NGOs working in the territory as well as by some key UN officials in the field, the Transitional Administration 'was ill-equipped for peacebuilding because it was structured as a peacekeeping operation'.[24] This was the controversial position of Jarat Chopra who resigned from his position as head of UNTAET's Office of District Administration in March 2000, only a few months into his appointment. In an outspoken article published the following year, Chopra argued that while UNTAET was part of a general trend towards a greater assertion of control by the UN in territories in which it was called on to intervene, 'the result will be merely another form of authoritarianism unless the transitional administrators themselves submit to . . . genuine accountability to the local people whom they serve . . . Thus far the UN has not done so in East Timor'.[25] The dispute, so far as it went beyond the common run of bureaucratic and personal rivalries that any large organisation is prey to, could be seen as a doctrinal schism; one with broad implications for multi-functional interventions by the UN.

On one side of this, represented by Chopra, the UN administration in East Timor had emerged as a semi-imperial autocracy. This sceptical view of UN interim administrations was not limited to the case of East Timor, of course. The Interim Mission in Kosovo which was also in existence at this time was subject to similar criticism. This UN imperium, in order to safeguard its own power and achieve a narrowly defined mandate, had exploited the concentration of power inherent in the 'vice-regal' status of the secretary-general's special representative. It had failed to make itself accountable to the Timorese, had excluded their political representatives from the administration and had failed in the essential task of the 'Timorisation' of administration. UNTAET, in short, had a 'preoccupation with control at the expense of the local community's involvement in government.'[26] This reflected the peacekeeping model of the DPKO but, according to Chopra, it was exacerbated by the personalities involved. Immediately prior to his East Timor posting, Vieira de Melo had been responsible for setting up the transitional administration in Kosovo. He now brought with him 'an inner circle from the Balkans, whose members projected a blunt, bullying style' inconsistent with a transparent and accountable transition process.[27] The centralising tendency associated with this seemed, in Chopra's view, to be merely replicating the authoritarianism of the decades of Indonesian rule.

The extent of Jarat Chopra's criticism and the terms in which it was made seem at times intemperate. But his basic position has been supported by other observers. In particular, the incompatibility of the 'operation accomplished' approach of the Department of Peacekeeping Operations with the complexities of the nation-building process has been commented on. Astri Suhrke argued that the mission suffered from this underlying contradiction: the 'institutional lead of the DPKO in planning and implementing the mission had significant consequences'. What was essentially a civilian operation 'was staffed and organised by, and ultimately responsible to, a department that had little experience of "governance missions", no country-knowledge of East Timor, and whose standard operation procedures were designed for military and preferably short-term operations'.[28]

One of the genuine dilemmas facing UNTAET, acknowledged by Suhrke, was the issue of mission neutrality. This, of course, is central in the classic peacekeeping model (along with consent and the non-use of force). But where was neutrality to be located in East Timor during the transition period? The various pro-independence parties and factions had subsumed themselves into a single organisation at the time of the referendum. This umbrella was the National Council of East Timorese Resistance (CNRT – *Conselho National de Resistência Timorense*). In one sense, of course, the CNRT was a 'faction'. But given that the territory was now, post-referendum, on a one-way road to independence and that UNTAET's mandate was to facilitate this, the CNRT could also reasonably be considered as a government-in-waiting. The UNTAET leadership, following the peacekeeping model, was reluctant to demonstrate such flexibility, however. As a result, the political process of Timorisation was fettered. A more 'situation-sensitive' and politically attuned approach (of the type associated with the Department of Political Affairs) might have been more creative in these circumstances.

Similarly, at the administrative level, the tendency of UNTAET was to assume that East Timor presented, in Suhrke's expression, a *terra nullis* – an empty space which could only be populated by international staff. This was not entirely the case, though after centuries of Portuguese colonialism and decades of Indonesian oppression there was an obvious education and skills shortfall. However, self-imposed pressure on UNTAET to 'get the job done' as efficiently as possible assigned a low priority to localisation of administration and the essential training functions that go with it.

Against these criticisms there are a number of arguments which relate to the realities of UNTAET's particular political and diplomatic setting and the demands of practicality. At the administrative level, there is an unavoidable tension between, on one hand, the efficient creation of structures which would enable a territory to become a sovereign state and, on the other, the training and preparation of the human resources able to take over the management of the state after independence. Training for localisation should clearly be a priority task for any international transitional process in a territory with no previous tradition of self-administration. In this situation the secretary-general's special representative, Vieira de Melo, faced an inevitable tension between the demands, on the one hand, for an efficient administration capable of delivering services and establishing social stability, and on the other for the preparation of an entire new national cadre of administrators and public servants. This is a difficult but essential circle to square. No nation-building project can expect to succeed if its processes excluded those whose nation is being built. In an ideal world, of course, there would be no tension between the two imperatives. But in East Timor there were serious resource constraints (the undertaking was paid for from the regular UN budget) which simply did not permit the expenditure in both time and money to realise this ideal. Moreover, in a transitional situation, the timing of the process is also affected by pressures from those who are poised to assume power. Paradoxically perhaps, the necessary patience required for the long-term process of administrative localisation is rarely displayed by those most likely to benefit from it. A protracted transitional period is prone to be denounced as an attempt to delay independence rather than embraced as an essential preparation for it. In the event, the approach taken in East Timor was for a relatively rapid move to formal statehood followed by a post-independence phase of intensive administrative support. In this way training and preparation for administrative localization became the responsibility, not of UNTAET but of the post-independence follow-on project, the Mission of Support in East Timor (UNMISET).

Beyond the largely technical process of administrative formation, UNTAET also faced very considerable political difficulties in its approach to the involvement of local parties and factions in the larger policy process. These difficulties had both external and internal dimensions. A glance at its location on the map, let alone a cursory knowledge of East Timor's history, should explain the first of these. The new state of East Timor had no choice as to its physical setting. Geographically it remained a part of the Indonesian archipelago and moreover continued to share a – very sensitive – land border with its huge neighbour. The new state could not possibly be viable if its relationship with Indonesia was a hostile one. The divisions which even just the prospect of independence had exposed in the Indonesian political and military elites had been horrifically evident during 1999. If the post-independence state was to succeed, extreme care had to be taken with Indonesian sensitivities during the transitional period. Rapid incorporation in 'government' of the leading local politicians by the Transitional Administration would in effect have meant the close embrace of the multiparty CNRT. The movements which comprised the CNRT had all been in some senses enemies of Indonesia and not, at least in the bitter aftermath of the 1999 violence, the most diplomatic of interlocutors. Ultimately UNTAET was, as its name makes clear, a United Nations Transitional Administration and, as such, best placed to negotiate with Indonesia as the representative of the international community rather than the voice of Timorese nationalism.

Internally, there was a different set of problems with political representation. The CNRT was an umbrella organisation whose capacity to act as a unified political force would certainly have been tested by access to significant levels of power. The danger of disintegration into factionalism was always present. Moreover, the East Timorese 'people' was not a unified entity. There were distinct regional cleavages between the eastern and western parts of the territory (which would become violently clear in the post-independence period). These tended to reflect different levels of nationalist commitment. Even among nationalist activists there were divisions, most notably between those who had stayed behind to organise and to fight with Falintil and those who had gone in to exile to agitate for East Timor abroad on behalf of Fretilin. There was a danger, therefore, that by pursuing a policy of deep and wide power-sharing with local political activists in the transitional period, UNTAET would have been importing potentially destructive factionalism into the process.

UNTAET's performance in this area did in fact improve under pressure from East Timor's emerging political class. The National Consultative Council (NCC) which had been established by UNTAET in December 1999 to 'shadow' the UN administration and advise on local complexities was overhauled in June 2000 with its membership more than doubled to thirty-three, drawn from set geographical, political and civil-society constituencies. In October 2000 former Falintil commander Xanana Gusmão, now leader of the CNRT, was elected president of the National Council. This was to form the new national legislature at independence. The skeleton of a post-independence democratic system thus began to emerge, even if it remained one weak on local administrative capacity.

None of this is to suggest that UNTAET's performance was exemplary and beyond criticism or that its relationship with the East Timor population was properly constructed. But the range of difficulties it faced in this respect was wide and complex. In many ways it was a matter of 'damned if it did and damned if it didn't'. A greater degree of administrative localisation would clearly have been desirable. But it would have been costly, time-consuming and, potentially, would have compromised the effectiveness of public administration at the point of independence. Pre-independence power-sharing with local political movements would have pre-empted accusations that the UN was acting as a colonial presence with an unaccountable pro-consul in charge. But this had to be weighed against the evolving relationship with Indonesia and the management of opposing factions within the nascent Timorese political culture at a time of great pressure on the transition process. Similarly, criticisms of the gulf between the conditions and remuneration enjoyed by UNTAET's 'internationals' and those of its local employees are wholly understandable.[29] But this is simply a feature of complex multilateral interventions such as that in East Timor. It is a problem without any obvious solution. The recruitment of effective technical expertise to work in physically dangerous and difficult conditions is perhaps only possible if competitive international rewards are offered. Similar levels of reward for locally recruited staff would be difficult to justify in value-for-money terms. This would also have a distorting effect on the local economy.

Finally, it is perhaps significant that much of the criticism of UNTAET came not directly from the Timorese themselves but from other foreign professionals both within and beyond the UN mission. Such tensions, whether based on genuine differences over policy, inter-agency rivalries, personality clashes or, most usually, a combination of these, tend to be a common feature of humanitarian interventions. We have already seen this in Somalia and Rwanda and it has certainly been present in more recent interventions from Kosovo to Darfur.

Generally, given the mapless diplomatic, political and constitu-tional terrain UNTAET had to negotiate and the inescapable cultural complexities which dog all multinational interventions, UNTAET's achievements were considerable. A working system of public admin-istration was put in place and at least the basis of a judicial system was created (with the Dili district court opening for business in May 2000).

The security sector, obviously among the most sensitive areas of preparation for independent statehood, was not neglected by UNTAET, but it was not developed with any great urgency, perhaps for sound political reasons. In September 2000 a putative national defence force came into being. About 3,000 strong at the outset, it had at its core, perhaps inevitably, former Falintil fighters. These were the only East Timorese (other than those compromised by service with the Indonesian army) with any military experience. This provenance was reflected in its double-barrelled title: *Falintil-Forças de Defesa de Timor Leste* (F-FDTL). The former Falintil guerrilla commander, Taur Matan Ruak, took charge of the new force with the rank of brigadier-general.

In general these developments in the provision of effective admin-istration and the preparations for sovereign statehood took place in a stable security environment guaranteed by UNTAET's military force. The one significant threat to this stability was located along the border with West Timor. Several thousand East Timorese refugees from the violence of the previous year still inhabited camps on the Indonesian side. These camps gave succour and cover to the remnants of the pro-Indonesian armed bands which had been primarily responsible for the trouble which had created the population movement in the first place. UNTAET forces had generally been effective in pursuing tactics which were both sensitive and, when necessary, robust in the management of this border area, but occasional incursions into East Timor and acts of targeted violence in West Timor itself continued. In September 2000, three members of the UN High Commission for Refugees staff working in the border camps on the West Timor side were killed by militia elements. This led to a strongly worded security council resolution insisting that Indonesia fulfil its responsibilities 'to disarm and disband the militia immediately, restore law and order on the affected areas of West Timor, ensure safety and security in the refugee camps, and prevent cross-border incursions into East Timor'.[30] The resolution went on to instruct UNTAET forces to 'respond robustly to the militia threat in East Timor'. More significantly, however, the security council called on Indonesia to 'take immediate and effective measures to ensure the safe return of refugees who choose to return to East Timor'.

Here, perhaps, can be discerned an awareness in the security council of the terrible precedent of the aftermath of the Rwanda genocide in 1994. There, many of the refugee camps on the Congo (then still Zaire) side of the border, populated mainly by Hutus escaping retribution from the now Tutsi-dominated regime in Rwanda, came under the control of former genocide militias. The orderly return of the refugees back to Rwanda was prevented by violence and threat as the one-time *génocidaires* sought to build up their forces and resources to maintain cross-border attacks into Rwanda and to spread their ethnic violence into eastern Congo. This was a situation which contributed greatly to the humanitarian disaster of the Congo over the following years and brought not just inter-ethnic civil war but region-wide external intervention. In 1999 the situation demanded the creation of MONUC, one of the UN's most complex, expensive and largely unavailing humanitarian interventions (see Chapter 4). Clearly, a calamity on that scale was not going to befall East Timor, but the dynamics of the two situations were very similar, and the potential of an unresolved cross-border refugee situation to sabotage progress towards sovereign independence for the territory was considerable. Although more than 150,000 refugees returned to East Timor in the first months of 2000, around 100,000 remained in the camps. Perhaps aware of the dangers to themselves of unmanaged and 'unofficial' violence in the West Timor border area, the Indonesian authorities were generally responsive to UN pressures. In January 2002 the Indonesian army and UNTAET forces agreed to a coordinated security operation on their respective sides of the common border which was effective in weakening the capacity of the militias.

The pace towards independence and the end of UNTAET's mandate quickened at the end of August 2001 on the second anniversary of the independence referendum. Elections for an eighty-eight-seat constituent assembly were held from which Fretilin (which contested the poll as a party in its own right after the dissolution of the umbrella CNRT) emerged clear winner with more than 57 per cent of the vote and 55 seats. A month later a twenty-four-member council of ministers – effectively the post-independence government in waiting – was sworn in. With a national constitution approved and adopted by the constituent assembly in February 2002, only the elections for the country's first president were necessary before the final acquisition of statehood. These took place in April, with Xanana Gusmão elected by a sweeping majority of over 82 per cent of the vote. Gusmão had contested the election only reluctantly and as an independent as his relations with his former resistance comrades in Fretilin had deteriorated after the disaggregation of the CNRT. This was not the best start for the constitutional democracy as Fretilin formed the majority in the constituent assembly. In the event, however, Gusmão was able to develop an effective working relationship with the Fretilin prime minister, Mari Alkitiri. Consequently, on 20 May 2002, in the presence of US president Bill Clinton and the new Indonesian head of state, Megawati Sukarnoputri, the territory became the independent state of Timor Leste, the 191st member of the United Nations.

Amidst the natural euphoria generated by the successful conclusion to Timor Leste's long, bloody struggle for independence there lurked some difficult questions, however. Timor Leste emerged to statehood by all significant indicators as the poorest country in Asia. Over 40 per cent of the population was illiterate. Unemployment stood at 70 per cent and the average annual income was $US200 dollars. Yet the new state was, in general, warmly welcomed into the international system with key aid donors agreeing to a package worth $US440 for the first three years of independence.

Continued engagement: the post-independence period

Reflecting the goodwill with which Timor's independence was greeted, a few days before the celebration of independence the security council had agreed to a continued UN presence. This, it was felt, would be essential if the new state were to become successfully established within the international system. On 17 May 2002 the council had voted to establish the Mission of Support in East Timor (UNMISET) to maintain some of the responsibilities of the now defunct Transitional Administration.[31] The Mission would include administrative support for the departments of the new government, but perhaps most importantly UNMISET's responsibilities were focused on the security sector. It was to have a major training role for local police and paramilitary forces. It would also guarantee internal and external security. This responsibility would be directed primarily at the border with West Timor where tensions remained despite a considerable improvement in government-to-government relations with Indonesia. UNMISET would have at its disposal military and police components broadly similar in size to those of UNTAET (and INTERFET before it). A 5,000-strong peacekeeping force and 1,250 international civilian police were to be provided. But UNMISET's force levels were to be dynamic. The intention was that virtually from the outset there would be a progressive reduction in the UN presence as a process of localisation brought a corresponding increase in Timorese responsibilities.

This process of localisation in the security sector was not without its difficulties. Tensions in the border area were much reduced in the immediate post-independence period. But the residual refugee population which remained in West Timor – about 30,000 strong at the beginning of 2003 – for the most part resisted repatriation. Many had good reason, having been members of pro-Indonesian militia groups or former officials of the occupation administration.[32] Occasional cross-border violence continued and it fell mainly to UNMISET to confront it, along with carrying out its principal function of the capacity-building of local institutions. The new national F-FDTL security force still had only limited operational capabilities in 2002 and 2003. The civilian national police force also faced major developmental problems, which were brought home in the aftermath of serious rioting in Dili in December 2002. This bout of violence was entirely home-grown in that it emerged from economic and social grievances and not from any residual anti-independence sentiment. It overwhelmed the national police and in the short term it led the security council to strengthen the police component of UNMISET.[33] In the longer term, this civil disorder was a harbinger of worse to come in the following years.

UNMISET ceased to exist in May 2005 after a deployment which, despite the slow and variable pace of capacity-building, was broadly successful in maintaining the necessary conditions of security to permit the new state to develop its institutions and consolidate its democratic system. The mission was immediately succeeded by another: the United Nations Office in Timor Leste (UNOTIL). UNOTIL's mandate was almost wholly political in its objectives in the sense that it was to be devoted to local capacity-building across the functions of the Timor Leste state. A peacekeeping force was no longer considered necessary.

The mission was also time-limited to twelve months.[34] In truth, the external security picture was now quite encouraging. Two months before the final draw-down of UNMISET, in March 2005, President Gusmão had visited Jakarta where with Indonesian President Yudhoyono he had agreed the creation of a joint Truth and Friendship Commission to investigate the violence around the referendum in 1999. The following month Yudhoyono was in turn received in Timor Leste where he made a well-judged and warmly received visit to the Santa Cruz cemetery, the scene of the 1991 massacre of Timorese demonstrators by Indonesian soldiers. More practically, the two heads of state signed an agreement definitively demarking the previously troubled border between Timor Leste and West Timor. This new international stability veiled growing internal tensions in Timor Leste, however.

In March 2006, just weeks before the scheduled completion of UNOTIL's mission, the capital Dili experienced disorder and factional violence which at times approached the intensity of that in 1999. The immediate cause was the dismissal, on the orders of Fretilin prime minister Mari Alkitiri, of about 600 members of the by then 1,400 strong paramilitary F-FDTL. Although the move was ostensibly supposed to be about essential budget-trimming in the security sector, ethnic and political factors seemed to be involved well. The demobilised troops were almost entirely from the west of the country, home to the Loromonu ethnic group. This was the part of the country adjacent to Indonesian West Timor and there had always been an element of suspicion of the Loromonu on the part of the nationalist movement. This result of the dismissals was to leave the defence force dominated by the Lorosau ethnic group from the east of the country which had been more prominent in Falintil during the liberation war. The Falintil influence in what was now in effect the national army had, of course, been acknowledged in its title and the mainly Lorosau ex-Falintil fighters also dominated the officer ranks of the F-FDTL. Already resentful at what they regarded as Lorosau arrogance in the force, the Loromonu element found itself excluded both professionally and, now unemployed, economically. Joining with Dili's large pool of jobless and disaffected youth, the aggrieved former soldiers caused mayhem. A further toxic ethnic element in the trouble was that many westerners, deterred by the dominance of the eastern Lorosau in the defence force, had sought careers in the civilian police. This, now in the front line of public order, was perceived by the easterners as Loromonu dominated and therefore sympathetic to the rioters. The violence reached a peak at the end of April 2005 when, at the request of the government and in an uncanny replay of September 1999, an Australian-led international force (the International Security Force – ISF) was once again deployed on the streets of Dili. As before, this was the only configuration of intervention capable of meeting the immediate and utterly dire situation in Timor Leste. No formalised UN operation could have been authorised, formed and deployed in the time available to prevent the situation deteriorating to the point of catastrophe.

The crisis on the streets was interwoven with a power struggle within the ruling elite. Despite an encouraging beginning, the relationship between the prime minister Mari Alkitiri and President Gusmão had deteriorated. Alkitiri had also become unpopular within his own Fretilin party. In particular he had attracted the disfavour of José Ramos-Horta, who like Gusmão had also broken with Fretilin and who was now Timor Leste's foreign minister. Together Gusmão and Ramos-Horta embodied the national struggle in the minds and hearts of the East Timorese and Alkatiri could not long resist their combined hostility. He resigned at the end of June and was replaced as prime minister by Ramos-Horta.

The latest international force – which grew to a strength of 2,200 – was more than capable of suppressing the violence and overseeing a return to at least a degree of normality. The death toll – around forty – was low compared with the level of violence in 1999. But the crisis was ominous for Timor Leste's long-term stability. Underlying tensions remained high, particularly in Dili. Again, following the narrative of 1999, the security council moved to replace the regional coalition of the willing which had responded to the immediate crisis with a formal UN intervention. This took the form of the Integrated Mission in East Timor (UNMIT). Now though, security council disagreements prevented the inclusion of peacekeeping troops within it.[35] UNMIT did, though, have a large and directly operational 1,600-strong UNCIVPOL – civilian police – element along with a military liaison unit responsible for working with the Indonesian authorities along the border.

This large-scale UN re-engagement with Timor Leste could not instantly solve its many political and social problems. Tensions remained and if anything they were heightened the following year when the country held its first round of elections since those which had selected the leadership of the post-independence state. These saw a straight exchange of positions after Xanana Gusmão announced that he would not seek re-election as head of state. Instead he would 're-form' the CNRT (though in reality it was to be a personal vehicle with an evocative title rather than, as originally, a nationalist umbrella movement) and join the parliament. Gusmão was now in a position to be elected to the legislature, which he was with a view to becoming prime minister. At the same time José Ramos-Horta indicated that he would run for the more ceremonial position of president. In this he was successful, with a landslide 70 per cent of the vote. The outcome for Gusmão was less clear-cut. Fretilin as a political movement still retained broad support in the country, and the 'new' CNRT, despite Gusmão's personal popularity, won only eighteen seats in the sixty-seven-seat parliament with Fretilin taking twenty-one. Nevertheless, with the support of his ally the new president, and with the crucial backing of the secretary-general's representative and head of UNMIT, he was judged to command the most viable coalition and was allowed to form a new administration.

These generally encouraging developments at governmental level – which left national policy in the mutually supportive hands of two highly respected national leaders – could not disguise the persisting tears in Timor Leste's social fabric. After their electoral success Gusmão and Ramos-Horta fell victim to co-ordinated assassination attempts led by the leader of the dissident F-FDTL faction (the former military police commander). Once again it was Australia rather than the UN that moved to meet the security threat.[36] On this occasion, though, it was Timorese security forces that dealt with the immediate crisis, capturing those responsible for the attacks. At all events there was no general breakdown in order. This was perhaps only limited progress but progress nevertheless.

The birth and infancy of Timor Leste: humanitarian intervention vindicated?

Assessments of the success of the complex of interventions which took place in East Timor (and then Timor Leste) were made at different points in the territory's varied fortunes and therefore could change with confusing speed. At the outset, the United Nations seemed to have acted with admirable responsiveness to Indonesia's acceptance of the principle of an independence referendum followed by the Portuguese–Indonesian agreement in May 1999. A convenient veil was drawn over the UN's relative inaction over the original Indonesian annexation in 1975 and the subsequent abuses inflicted on the Timorese. The creation and deployment of UNAMET, despite the tight timetable that it was required to follow, showed that the international community could act through the UN to right international injustices in the post-cold war years. It served as at least a partial corrective to the plainly deficient interventions from Rwanda to Bosnia. In other words, these did not necessarily reflect an emerging pattern. The violence which surrounded the referendum campaign, especially after the vote itself, changed that perception. Once again, it seemed, an inadequate UN mission had failed to complete its task amidst the intensification of the conflict it was put in place to resolve.

Then the rapid success of the INTERFET, the Australian-led coalition of the willing, reversed perceptions once again. Tellingly, perhaps, though INTERFET was not a 'UN' force as such, there was little sign that its performance was held against the UN as proof that only robust 'national' forces could be effect humanitarian interveners. This was in contrast to the deployment of the US Unified Task Force in Somalia in December 1992. 'Operation Restore Hope' was seen by a large public as a rebuke to the ineffectual UN force (UNOSOM-I) that had originally been put in place. Clearly, UNAMET did not have the military functions of UNOSOM, but nevertheless there seemed to be a greater association between the INTERFET intervention and the UN as its legitimising agency than there had been in the case of Somalia. In large part, of course, this was due to different perceptions of American and Australian national power in relation to the UN. This may be of significance to the broader question of the UN's use of coalitions of the willing. The importance to the United Nations of the 'middle power' as intervener did not wholly disappear with the end of the cold war; the credibility of the UN is closely tied to the perception of the intervening powers which it legitimises.

Assessments of the intervention changed again, at least in some circles, during the UN's transitional administration. Now it was the United Nations itself in the form of UNTAET that became the object of criticism for its alleged insensitivity to local needs and its flawed approach to nation-building. The apparent success of the territory's transition to independence in May 2002, however, was greeted with general enthusiasm across the world and the essential role of the United Nations intervention in the process was widely applauded. But the general climate of opinion changed again when the post-independence violence and political instability appeared to reflect poorly on both the UN's broad nation-building project in Timor and also, within this, its capacity-building efforts on behalf of the country's administrative and security functions. Subsequently, with Timor Leste returning to a reasonable level of stability, the view was modified yet again.

Is it possible to tunnel through the peaks and valleys of this shifting assessment towards a viable judgement? Firstly we must enter once again the crucial caveat that there are simply limits to what can be achieved by any external intervention in a situation of humanitarian need and violent conflict when the local dynamics of that conflict are simply unready for resolution. There was little that could be done over the short or even medium term to address the underlying problems of poverty and the shortcomings in education and training of the population. But the limitations set on the management of violence will always be set most forcefully by the nature of the particular conflict and its immediate regional diplomatic setting.

In this respect the situation in East Timor and then Timor Leste was far from as grave as in other areas of United Nations intervention; conditions were in fact relatively propitious for the success of intervention. For one thing, the small scales of both area and of population size involved meant that the challenges faced in securing the territory were neither enormous nor massively expensive. Clearly, some of the terrain of East Timor, along with prevailing climatic conditions, were militarily challenging. The Indonesian army could certainly testify to this from the bitter experience of the liberation war. But for the various phases of the humanitarian intervention – from the deployment of INTERFET to the emergency return of Australian-led forces after the violence of 2005 – the points of greatest threat were either in urban areas or along the border with West Timor rather than in the mountains of the interior where Falintil had pursued the major part of its campaign during the Indonesian occupation.

Crucially too, the political and regional divisions that existed within East Timor, though real and momentarily lethal, were neither deep-rooted nor of long historical duration in comparison to those faced by the UN in other interventions. The differences between the Loromonu of the west and the Lorosau of the east were hardly those of Hutu and Tutsi in Rwanda or even those of the clans of Somalia. The divisions generated during the war against Indonesia and its aftermath were bitter and aggravated by social and economic conditions. But with sufficient external support they were certainly not insurmountable.

Beyond the territory itself, the Indonesian regime in 1999, despite its internal divisions and its limited capacity to control its own military, simply was in no position to stand out against the enormous diplomatic pressure it faced, not just from the United Nations but from the United States, Europe and the Bretton Woods institutions as well. Jakarta had little choice not only to acquiesce to humanitarian intervention but also to support its objectives so far as it was able to do so.

This situation would not have existed in 1969 or 1979 when Indonesia had a powerful diplomatic hand to play as an ally of the west in a region of cold war contestation. In that earlier period Indonesia was also a formidable actor in the global economy with strong trade-based leverage as one of the most powerful of the so-called 'Asian tigers'. But in 1999 none of this applied any more. The old regime in Indonesia had fallen amidst the changed rules of global diplomatic engagement and its failure to manage recent shocks to the tiger economies.

Indonesia's position of relative weakness was matched by the relative strength of Australia across the Timor Sea. The crisis in East Timor unfolded within a few hundred kilometres of a regional actor which was willing and able to provide the lead in a humanitarian intervention. Not only was Australia a regional power with a legitimate interest in the outcome in East Timor; it was also an experienced and respected peacekeeping contributor of long standing. This status was acknowledged throughout the states and organisations pressing Indonesia to accept an intervention (though less so among Indonesia's ASEAN partners). Moreover, the ultimate destination of East Timor was clear to all, regardless of the different levels of enthusiasm with which the truth was embraced by the various actors. After the UN-sponsored referendum of 1999 the territory was, quite simply, bound for sovereign statehood. No serious actor in the drama could have doubted this, and national policies had to be shaped to accommodate inescapable reality.

On the scale of comparisons with other crises addressed by the United Nations in the post-cold war years, therefore, assessment of the multiple interventions in East Timor/Timor Leste would lie well to the positive end of the scale. The extent to which this can be attributed to any deliberate strategy formulated and pursued by the United Nations as an institution, however, is far from clear. Although the outcomes may have been much more positive than those in various previous interventions from Africa to central Europe, the nature of local circumstances beyond the control of the UN must in this be given their proper, perhaps dominant, role.

Notes

1. An account of East Timor's history up to the Indonesian annexation (which is sympathetic to the popular aspiration for self-determination) is provided by Jill Joliffe, *East Timor: Nationalism and Colonialism* (St Lucia: Queensland University Press, 1978).
2. Security council resolution S/RES384(1975), 22 December 1975. The

resolution also criticised Portugal for failing properly to discharge its responsibilities as administering power of a non-self-governing territory.

3. Article 73 of chapter XI of the charter (Declaration Regarding Non-Self-Governing Territories) requires 'Members of the United Nations which have or assume responsibilities for the administration of territories whose peoples have not yet attained a full measure of self-government . . . to develop self-government, to take due account of the political aspirations of the peoples, and to assist them in the progressive development of their free political institutions.'

4. General assembly resolution, A/37/30, 23 November 1982.

5. Issued as security council document S/1999/513 annexes, 5 May 1999.

6. Security council resolution S/RES/1246(1999), 11 June 1999.

7. Alan Ryan, 'The Strong Lead-Nation Model in an ad hoc Coalition of the Willing: Operation Stabilise in East Timor', *International Peacekeeping* 9(1) (2002), p. 27.

8. Quoted in Nicholas J. Wheeler and Tim Dunne, 'East Timor and the New Humanitarian Intervention', *International Affairs*, 77(4) (2001), p. 818.

9. Ibid., p. 819.

10. Among the major UN operations that Australia had contributed to were those in Cambodia, Cyprus, Congo, Golan Heights, Lebanon, Palestine, Somalia, Yemen and former Yugoslavia. Its non-UN operations included the Commonwealth Monitoring Operation in Rhodesia/Zimbabwe, the Multinational Force and Observers in Sinai and IFOR in Bosnia.

11. The membership of ASEAN comprises Burma, Brunei, Cambodia, Indonesia, Laos, Malaysia, Philippines, Thailand and Vietnam. Originally founded in 1967, it had no clear role until a 'relaunch' in 1975 brought about a focus on economic and commercial relations. Membership expanded in the 1990s after the end of the cold war to include the former communist regimes of Indo-China.

12. Moreen Dee, '"Coalitions of the Willing" and Humanitarian Intervention: Australia's Involvement with INTERFET', *International Peacekeeping* 8(3) (2001), p. 16.

13. Ryan, 'The Strong Lead-Nation Model', pp. 24–5.

14. Security council resolution S/RES/1264(1999), 15 September 1999.

15. A detailed list of contributions and pledges made at the point of deployment is provided by Adam Cobb in an official Australian Foreign Affairs department brief, 'East Timor and Australia's Security Role: Issues and Scenarios'. Found at: http://www.aph.gov.au/library/pubs/CIB/1999-2000/2000cib03.htm

16. Dee, 'Coalitions of the willing', p. 10.

17. Security council resolution S/RES/1264(1999), operative paragraph 3.

18. As it was, the Thai deputy force commander, General Songkitti Jaggabatarara, was not even located in the INTERFET command headquarters. Ryan, 'The Strong Lead-Nation Model', p. 31.

19. Security council resolution S/RES/1264(1999), 15 September 1999, operative paragraph 10.

20. Security council resolution S/RES/1272(1999), 25 October 1999.

21. See Simon Chesterman, 'East Timor in Transition: Self-Determination, State-Building and the United Nations', *International Peacekeeping*, 9(1) (2002), p. 46.

22. Ibid., p. 62.

23. Ian Martin and Alexander Mayer-Rieckh, 'The United Nations and East Timor: From Self-Determination to State-Building', *International Peace-keeping*, 12(1) (2005), p. 136.

24. Oliver P. Richmond and Jason Franks, 'Liberal Peacebuilding in Timor Leste: The Emperor's New Clothes?', *International Peacekeeping*, 15(2) (2008), p. 190.

25. Jarat Chopra, 'The UN's Kingdom of East Timor', *Survival*, 42(3) (autumn 2000), p. 27.

26. Ibid., p. 30.

27. Ibid., p. 33.

28. Astri Suhrke, 'Peacekeepers as Nation-Builders: Dilemmas of the UN in East Timor', *International Peacekeeping*, 8(4) (2001), p. 7.

29. See, for example, Chopra, 'The UN's Kingdom of East Timor', p. 33.

30. Security council resolution S/RES/1319(2000), 8 September 2000.

31. Security council resolution S/RES/1410(2002), 17 May 2002.

32. See Katsumi Ishizuka, 'Peacekeeping in East Timor: The Experience of UNMISET', *International Peacekeeping*, 10(3) (2003), p. 47. The UNHCR withdrew formal refugee status from those still displaced in West Timor in January 2003.

33. Security council resolution S/RES/1473(2003), 4 April 2003.

34. UNOTIL was established by security council resolution S/RES/1599 (2005), 28 April 2005.

35. The security council created UNMIT by resolution S/RES/1704(2006), 25 August 2006, following a detailed report on the situation by secretary-general Kofi Annan (security council document S/2006/626, 8 August 2006).

36. Gusmão was seriously wounded and evacuated to Australia for treatment. Ramos Horta escaped largely unscathed.

Chapter 7

Is it worth it? Success and failure in UN intervention

So far we have explored the conceptual and the ethical aspects of armed humanitarian intervention by the United Nations. We have also looked at the practice across the world as revealed by specific interventions. But a very fundamental question has yet to be directly confronted. Quite simply, as a *general* project in conflict management and resolution, does it work? Is there a convincing justification for the outlay of the vast – and limited – human, material and political capital that the United Nations undertakes when the security council mandates an operation? At the extreme, it can be asked, is humanitarian intervention even counterproductive to long-term domestic and international stability? Might intervention in fact cost more lives and bring more destruction than non-intervention? Assuming that this is not – or not necessarily – so, what is 'success' in humanitarian intervention? What, in short, do we expect it do and how good is the United Nations at doing it?

Giving war a chance: does intervention exacerbate rather than resolve conflict?

In a famous (in some views, notorious) article in *Foreign Affairs* in 1999, provocatively titled 'Give War a Chance', the American commentator Edward Luttwak argued against the entire concept of armed humanitarian intervention. Writing at the time of the Kosovo campaign he insisted that 'although war is a great evil, it does have a great virtue: it can resolve political conflicts and lead to peace . . . when all belligerents become exhausted or when one wins decisively'. But 'war brings peace only after passing a culminating phase of violence'.[1] Well-intentioned interference therefore only intensifies and prolongs struggles. Intervention by the United Nations or other external actors, in other words, tends to exacerbate rather than resolve conflict in the medium and long term:

> Since the establishment of the United Nations and the enshrinement of great-power politics in its Security Council, however, wars among lesser

powers have rarely been allowed to run their natural course. Instead, they have typically been interrupted early on, before they could burn themselves out and establish the preconditions for a lasting settlement. Cease-fires and armistices have frequently been imposed under the aegis of the Security Council in order to halt fighting . . . But a cease-fire tends to arrest war-induced exhaustion and lets belligerents reconstitute and rearm their forces. It intensifies and prolongs the struggle once the cease-fire ends – and it does usually end. [2]

By the last year of the last decade of the twentieth century when his article was published, Luttwak's point seemed to have some force. The outcome of the Kosovo intervention was not yet clear. The Bosnian war, and its terrible apotheosis at Srebrenica, remained a stain on the record of UN intervention. The more or less successful operation in East Timor was just beginning while sub-Saharan Africa offered a litany of apparently doomed interventions over the previous decade, with those in Somalia, Rwanda, Liberia and Angola only the most dramatic examples. Although presented from a different perspective, Luttwak's argument recalls in some ways John Stuart Mill's similarly pragmatic rejection of intervention nearly a century-and-a-half before:

> . . . the evil is that if they [the victims] have not sufficient love of liberty to be able to wrest it from merely domestic oppressors, the liberty which is bestowed on them by other hands than their own, will have nothing real, nothing permanent. No people ever was and remained free, but because it was determined to be so; because neither its rulers nor any other party in the nation could compel it to be otherwise.[3]

Both Mill and Luttwak suggest from their different historical and political standpoints that only a 'natural' resolution of conflicts by those directly party to them will be sufficiently 'authentic' to endure. Externally imposed settlements are unlikely to be permanent. It is extremely difficult, if not impossible, to refute this point of view with any certainty. On either side the counterfactuals, the 'what ifs' (what if there had been intervention when there was none, or what if there had be no intervention when there had been?), are enormous and beyond what might be described as experimental control.

This is not to say that the attempt has not been made. In a detailed, statistically sophisticated article published in 2004, Virginia Page Fortna ranged over a broad sample of conflicts and differing modes of intervention.[4] Her fundamental research question was whether particular types of intervention in different categories of conflict could be related to the durability or absence of violence in the post-conflict phase. Fortna noted that external military intervention, like forms of radical medical intervention, tends to be directed at the more difficult and intractable cases and this distorts judgement of success and failure (open heart surgery is obviously more problematic in its outcomes than chiropody). Her conclusion was that 'despite a number of well-publicized peacekeeping fiascos in the early and mid-1990s, peacekeeping is an effective conflict management tool'.[5] Empirical rigor, in other words, challenges Luttwak's seductive but broad-stroke assertions.

It is possible to find virtue in the conclusions both of Luttwak and his opponents if the terms of the debate are shifted slightly. Each of the opposing positions tends to the reductive. Either all conflicts need to run their course within their own natural 'ecology' or all conflicts are amenable to resolution by external intervention if the correct tools are used in the effort. If, however, conflicts are explored in terms of their own unique settings and the social and political dynamics that drive them, it is reasonable to conclude – as we have already in some of the cases we have explored – that some conflicts do indeed 'need' to run their course without external intervention. Moreover, misguided intervention (or 'premature peacemaking' as Luttwak calls it) might indeed do more harm than good.

However, it can be argued that conflicts may reach a stage of their 'natural' development at which external intervention becomes an essential part of the resolution process. This in some ways takes us back to the earliest episodes of UN peacekeeping where the confidence provided to each side in a conflict by the presence of military observers (as in Kashmir and Palestine) or of an interposition force (as in Suez) literally 'keeps the peace' towards which the conflict has naturally gravitated. In this view, the evident failure of the UN interventions in the Rwanda genocide, Somalia and even Bosnia in the early 1990s may have been foreordained in that in none of those conflicts were the local dynamics amenable to successful intervention. In East Timor, in contrast, where the basis of the conflict was 'right' for resolution, there may have been no way forward for the territory without external intervention.

The difficulty here is that it is not – or not always – clear to even the closest observer which category a particular conflict might be in. The tendency therefore is to assume the desirability of humanitarian intervention as the default. This is a position bolstered by the basic *raison d'être* of the United Nations – preventing 'the scourge of war'. More immediately, it is also encouraged by the operation of what we loosely describe as the CNN effect operating on public opinion in UN member states.

External intervention and internal dynamics: the cases of Angola and Mozambique

The contrasting examples of Angola and Mozambique are revealing here. At first (or even second) glance the post-independence civil wars that afflicted both countries were strikingly similar in their origins and development. On this basis, the interventions that the UN undertook in each during the 1990s would have been expected to follow a similar pattern and end with similar outcomes. Both Angola and Mozambique became independent in 1975 after the military coup in Portugal the previous year. The new regimes in both countries were formed by the liberation movements which had been fighting against the Portuguese army since the early 1960s: the MPLA in Angola and Frelimo in Mozambique. Both attempted to form their new states on the basis of their shared 'Afro-Marxist' ideology. The legitimacy of the two regimes was challenged internally on regionalist and ethnic grounds as well as ideological ones. Externally, both were forced to co-exist in the southern African sub-region which was dominated by a hostile and aggressive white-ruled South Africa. Globally, the two countries were effectively part of the Soviet bloc. The two movements at war with the governing regimes – UNITA in Angola and Renamo in Mozambique – reflected the regionalist and ethnic divisions in their countries and both were supported militarily by South Africa. Unsurprisingly, therefore, the UN's interventions in both countries were broadly similar in their approach and aims. Negotiated ceasefires were followed by parliamentary and presidential elections while both government and rebel fighters undertook to cooperate with a UN-supervised process of demobilisation, disarmament and reintegration into civilian society (the DDR process, which became almost standard operating procedure in UN interventions after the cold war). In both countries the extent of the UN military presence was broadly similar.[6]

Yet despite these close similarities between the origins and nature of the conflicts and the UN's approach to their resolution, the outcomes of the two interventions were dramatically different. The reasons for this lay in a myriad of factors relating to personalities, politics, diplomacy and economics which was woven through the quite striking similarities just listed.

Yes, both UNITA and Renamo had regional and ethnic roots, but their respective histories were quite different. UNITA, which had its main support in the central plateau of Angola, had been involved in the original liberation war against the Portuguese (albeit to a very limited extent) and it had fought the MPLA for control of the state even before the country's independence. Renamo, in contrast, drew less solid support from the central region of Mozambique and had emerged as a movement only after independence with encouragement and support from outside the country (originally from white Rhodesia and then from South Africa). It was consequently vulnerable to changes in this international setting. The end of white rule in Rhodesia with the advent of Zimbabwe in 1980 saw South Africa step in to fill the resulting void in support. But when South Africa itself began to move to majority rule in the early 1990s, Renamo's prospects deteriorated sharply. While UNITA also had the support of South Africa, it could still pursue its war against the Angolan government without it. Both the internal politics and the international relations around the two conflicts therefore were less similar than they appeared.

This situation was reflected in the very different military capacities of UNITA and Renamo. UNITA was a much more formidable fighting force than Renamo, capable of mounting extensive conventional (as opposed to limited guerrilla) operations against government forces. Renamo was more fragmented and much less well trained and equipped. This allowed UNITA to return to war after the electoral process, constructed and supervised by the UN in Angola in 1992, went against it. Renamo, in contrast, once it had stood down to make way for the almost identical electoral process in Mozambique, would probably have been incapable of returning to war. Leadership personalities came into play in this. UNITA's leader was Jonas Savimbi who had founded the movement in the mid-1960s. Violent, unpredictable but undoubtedly charismatic, he was utterly uncompromising in his pursuit of victory over the MPLA and exerted the tightest control over his fighters. Renamo's Afonso Dhlakama, in contrast, was a much less impressive figure whose hold over the movement was never complete. Defeated in the electoral process, therefore, Renamo had little option but to accept a new role as the opposition in a multiparty democracy – something that Savimbi would never countenance and did not have to.

The final contrast between the conflicts in Angola and Mozambique – and perhaps the critical one – was economic. Control of the state in each country held out the promise of very different rewards. During the colonial period both countries had contributed to the imperial economy in different ways. Both had been colonies of settlement for excess population from Portugal, but beyond this Mozambique had provided port, road and railway facilities for a large part of east and central Africa. Angola, for its part, had greater mineral resources. By the time of independence and in subsequent years it was these – and particularly off-shore oil and the diamond mines of the north – that provided the prize in the civil war. Mozambique, in contrast, had been reliant for its national economic base on a transport infrastructure which had itself been degraded by the war. The spoils of civil war, in other words, were very different in each country and this affected the determination with which the two wars were fought.

Within these sets of specific factors in two otherwise very similar conflicts lay the explanation of the very different outcomes of intervention. In Mozambique, UN-organised and supervised elections in 1994 led, despite some last-minute difficulties, to the establishment of an enduring peace based on a new pluralist constitution. In the meantime in Angola a similar electoral process in 1992 which was the centrepiece of a very similar peace process had simply been disregarded by the losers (UNITA), who returned to war. For the following ten years Savimbi rejected repeated attempts by the UN to bring him back into the process and pursued an ultimately doomed strategy of total victory. These attempts by UN mediators, however, themselves served to validate his claims to the status of putative national leader rather than that of violent rebel who had blatantly reneged on an agreement to follow the democratic process. UNITA was thus given an international profile as an interlocutor in the peace process, giving the war, which the UN's intervention was designed to end, an artificial legitimacy. At the same time, UN-brokered ceasefires, while never likely to become permanent, allowed the sides to regroup, rearm and refresh their capacity to continue the war. Simultaneously, the international humanitarian effort ameliorated the most horrific effects of the war which might otherwise have built a greater momentum to finish it.

Only Savimbi's death at the hands of government forces in 2002 brought a final end to the war which UNITA had in fact been losing for some time. This was not, of course, part of the UN's script for Angola but it was the critical event in bringing peace. Subsequently, Angola was able to follow Mozambique into a more or less stable post-war phase of reconstruction within a constitutional structure. UNITA now followed Renamo in Mozambique in converting itself into a political party providing the parliamentary opposition.

Angola, therefore, appears to fully validate the Luttwak's argument that humanitarian intervention perpetuates civil wars by blocking 'the transformative effects of both decisive victory and exhaustion' which would in the natural order bring an enduring end to the conflicts.[7] Yet the situation in Mozambique was quite different. There, violence and destruction would almost certainly have dragged on far beyond the point where 'victory' had any meaning. The war had truly reached stalemate in Mozambique when the UN intervention began. But Luttwak's desired options of exhaustion or decisive victory would probably have resulted in hundreds of thousands of deaths in the future in the absence of that intervention. The mechanisms of civil society that might have been capable of driving a peace process in Mozambique were non-existent. Circumstances brought the end of the war within reach – but it required the services of an external intervention to grasp it.

What *is* effective intervention?

Even before judgements about the point or pointlessness of intervention are sought, there is a major prior question to be resolved. Quite simply, what constitutes success? Virginia Page Fortna's criterion was relatively simple: the resumption or non-resumption of local fighting. But while this meets the purpose of refuting the idea of peacekeeping and humanitarian intervention as fundamentally useless, explanations and therefore expectations of its 'usefulness' can vary widely. As a result, discussions of whether or not intervention 'works', and if so how well, can be complicated by fundamental differences in the expectations with which they begin.

It is possible to identify three major sets of assumptions about success and failure in humanitarian intervention. In several specific cases of intervention we can arrive at wholly different judgements about effectiveness depending on which perspective is applied.[8] The three contending bases of assessment can be characterised as, firstly, the idea of intervention as 'process', secondly as 'deep resolution' and thirdly as 'system management'. These are widely drawn categories without hard borders between them, but in their essential starting points each of them presents significantly different perspectives on what constitutes effectiveness in a United Nations military intervention. Each too has a significantly different interpretation of the humanitarian good to which an effective operation should aspire.

Intervention as 'process'

Verdicts on interventions based on their success as discrete processes focus on administrative, tactical and legal criteria The concern here is essentially the fulfilment of the terms of the mandate set for an operation (usually by the security council). So to speak, does the mission 'do what it says on the tin'? Most fundamentally, does the mission reduce violence on the ground during the term of deployment? In other words, do the means employed by the operation produce intended ends in the short term? The important judgement here is based on comparisons of the 'before' and the immediate 'after' of an operation. This is not to ignore the longer-term impact of an intervention, but simply to recognise the difficulty, if not the impossibility, of reaching fair and reliable judgements for the long term in what are usually highly complex conflict situations.

In this sense the process perspective is the most practical and focused of the three. It takes a highly empirical approach to arriving at judgements rather than engaging in speculative and contestable interpretations of conflicts and their resolution. This is reflected, for example, in the work of Virginia Page Fortna which we have just discussed. In some respects, the process viewpoint looks back to the traditional peacekeeping model which evolved in the 1950s with its 'holy trinity' of characteristics: consent; impartiality; and force only in self-defence. 'Peacekeeping' is related to but separate from both peacemaking and peace-building and can be judged as such.[9]

Intervention as 'deep resolution'

In contrast to the process approach, judgements of an intervention's effectiveness made from the perspective of 'deep resolution' look much further than to just the completion of a set operational mandate and the short-term management of violence. In this perspective humanitarian intervention embraces not just a temporary military peacekeeping presence but also a much larger, longer-term and further-reaching engagement in which post-conflict peace-building is at least as important as military interposition, observation and ceasefire brokerage. The 'point' of UN intervention in this view goes far beyond ticking the boxes of mandate completion by checking off the operative paragraphs of security council resolutions against tangible outcomes. The control of immediate violence that the process viewpoint tends to base its judgements on is just the starting point here. Verdicts, while to some degree evidence-based, will also draw on wider judgements about the breadth and depth of the long-term peace achieved.

The distinction between two different conceptualisations of 'peace' are important to an understanding of the difference between assessments of interventions using this model and the previous, process-based one. The first conceptualisation, 'negative peace', is indicated by the simple absence of physical violence (the principal evidence adduced by those assessing missions from the process perspective). 'Positive peace', in contrast, is evidenced, not just by an absence of violence, but also by the creation of long-term harmonious social relations and by political and economic equity in the post-conflict society. Humanitarian intervention, therefore, must involve a more complex, varied and long-term commitment than traditional notions of peacekeeping. It must be judged against much more demanding criteria, which may be difficult to test on the ground until long after the immediate violence has been brought under control. This perspective is often informed by a cosmopolitanist worldview (see Chapter 2). It sets out universal norms for a truly peaceful society. Intervention in this view is at the service of the UN's responsibilities for the provision of 'global governance' which must foster and safeguard universal rights and values.

In this sense the deep resolution perspective is profoundly post-Westphalian in that the traditional peacekeeping rules of consent and neutrality do not feature. Respect for state sovereignty (central to the Westphalian position) simply does not apply if that sovereignty cuts across the responsibilities of global governance and is used to obstruct the implantation of the universal values essential to achieving positive peace.[10]

Intervention as 'system management'

Judgements of the success of interventions from the system management perspective in contrast are deeply Westphalian in character. The fundamental purpose of UN military interventions in this view is to maintain and promote the stability of the international state system as a whole and its regional sub-systems. The 'humanitarian' element of interventions, therefore, though still the ultimate priority, tends to be long range and indirect rather than immediate. The fate of local populations is weighed against broad assessments of the well-being of much more widely dispersed states and nations.

This is intervention as 'high politics' with a view to the longer horizons of the international system. It is Westphalian in that it is concerned with the smooth and effective workings of a world politics based primarily on relationships between territorially based states with sovereign power. In this sense it lies close to the classic Hammarskjöldian model of peacekeeping. Local intervention by the United Nations is designed to serve the larger interests of the organisation's members by containing and resolving violence at the local level before it can infect the surrounding sub-systems and ultimately the international system as a whole. The metaphor here is that of immunisation: local conflicts are quarantined and the larger system inoculated against infection by them.[11] Hammarskjöld himself, it will be recalled, described his approach to peacekeeping as 'preventive diplomacy' (see Chapter 1).[12]

'Trial by perspective'

A fuller sense of the differences in the perspectives comes when we apply them to actual operations. To this end we can return to a range of interventions already explored in some detail and subject them to this further level of analysis. Two of these are cold war/decolonisation operations of the 1960s. One transcends the cold war/post-cold war period. Two were ventures in the 'new peacekeeping' of the 1990s. They are the first UN operation in the Congo which lasted four years from 1960 (see pages 25 to 30), the temporary administration in Irian Jaya (West New Guinea), also in the early 1960s (see pages 30 to 33), and the UN force in Cyprus which has been in place since 1964. Finally, we take a last look at the two interventions we have just contrasted in relation to Luttwak's ideas: those in Angola and Mozambique.

The UN operation in the Congo (ONUC), 1960–4

The Congo operation was by far the largest to be undertaken by the United Nations when it was established in 1960. It was also the most damaging for the UN, with high casualty rates among the force (it also, of course, cost the life of Dag Hammarskjöld himself).

Designed to ease the Congo's passage to independence and to exclude cold war rivalries from the sub-Saharan African region, ONUC would be judged a failure from all three of our perspectives. It failed to fulfil successive mandates which themselves were altered by the security council in a vain attempt to keep up with a rapidly changing crisis which moved from one of foreign intervention to one of state collapse and humanitarian disaster. In this sense it utterly failed to meet even the basic requirements of success as a 'process'.

Nor could ONUC be said to have come anywhere close to the much more demanding criteria of deep resolution. The UN force departed from the Congo virtually at the first point possible without the withdrawal appearing to be an obvious retreat. The following decades in the country were marked by intermittent civil war, dictatorship and the most appalling levels of poverty and corruption. If any more conclusive evidence of the failure of the intervention to bring 'positive peace' were needed then the necessary return of UN forces to the country in

1999 provided it. MONUC was in a very real sense required to confront deep social and political problems which had simply been left to ferment by the UN's departure and which had once again flared into nation-wide violence.

Did ONUC fare any better from the system management perspective? It did not – either in its immediate context of cold war and global bipolarity or in the longer-term stabilisation of regional international relations in the Central Africa–Great Lakes area. Far from beating out a local brushfire, or quarantining the Congo from broader global hostilities, it could be argued that ONUC and its management from New York instead actively exacerbated East–West tensions. The conduct of ONUC amidst the chaos of the Congo simply invited Soviet accusations of neo-colonialism and of the co-option of the UN for the pursuit of pro-western policies in the region. And, once again, the reappearance of UN forces in the Congo thirty-five years after the end of ONUC underlines the failure of the earlier intervention to stabilise the Westphalian order even at the regional level. The crisis which overtook the Congo in the late 1990s was at least as much regional as national. It was precipitated by multiple invasions from the Congo's neighbours (most notably post-genocide Rwanda) either in an effort to impose stability or in an opportunistic attempt to exploit the chaos in the Congo for their own political and economic benefit. The description of the Congo conflict at this time as 'Africa's first world war' was apposite.

From all three perspectives, therefore, the UN operation in the Congo in the early 1960s, despite the (then) unprecedented resources devoted to it and the breadth of activities that it ultimately involved, would be judged a comprehensive failure.

The UN Temporary Executive Authority and Security Force in West New Guinea/Irian Jaya (UNTEA-UNSF), 1962–3

The intervention in West New Guinea, which took place within the time span of the first Congo operation, offers a more revealing subject, with different verdicts produced by the different perspectives. Like the Congo mission, the operation in West New Guinea emerged from a crisis of decolonisation – though in this case it was a matter of a contested decolonisation rather than an under-prepared one. From the process perspective the operation in Irian Jaya was a textbook success. The mandate set by (unusually in this case) the general assembly was fully and efficiently carried out within the time-frame set. The immediate violence ended as the international conflict was resolved.

The view from the deep resolution perspective, however, could not be more different. The UN withdrew in 1963 leaving huge political, cultural and ethnic divisions which would smoulder and spark into violence at various points over the coming decades. Social and economic equity and the consensual government necessary to create it were not even distant prospects amidst authoritarian Indonesia's 'internal colonisation' of the territory. Moreover, this was in many ways the direct consequence of the UN intervention and the transfer of power from the Netherlands to Indonesia that it supervised. To this extent, far from advancing 'peace', the intervention made it more unlikely. The 'act of free choice' which was supposed to affirm local acceptance of the territory's status was a sham. And, having failed in bringing positive peace to Irian Jaya, the UN intervention did not even produce a meaningful negative peace in the form of an end to routine violence.

The assessment from the system management perspective would be less definite than the judgements of the process and the deep-resolution viewpoints. The intervention evidently helped end an international conflict – between Indonesia and the Netherlands – which had secondary implications for the stability of the cold war system. By resolving a confrontation over 'imperialism', the intervention removed the potential for an East–West dispute. In this sense the 'brushfire' was stamped out by the UN in a classic exercise of 'preventive diplomacy'. The diplomatic face-saving function of UN intervention had also been successful in that, although the Netherlands had given up Irian Jaya, it had not ceded it directly to Indonesia (even though that was the practical effect). However, this victory for the aggressively nationalist Sukarno regime in Indonesia did not contribute to stability at the regional level where a triumphalist Indonesia was viewed with renewed wariness by its neighbours. Relations between Indonesia and Australia, the two regional superpowers of the Asia-Pacific interface, were affected negatively for decades, particularly as Irian Jaya shared the island of New Guinea with the Australian trust territory (later dependant neighbour) Papua New Guinea. Indonesia's behaviour in Irian Jaya would later affect perceptions of its good faith in East Timor, as we saw in the previous chapter.

The outcomes of that single and relatively short-lived intervention, therefore, can draw radically different evaluations of success and failure depending on the assumptions brought to the judgement.

The UN Force in Cyprus (UNFICYP), 1964–

The case of Cyprus brings a similar, though perhaps less sharply contrasting, set of assessments of success. Certainly the moral and ethical issues would be less raw than in Irian Jaya. The fact that the Cyprus operation was established in 1964 and the problem it addressed remains unresolved in the second decade of the twenty-first century might in some views clinch any debate about its success and failure before it begins. In fact, from the process position, with its focus on mandate performance and the control of immediate violence, the Cyprus operation could be judged a success. Unquestionably, peacemaking has not been successful, but UNFICYP has consistently carried out the instructions of the security council by providing an interposing presence between the two communities in conflict – which it has done through all the vicissitudes of the long crisis. The original security council resolution instructed the force to use 'its best efforts to prevent a recurrence of fighting and, as necessary, to contribute to the maintenance and restoration of law and order and a return to normal conditions', and this is precisely what it has done across the decades of its existence.[13] The intervention has proved remarkably adaptable in this, absorbing the impact of the Turkish invasion of 1974 and reconfiguring itself in the aftermath.

Cyprus would assuredly not, however, be considered a successful UN intervention from the perspective of deep resolution. The holistic approach to conflict resolution sees the management of violence as inseparable from the larger process of peacemaking and peace-building. Self-evidently, a country which remains physically divided and 'peaceful' only by virtue of the presence of an interposition force in place for decades is not enjoying positive peace. Indeed, the intervention force itself could be considered as part of the problem rather than the solution. Its presence, now institutionalised, has become a fixed feature of social relations on the island and poses an obstruction to a deep, demilitarised resolution.

The performance of UNFICYP in system management terms has been much more successful. As we have described it, this perspective is not focused primarily on the day-to-day experience of local populations, but on the stability of the larger system. While it is obviously unfortunate that the Greek and Turkish ethnic communities in Cyprus remain physically divided, the presence of UN forces on the island has had a restraining effect on the bigger regional actors in the eastern Mediterranean, Greece and Turkey themselves. The initial intervention in 1964 ended, at least for a decade, the danger of attempts either to bring about a forcible union with Greece (*enosis*) or a partition of the island into client statelets of the two big regional powers. When, ten years later, regional politics produced an attempted *enosis* and partition followed, it is almost certain that the UN's decision to maintain its presence on the island helped contain the local violence and prevent a war between Greece and Turkey. Regrettable as the absence of a permanent Cyprus-wide solution may be, therefore, the regional international system has benefitted enormously from the long-term presence of the UN force.

The second UN Verification Mission in Angola (UNAVEM-II), 1991–5

In all, four UN operations were deployed in Angola in the ten years between January 1989 and February 1999. The first of these, the UN Verification Mission (UNAVEM-I), was a military observer operation responsible for supervising the withdrawal of Cuban troops from the country as part of the linked agreement over the independence of neighbouring Namibia from South Africa (see Chapter 4). The success of that mission led to the immediate creation of UNAVEM-II in 1991. This was charged with the much more complex and onerous task of overseeing an externally organised peace process aimed at ending Angola's own civil war between the governing MPLA and the rebel UNITA movement which had been underway since before the country's independence in 1975. Specifically, UNAVEM-II was to establish and implement a programme of disarmament, demobilisation and reintegration of combatants and to supervise presidential and legislative elections within a new constitutional framework.[14] When UNITA refused to accept its evident defeat in the 1992 elections, the war resumed. UNAVEM-II remained deployed until the beginning of 1995, but failed to make any impact either on the political process or the war itself. Two further UN operations, the third Verification Mission (UNAVEM-III from 1995 to 1997) and the Angola Observation Mission (MONUA from 1997 to 1999) succeeded it. As we have seen, however, the war ended and the political process began only with the death of UNITA leader Jonas Savimbi in 2002, three years after the UN had withdrawn its military presence. The three different perspectives of judgement would, as in the case of the Congo operation in the early 1960s, return a unanimous verdict of failure on UNAVEM-II, though of course on quite different grounds.

The failure from the process perspective would have begun even before the UN force was mandated and deployed. The United Nations had not been directly involved in the peace negotiations or the shape of the agreement that emerged from them (the international driving force in this had been an informal troika of the United States, the Soviet Union and Portugal). The agreement itself was flawed, involving elections within an unrealistic time-scale and imposing a 'winner-takes-all' outcome on them. Therefore any mandate which required a UN presence to implement this arrangement would be difficult to fulfil. The security council itself, however, compounded this problem by providing only limited resources. The ease with which UNAVEM-I had fulfilled its – quite different – mandate may have misled the security council into underestimating the practical and political problems the intervention would face. Therefore a task which was unlikely to succeed even in favourable conditions was mandated to a force of barely 500 military and police personnel.[15]

Unsurprisingly, the performance of UNAVEM-II would not impress those viewing it from the deep resolution perspective. The UN presence had failed not only to foster a positive peace in the country: it had failed completely to maintain even a negative peace in the form of a cessation of fighting. Moreover, the attempt to impose an externally imposed peace settlement with a competitive electoral process as its centrepiece may simply have exacerbated the deep-rooted ethnic and regional divisions within Angola. At best it could only move these divisions from the military to the political sphere; it did nothing to challenge their deep roots.

A separate set of flaws would lead to a negative overall judgement from the system management perspective. At the level of international politics the success of UNAVEM-I in overseeing the withdrawal of Cuban forces from Angola added credence to an interpretation of the Angolan civil war which saw it essentially as an externally driven product of the cold war with the west supporting UNITA and the Soviet bloc backing its MPLA ally. It should therefore have been axiomatic that the end of the cold war would lead to the easy resolution of such proxy conflicts. The politics of the Angolan conflict were, however, complex and its roots largely endogenous. Whatever the external role in feeding the conflict during the cold war, it had a powerful internal momentum which would ensure that it would continue with or without support from foreign patrons.

Paradoxically, however, for these very reasons the system management function of the intervention in Angola was perhaps not as urgent as external observers may have calculated. If the Angolan civil war was indeed driven by essentially internal dynamics, the prospects of it 'infecting' global politics or even the southern African region were limited. For one thing, the cold war was over and whatever happened in Angola was unlikely to have an impact on big power relations. In Africa the transition to majority rule in South Africa had a profoundly stabilising effect on regional international relations. If the Angolan conflict was a 'brushfire', in other words, it was one well contained behind its own fire-breaks. None of this, however, was the achievement of UNAVEM-II which, if not an actual failure from the system management perspective, was of only limited relevance.

The UN operation in Mozambique (ONUMOZ), 1992–4

We have already explored the contrasts between the interventions in Angola and Mozambique from a more general standpoint of success and failure. Angola, as we have just seen, fails comprehensively across the three perspectives. How does Mozambique, with all its apparent similarities, perform against the same sets of criteria?

The security council mandate given to the UN operation in Mozambique at the end of 1992 was very similar to that set for UNAVEM-II a year and a half previously.[16] The UN was to establish and conduct a DDR process among former combatants and supervise presidential and legislative elections. These responsibilities were successfully carried out by ONUMOZ, which was withdrawn at the end of 1994 after the establishment of a new parliamentary government. Only isolated and minor episodes of violence occurred during the period of ONUMOZ's deployment. From the process vista, therefore, the operation proved to have been an almost complete success.

In our earlier analysis of the conflict dynamics in Mozambique, however, we pointed up the contrasts with the superficially similar situation in Angola. Yes, the process of intervention in Mozambique was remarkably successful, but it is essential never to lose sight of the importance of the conditions, political and military, in which the UN intervenes. At risk of excessive repetition, the point has already been made that UN interventions do not operate in a vacuum where success or failure depends simply on the application of set techniques by personnel on the ground. The contrast in the process-level judgements between UNAVEM-II in Angola and ONUMOZ in Mozambique provide particularly sharp illustrations of this essential truth.

The deep resolution position, difficult to satisfy as always, would tend to view the performance of ONUMOZ in Mozambique as only the beginning of the 'real' peace process there. The measurements against mandate-fulfilment which underlie the judgement of the process perspective would not in themselves constitute success when the criterion is the establishment of positive peace. After the end of the fighting and the creation of a functioning party-based government, the social and economic conditions of the majority of Mozambicans remained very bad. The country continued to appear in the lowest percentiles of standard development indices. Democracy or not, political and economic corruption grew at a startling pace in the new Mozambique and inequalities deepened. The long-term impact of the UN intervention therefore – and that is the only one considered by the deep resolution perspective – has been far from wholly positive.

As in Angola, the benefits of intervention from the system management perspective were unclear. Both countries share the same southern African region and unrelated developments there – principally the end of apartheid South Africa – meant that the quarantining role of the UN operation was largely unnecessary. The end of the cold war pointed to the same conclusion at the global level.

In one respect, however, the resolution of the Mozambique conflict had an important regional benefit which, though economic, had longer-term implications for stability and co-operation at the political level too in southern Africa. As we noted, Mozambique's potential wealth was small in comparison to that of Angola (and that affected the different narratives of the respective conflicts). But while Angola's mineral resources were fundamentally a national concern, Mozambique's economy, from colonial times forward, was based on the provision of regional infrastructure. During the civil war there, roads and railways which had served almost all the landlocked countries of the region as well as South Africa quickly became unusable. The ports through which the imports and exports of those countries passed became largely redundant. The repair of this infrastructure and the resumption of regional traffic through the ports had an obvious benefit to regional co-operation. To this extent, the system management function of the intervention could be counted as a success, however indirectly.

	Process	Deep resolution	System management
Congo (1960–4)	Failure	Failure	Failure
Irian Jaya (1962–3)	Success	Failure	Limited success
Cyprus (1964–)	Success	Failure	Success
Angola (1992–5)	Failure	Failure	Limited relevance
Mozambique (1992–4)	Success	Very limited success	Indirect success

Table 7.1 Judgements of UN interventions from three perspectives

The analysis of these selected UN interventions could be applied to any other group of operations and produce broadly similar results. They merely confirm what experience and political common sense indicate: that intervention in a conflict by UN forces does not provide a panacea but will frequently result in an improvement in local and even international conditions. This is hardly a ringing endorsement, of course, and comes nowhere near the expectations of those who look to the UN to bring deep enduring holistic solutions to the conflicts it engages with. But such expectations themselves have an air of 'impossibilism' about them. Humanitarian intervention may attract evangelism but it does not provide fertile ground for it. It is unclear whether the direction of travel in international relations is towards a post-Westphalian world in which the cosmopolitan ideal of global governance transcending the power of states will prevail. If this is indeed the ultimate destination of world politics, and that is far from certain, then assuredly we are still in the earliest stages of a long journey.

If the end of the global divisions of the cold war are taken to signify the beginning of this passage (as it frequently is), then we have already wandered from the path. The failures of UN interventions in the 1990s, from Africa to Europe, proved an obstacle on the way. They deflated some of the more euphoric assumptions about multilateralism in a post-bipolar world. More barriers on the route emerged after the military interventions by big powers in the new century, most obviously that in Iraq. The general opprobrium which attached to this seeped across conceptual boundaries to pollute perceptions of all intervention by armed forces, on grounds of morality, practicality and national self-interest.

Intervention by UN forces will continue, new operations will be mounted. But to appreciate their value it is necessary to accept that their prospects of success will be shaped by certain inescapable realities. For one thing, the power of states and the national interests they represent endures in the international system, whether or not it is diminishing over a long historical cycle. This will continue to determine decisions about the location of interventions, the mandates they are given and their duration. These decisions will not always be either rational or wise; that is in the nature of national politics at the United Nations. Secondly, whatever the intended aims of an intervention and however these are expressed by the security council, the major determinant of outcomes is not the operation itself and how it is managed, but the nature of the specific crisis it is engaged with. However well resourced, manned and led a UN operation may be, it will fail unless the dynamics of the conflict it is addressing are at a point where there is an evident opportunity and role for external help towards a resolution. To acknowledge this does not mean an acceptance of Luttwak's arguments on the natural ecology of conflict, but simply acknowledgement that without the correct balance of incentives and disincentives for peace, conflict will continue under its own momentum. The matched pair of Angola and Mozambique provides one of the sharper illustrations of this. United Nations missions may not need a fully open door to succeed, but it has to be at least ajar.

These fundamental points are more widely accepted now than they were even a few years ago. Certainly there is not likely to be any return to the blizzard of interventions established in the 1990s. This is only in small part due to the existence of a relatively more secure international system after the inevitable instabilities of the immediate post-cold war period. It is mainly a result of more realistic assessments of the possibilities of intervention shaped by an acknowledgement of the realties just outlined. Had the convulsion of massacres and ethnic cleansing that beset Kyrgyzstan in the middle of 2010, for example, taken place say fifteen years previously, then a UN intervention would probably have been undertaken to meet the obvious humanitarian threat. As it was, the calls of the Kyrgyzstan government itself for intervention were ignored when states viewed the crisis through the lenses both of their national interests and the prospect of clear success.

The 'whats', 'wheres' and the 'hows' of humanitarian intervention are therefore problematic. But the 'who' should be clear. The United Nations remains by far the best agent of intervention. However effective in resource terms a single state or even a coalition of the willing may be, without at least the legitimisation of the UN their efforts will be politically contestable and consequently less likely to succeed. The manifest weaknesses in the UN system cannot be ignored. Military activity is subject to security council approval with all that means in the context of a body subject to multiple veto. Its machinery is slow and steady, offering only limited possibilities of rapid reaction. The forces it deploys are often multinational in the broadest, most haphazard sense. Yet these are at least as much strengths as weaknesses. They give a legitimacy and solidity which can be provided by no other international actor. In the uncertain and complex field of armed humanitarian intervention it is reasonable to describe the United Nations as the worst possible option – apart from all the others.

Notes

1. Edward N. Luttwak, 'Give War a Chance', *Foreign Affairs*, 78(4) (1999), p. 36.
2. Ibid.
3. John Stuart Mill, 'A Few Words on Non-Intervention', originally published in *Fraser's Magazine* (1850). Found at http://www.libertarian.co.uk/lapubs/forep/forep008.pdf
4. Virginia Page Fortna, 'Does Peacekeeping Keep Peace? International Intervention and the Durability of Peace after Civil War', *International Studies Quarterly*, 48 (2004), pp. 269–92. Fortna later expanded her discussion in a book: *Does Peacekeeping Work?* (Princeton NJ: Princeton University Press, 2008).
5. Ibid., p. 288.
6. For a fuller account of the conflicts in Angola and Mozambique and the UN's response to them see Norrie MacQueen, *United Nations Peacekeeping in Africa since 1960* (London: Longman, 2003), pp.122–67. The two interventions are also examined by Dennis C. Jett in *Why Peacekeeping Fails* (London: Palgrave, 2001).
7. Luttwak, 'Give War a Chance', p. 44.
8. I explore these contending approaches to assessing intervention in greater detail (and using slightly different terminology) in 'Judging Peacekeeping Outcomes: Three Perspectives on UN Operations', in H. J. Langholtz, B. Kondoch and A. Wells (eds), *The Yearbook of International Peace Operations* (The Hague: Martinus Nijhoff, 2008), pp. 1–21.
9. Like Fortna, writers and works which adopt this position on mission assessment are predominantly North American. Loosely categorised, they would include: William J. Durch (ed.), *The Evolution of UN Peacekeeping* (New York: St. Martin's Press, 1993); Paul F. Diehl, *International Peacekeeping* (Baltimore MD: Johns Hopkins University Press, 1993). One British author who writes from this perspective is N. D. White whose *Keeping the Peace: The United Nations and the Maintenance of International Peace and Security* (Manchester: Manchester University Press, 1997) approaches the issue of intervention from a largely legal standpoint.
10. The deep resolution model of intervention is perhaps more closely associated with the discipline of peace studies rather than politics or international relations. Works from this general perspective include A. B. Fetherston, *Towards a Theory of United Nations Peacekeeping* (London: Macmillan, 1994); Tom Woodhouse and Oliver Ramsbotham, *Peacekeeping and Conflict Resolution* (London: Cass, 2000); Oliver Richmond, *Maintaining Order, Making Peace* (London: Palgrave, 2002); Mary Kaldor, *Human Security* (Cambridge: Polity, 2007).
11. An alternative metaphor for this view of intervention is the familiar one

of the containment of a grass fire to prevent it becoming a full-scale forest fire. This was employed by the political journalist Joseph Lash in his study of Hammarskjöld published in the year of the latter's death: *Dag Hammarskjöld: Custodian of the Brushfire Peace* (New York: Doubleday, 1961).

12. Writers in this perspective include the British scholar of peacekeeping, Alan James, who first engaged with the subject in the 1960s. See, for example, his *The Politics of Peacekeeping* (London: Chatto and Windus, 1969) and *Peacekeeping and International Politics* (London: Macmillan, 1990). The late Sir Antony Parsons, a former British ambassador to the UN, adopted a similar position in his *From Cold War to Hot Peace: UN Interventions 1975–1995* (Harmondsworth: Penguin, 1995).

13. Security council resolution S/RES/186(1964), 4 March 1964, paragraph 5.

14. The mandate of UNAVEM-II was set out in security council resolution S/RES696(1991), 30 May 1991.

15. These were points made by the secretary-general's representative Margaret Anstee in *Orphan of the Cold War*, her own account of the debacle.

16. The Mozambique operation was mandated by security council resolution S/RES/797(1992), 16 December 1992.

Further reading

Abiew, Francis Kofi, *The Evolution of the Doctrine and Practice of Humanitarian Intervention* (Leiden: Brill, 1999).

Abi-Saab, George, *The United Nations Operation in the Congo, 1960–1964* (London: Oxford University Press, 1978).

Adelman, Howard, *The Ethics of Humanitarian Intervention* (Aldershot: Ashgate, 2004).

Anstee, Margaret, *Orphan of the Cold War: The Inside Story of the Collapse of the Angolan Peace Process, 1992–93* (London: Macmillan, 1996).

Appiah, Kwame Anthony, *Cosmopolitanism: Ethics in a World of Strangers* (London: Allen Lane, 2006).

Archibugi, Daniele (ed.), *Debating Cosmopolitanism* (London: Verso, 2003).

Barnett, Michael, *Eyewitness to Genocide: The United Nations and Rwanda* (Ithaca NY: Cornell University Press, 2002).

Bass, Garry J., *Freedom's Battle: The Origins of Humanitarian Intervention* (New York: Knopf, 2008).

Bellamy, Alex, *Kosovo and International Society* (London: Palgrave, 2002).

Bellamy, Alex and Williams, Paul, *Understanding Peacekeeping* (2nd ed.) (Cambridge: Polity, 2009).

Berman, Eric G. and Sams, Katie E., *Peacekeeping in Africa, Capabilities and Culpabilities* (Geneva: United Nations Institute for Disarmament Research, 2000).

Boutros-Ghali, Boutros, *An Agenda for Peace* (New York: UN, 1982).

Boutros-Ghali, Boutros, *Unvanquished: A US–UN Saga* (New York: Random House, 1999).

Chesterman, Simon, *Just War or Just Peace? Humanitarian Intervention and International Law* (Oxford: Oxford University Press, 2006).

Cooper, John M., *Breaking the Heart of the World: Woodrow Wilson and the Fight over the League of Nations* (Cambridge: Cambridge University Press, 2001).

Coulon, Jocelyn, *Soldiers of Diplomacy: The United Nations, Peacekeeping and the New World Order* (Toronto: University of Toronto Press, 1998).

Crawford, Neta, *Argument and Change in World Politics: Ethics, Decolonization, and Humanitarian Intervention* (Cambridge: Cambridge University Press, 2002).

Daalder, Ivo H., *Getting to Dayton: America's Bosnia Policy* (Washington DC: Brookings Institution, 2000).

Dallaire, Roméo, *Shake Hands with the Devil: The Failure of Humanity in Rwanda* (London: Arrow Books, 2005).

Diehl, Paul F., *International Peacekeeping* (Baltimore MD: Johns Hopkins University Press, 1993).

Durch, William (ed.), *The Evolution of UN Peacekeeping: Case Studies and Comparative Analysis* (New York: St. Martin's Press, 1993).

Durch, William (ed.), *UN Peacekeeping, American Politics and the Uncivil Wars of the 1990s* (New York: St. Martin's Press, 1996).

Falk, Richard, *Law in an Emerging Global Village: A Post-Westphalian Perspective* (Amsterdam: Hotei-Brill, 1998).

Fetherston, A. B., *Towards a Theory of United Nations Peacekeeping* (London: Macmillan, 1994).

Findley, Trevor (ed.), *Challenges for the New Peacekeepers* (Oxford: Oxford University Press, 1996).

Fortna, Virginia Page, *Does Peacekeeping Work?* (Princeton NJ: Princeton University Press, 2008).

Frye, Alton, *Humanitarian Intervention: Crafting a Workable Doctrine* (Washington DC: Brookings Institution, 2000).

Furley, Oliver and May, Roy (eds), *Peacekeeping in Africa* (Aldershot: Ashgate, 1998).

Glenny, Misha, *The Fall of Yugoslavia* (3rd ed.) (Harmondsworth: Penguin, 1999).

Gourevitch, Philip, *We Wish to Inform You That Tomorrow We Will Be Killed With Our Families* (London: Picador, 1999).

Harriss, John, *The Politics of Humanitarian Intervention* (New York: St. Martin's Press, 1995).

Hehir, Aidan, *Humanitarian Intervention after Kosovo: Iraq, Darfur and the Record of Global Civil Society* (London: Palgrave, 2009).

Heinze, Eric A., *Waging Humanitarian War: The Ethics, Law, and Politics of Humanitarian Intervention* (Albany NY: State University of New York Press, 2009).

Higate, Paul and Henry, Marsha, *Insecure Spaces: Peacekeeping in Liberia, Kosovo and Haiti* (London: Zed Books, 2009).

Hoffmann, Stanley, *The Ethics and Politics of Humanitarian Intervention* (Notre Dame IN: University of Notre Dame Press, 1996).

Holzgrefe, J. L. and Keohane Robert, O. (eds), *Humanitarian Intervention* (Cambridge: Cambridge University Press, 2003).

Howard, Lise Morje, *UN Peacekeeping in Civil Wars* (Cambridge: Cambridge University Press, 2007).

Huntington, Samuel P., *The Clash of Civilizations and the Remaking of the Modern World* (New York: Simon and Schuster, 1996).

Huth, Paul K. et al., *The Democratic Peace and Territorial Conflict in the Twentieth Century* (Cambridge: Cambridge University Press, 2003).

Ignatieff, Michael, *Virtual War* (London: Vintage, 2001).

Ignatieff, Michael, *Empire Lite: Nation-Building in Bosnia, Kosovo and Afghanistan* (London: Vintage, 2003).

James, Alan, *Peacekeeping in International Politics* (London: Macmillan, 1990).

Janzekovic, John, *The Use of Force in Humanitarian Intervention* (Aldershot: Ashgate, 2006).

Jett, Dennis C., *Why Peacekeeping Fails* (London: Palgrave, 2001).

Joliffe, Jill, *East Timor: Nationalism and Colonialism* (St Lucia: Queensland University Press, 1978).

Juddah, Tim, *Kosovo: War and Revenge* (2nd ed.) (London: Yale University Press, 2002).

Kabia, John M., *Humanitarian Intervention and Conflict Resolution in West Africa* (Aldershot: Ashgate, 2009).

Kaldor, Mary, *Human Security* (Cambridge: Polity, 2007).

Kant, Immanuel, *Perpetual Peace: A Philosophical Sketch (1795)* (New York: Cosimo Classics, 2005).

Kondoch, Boris, *International Peacekeeping* (Aldershot: Ashgate, 2007).

Kuperman, Alan J., *The Limits of Humanitarian Intervention* (Washington DC: Brookings Institution, 2001).

Kuperman, Alan and Crawford, Timothy, *Gambling on Humanitarian Intervention* (London: Routledge, 2006).

Lash, Joseph P., *Dag Hammarskjöld: Custodian of the Brushfire Peace* (London: Cassell, 1962).

Lepard, Brian D., *Rethinking Humanitarian Intervention* (Philadelphia PA: Pennsylvania State University Press, 2003).

Lillich, Richard B., *Humanitarian Intervention and the United States* (Charlottesville VA: University of Virginia Press, 1988).

Linklater, Andrew, *The Transformation of Political Community: Ethical Foundations of the Post-Westphalian Era* (Columbia SC: University of South Carolina Press, 1999).

Luard, Evan, *A History of the United Nations: Vol. I: The Years of Western Domination, 1945–55* (London: Macmillan, 1982).

Luard, Evan, *A History of the United Nations: Vol. II: The Age of Decolonization, 1955–65* (London: Macmillan, 1989).

Luttwak, Edward, 'Give War a Chance', *Foreign Affairs*, 78(4) (1999).

MacKenzie, Lewis, *Peacekeeper: The Road to Sarajevo* (Toronto: HarperCollins, 1994).

MacKinnon, Michael G., *The Evolution of US Peacekeeping Policy under Clinton* (London: Cass, 1999).

MacQueen, Norrie, *Peacekeeping and the International System* (London: Routledge, 2006).

MacQueen, Norrie, *United Nations Peacekeeping in Africa since 1960* (London: Longman, 2002).

Malcolm, Noel, *Bosnia* (London: Pan, 2002).

Malcolm, Noel, *Kosovo: A Short History* (London: Pan, 2002).

Martin, Ian, *Self-determination in East Timor: The United Nations, the Ballot, and the International Intervention* (London: Lynne Rienner, 2001).

Mayall, James (ed.), *The New Interventionism 1991–1994: United Nations*

Experience in Cambodia, Former Yugoslavia and Somalia (Cambridge: Cambridge University Press, 1996).

McQueen, Carol, *Humanitarian Intervention and Safety Zones* (London: Palgrave, 2005).

Melvern, Linda, *A People Betrayed: The Role of the West in Rwanda's Genocide* (London: Zed, 2000).

Murphy, Ray, *Peacekeeping in Lebanon, Somalia and Kosovo* (Cambridge: Cambridge University Press, 2007).

Murphy, Sean D., *Humanitarian Intervention* (Philadelphia PA: University of Pennsylvania Press, 1996).

Nardin, Terry and Williams Melissa, S. (eds), *Humanitarian Intervention* (New York: New York University Press, 2006),

Neuman, Johanna, *Lights, Camera, War: Is Media Technology Driving International Politics* (New York: St. Martin's Press, 1996).

Newman, Michael, *Humanitarian Intervention* (London: Hurst, 2009).

Northedge, F. S., *The League of Nations: Its Life and Times, 1920–1946* (Leicester: Leicester University Press, 1985).

Obiaga, Ndubisi, *The Politics of Humanitarian Organizations Intervention* (Lanham MD: University Press of America, 2004).

O'Brien, Conor Cruise, *To Katanga and Back: A UN Case History* (London: Hutchinson, 1962).

O'Hanlon, Michael E., *Expanding Global Military Capacity for Humanitarian Intervention*, (Washington DC: Brookings Institution Press, 2003).

Orford, Anne, *Reading Humanitarian Intervention* (Cambridge: Cambridge University Press, 2007).

Parsons, Anthony, *From Cold War to Hot Peace: UN Interventions 1975–1995* (Harmondsworth: Penguin, 1995).

Phillips, Robert L. and Cady, Duane L., *Humanitarian Intervention* (Lanham MD: Rowman and Littlefield, 1995).

Prunier, Gerard, *Rwanda in Zaire: From Genocide to Continental War* (London: Hurst, 2000).

Prunier, Gerard, *The Rwanda Crisis: History of a Genocide* (London: Hurst, 2002).

Pugh, Michael (ed.), *The UN, Peace and Force* (London: Cass, 1997).

Ramsbotham, Oliver and Woodhouse, Tom, *Humanitarian Intervention in Contemporary Conflict* (Cambridge: Polity, 1996).

Richmond, Oliver, *Maintaining Order, Making Peace* (London: Palgrave, 2002).

Rubinstein, Robert, *Peacekeeping Under Fire* (Boulder CO: Paradigm, 2008).

Russell, Ruth B., *A History of the United Nations Charter* (Washington DC: Brookings Institution, 1958).

Russett, Bruce M., *Grasping the Democratic Peace* (Princeton NJ: Princeton University Press, 1994).

Scholte, Jan Aart, *Globalization: A Critical Introduction* (2nd ed.) (London: Palgrave, 2005).

Seybolt, Taylor B., *Humanitarian Military Intervention* (Oxford: Oxford University Press, 2008).

Shawcross, William, *Deliver Us from Evil: Warlords and Peacekeepers in a World of Endless Conflict* (London: Bloomsbury, 2000).

Smith, Michael G. and Dee, Moreen, *Peacekeeping in East Timor* (London: Lynne Rienner, 2003).

Teson, Fernando R., *Humanitarian Intervention* (Leiden: Brill, 2005).

Thakur, R. C. and Thayer, C. A. (eds), *A Crisis of Expectations: UN Peacekeeping in the 1990s* (Boulder CO: Westview, 1995).

Thakur, Ramesh, *Kosovo and the Challenge of Humanitarian Intervention* (Tokyo: United Nations University, 2000).

Thant, U, *View from the UN: the Memoirs of U Thant* (New York: Doubleday, 1978).

Urquhart, Brian, *Hammarskjöld* (London: Bodley Head, 1973).

Verrier, Anthony, *International Peacekeeping: United Nations Forces in a Troubled World* (Harmondsworth: Penguin, 1981).

Waldheim, Kurt, *In the Eye of the Storm: A Memoir* (London: Weidenfeld and Nicolson, 1985).

Walters, F. P., *A History of the League of Nations* (London: Oxford University Press, 1960).

Watanabe, Koji, *Humanitarian Intervention* (Washington DC: Brookings Institution, 2003).

Weiss, Thomas G. and Collins, Cindy, *Humanitarian Challenges and Intervention* (Boulder CO: Westview, 2000).

Weiss, Thomas G., *Humanitarian Intervention* (Cambridge: Polity, 2007).

Welsh, Jennifer M., *Humanitarian Intervention and International Relations* (Oxford: Oxford University Press, 2006).

Wesley, Michael, *Casualties of the New World Order: The Causes of Failure of UN Missions to Civil Wars* (London: Macmillan, 1997).

Wheeler, Nicholas J., *Saving Strangers: Humanitarian Intervention in International Society* (Oxford: Oxford University Press, 2000).

White, N. D., *Keeping the Peace: The United Nations and the Maintenance of International Peace and Security* (2nd ed.) (Manchester: Manchester University Press, 1997).

Williams, Michael, *Civil–Military Relations and Peacekeeping* (Oxford: Oxford University Press, 1998).

Woodhouse, Tom, Bruce, Robert and Dando, Malcolm (eds), *Peacekeeping and Peacemaking: Towards Effective Intervention in Post-Cold War Conflicts* (London: Macmillan, 1997).

Woodhouse, Tom and Ramsbotham, Oliver, *Peacekeeping and Conflict Resolution* (London: Cass, 2000).

Woodhouse, Tom and Ramsbotham, Oliver, *Peacekeeping in the 21st Century* (London: Routledge, 2009).

Index

Abyssinia, 8, 103, 122; *see also* Ethiopia
Adriatic, 144
Afghanistan, 36, 62, 80, 83
Africa, 11, 36, 46, 55, 58, 60, 89, 94–137,
     177, 178, 204, 208, 224
   Central, 76, 122, 123, 211, 217
   East, 211
   Horn of, 68, 104, 106, 114
   Portuguese-speaking, 36, 55, 95, 96, 102
   scramble for, 99, 115
   southern, 210, 221
   sub-Saharan, xv, 68, 82, 94, 97, 104, 114,
     119, 130, 133, 208, 216
   West, 11, 61, 129, 135
African Union, xii, 103, 116, 132, 134, 135,
     136
African Union Mission in Sudan *see* AMIS
Afro-Asian bloc (in UN), 22, 27–8, 31, 27, 31
Afro-Marxism, 36, 102, 210
Agenda for Peace (1992), 50–60, 87, 148
Ahtisaari, Martii, 170
Aideed, Mohamed Farah, 107, 110, 111, 113
Akashi, Yasushi, 153
Albania, 142, 156–7, 158, 162, 164, 167, 168,
     170, 171; *see also* Kosovars
Algeria, 74, 106
Alkitiri, Mari, 197, 199, 200
Allenstein and Marienwerder, 9
Amazon, 10
AMIS, 129, 132, 133, 134, 136
Anglo-Sudanese war, 130
Angola, xiv, 52, 55, 57, 58, 75, 95, 96–7, 99,
     101, 108, 117, 118, 119, 128, 137, 148,
     178, 208, 210–12, 216, 220–2, 223, 225
Annan, Kofi, 54, 72–4, 76, 79, 86, 121, 124,
     127, 128, 132
   and East Timor, 181, 182, 185, 186, 189
Aouzou Strip, 97
apartheid, 78, 96, 223
APODETI, 178–9
Arab countries, 21, 24, 25, 34, 46, 130
Arabian Gulf, 103, 104
Arusha, 43, 116
   agreement (Rwanda), 116, 117, 118, 119,
     120, 121, 124
ASEAN, 184, 187, 204
Asia, 7, 17, 18, 19, 46, 89, 94, 183, 197, 204
   central, 49
   Pacific

south, 21, 37, 95
southeast, 36, 38, 180
Association of Southeast Asian Nations *see*
     ASEAN
Aswan dam, 21
Atlantic, Charter, 11–12
Atlantic alliance, 22, 149; *see also* NATO
Australia, xii, 76, 218
   and East Timor, 73, 85, 126, 183–8, 201,
     202, 203, 204
   Northern Territory of, 183
Austria, 9; *see also* Austria-Hungary
Austria-Hungary, 5, 141; *see also* Austria

Baghdad, 48
Bakongo, 99
balance of power, 4
Balkans, 4, 5, 9, 141–73, 191
Baltic, 9, 141
Bangladesh, 91, 118–19, 186
Beijing, 130
Beirut, 25, 38
Belgium, 9, 11, 26, 59, 101, 112, 152
   and Rwanda, 115, 116, 118, 120, 121–2,
     124, 127
Belgrade, 143, 145, 146, 147, 156, 157, 158,
     162, 164, 165, 166, 167
Bellamy, Alex, 157–8
Belo, Archbishop Carlos, 180
Belorussia, 141
Berlin, 10
   Wall, 141
Berlin, Isaiah, 19
Biafra, 94
Bicesse agreement, 117
Blackhawk Down, 111, 114
Blair, Tony, 80, 161, 164
   Chicago speech, 159–61, 164, 165–6
Blondin Beye, Alioune, 108
Bosnia, xii, xiv, 51, 55, 57, 62, 79, 86, 117,
     145–55, 156, 158, 165, 171, 172, 173,
     177, 187, 202, 208, 209
   Herzogovina, 145, 147, 155
Bosniaks, 145, 146
Boutros-Ghali, Boutros, 50, 51, 64, 74, 77, 83,
     122
   and *An Agenda for Peace*, 50–60, 75
   and Bosnia, 148, 153
   and Rwanda, 118, 121, 123, 124

and Somalia, 106–8, 110, 112
Brahimi, Lakhdar, 74
  Report, 74–6, 77, 79–80, 82, 134, 135, 136
Brazil, 177, 186
Bretton Woods institutions, 182, 203
Britain, 4, 7, 8, 9, 10, 11, 13, 46, 81, 85, 122,
    126, 130, 164, 187
  and Africa, 94, 95, 101–2, 103–4, 136
  and Bosnia 144, 148, 149, 150–1, 153
  and Kosovo, 160–1, 163
  and Suez, 21–3
British Somaliland, 103, 104; see also
    Somaliland
Brookings Institution, 86
Bulgaria, 142
Burma, 78
Burundi, 11, 98, 101, 115, 121
Bush, President George W., 80, 88, 161, 164
Bush, President George H. W., 42, 86, 108, 149

Cable News Network see CNN
Cambodia, 10, 30, 58, 62, 64, 118, 148, 167,
    189
Cameroon, 11
Camp David agreement, 34, 38
Canada, 22, 74, 76, 89, 91, 106, 119, 135, 168
Canberra, 185
Caribbean, 4
Catholic church, 2, 3
Central African Republic, 97, 98, 101, 129,
    130, 131, 136
Central America, 62
Chad, 97, 98, 101, 129, 130, 131, 136
Chamoun, Camille, 25
China, 8, 13, 20, 44, 81–2, 122, 125
  and Darfur, 72, 82, 130, 132
  and Gulf war, 46, 47, 48
  and Korean war 20
  and Kosovo, 162, 163, 166, 172
Chirac, Jacques, 153
Chopra, Jarat, 190–1
Christendom, 2–3
Christianity, 3
Churchill, Winston, 11
Claes, Willy, 152
Clinton, President Bill, 51, 86, 88, 108, 112,
    164, 182, 197
  and Bosnia, 149, 150–1, 154, 155
  and Kosovo, 80, 164
  and Rwanda, 123, 128
  and Somalia, 86, 108–14, 130
CNN effect, 83–7, 124, 133, 149, 159, 166,
    185, 209
  in Rwanda, 83, 85, 86, 122, 124
  in Somalia, 85, 102, 104, 108, 109, 112
CNRT, 191–2, 193, 194, 197, 200, 201
cold war, xi, xii, xiii, xv, 17, 21, 71, 72, 87,
    119, 143, 147, 180, 217, 218, 221, 224

'first', 23
'second', 38, 49
  end of, vi, 1, 7, 19, 28, 33, 42, 48–50, 54,
    57, 60, 61, 62, 69, 81, 83, 89, 90, 96, 102,
    104, 113, 141, 171, 180, 202, 221, 223
  post-, 43–4, 50–5, 60, 64, 67, 76, 81–2, 83,
    89, 97, 122, 124, 145, 149, 152, 159,
    201, 204, 210, 216, 225
collective security, 6, 7–8, 11, 13, 14, 15, 19,
    24, 44–6, 48, 52–3, 54, 76, 164
Colombia, 10
colonialism, 11, 31, 100, 192; see also
    imperialism; decolonisation
  neo-, 72, 99–100, 217
Commission on Human Rights (UN), 18, 43,
    180
Commonwealth, 94, 95, 126
Commonwealth of Independent States, 126
Communism, 18, 43, 72, 143
Concert of Europe, 4, 7
Conference on Security and Cooperation in
    Europe see CSCE
Congo, 23, 25–30, 31, 36, 56, 57, 61, 63, 64,
    94–5, 97, 98, 99, 101, 102, 121, 186,
    196, 216–17, 223
  Belgian, 25, 103
  Democratic Republic of, 25, 28, 68, 101,
    115, 123, 128–9, 136
consent (to intervention), 21, 24, 29, 64, 71,
    74, 77, 120, 126, 127, 130, 185, 191, 214
  host state, xiii, 24, 27, 75, 106, 145, 183, 186
Conservative party (Britain), 144, 159
Contact Group (Balkans), 158, 163, 165, 166,
    172
Cosmopolitanism, 69–72, 89–90, 215, 224
Côte d'Ivoire, 61–2, 101, 129
Croatia, 57, 62, 142, 143, 144–5, 158, 171
  and Bosnian war, 146, 147, 155
Crusades, 1, 2, 3
CSCE, 158
Cuba, 97, 117, 220, 221
Cyprus, 23, 29–30, 37, 56, 61, 171, 216, 218–
    20, 223
Czech Republic, 141
Czechoslovakia, 141

Dallaire, General Roméo, 119, 120–1, 125–6
Damascus, 34
Darfur, xii, 72, 82, 97, 98, 101, 103, 128–33,
    134, 135, 136, 195
Darwin, 183
Dayton agreement (Bosnia), 155
DDR process, 57, 210, 222
decolonisation, 21, 22, 25, 30–1, 94–5, 97–9,
    103, 115, 181, 216–17
Deliver Us from Evil, 128
Democratic party (US), 7, 11
Democratic Party of Kosovo, 170

democratic peace theory, 68
Denmark, 9, 149
Department of peacekeeping Operations *see* DPKO
Department of Political Affairs (UN), 190, 192
dependency theory, 99–100
détente, 33–7, 38, 49
Dhlakama, Afonso, 211
diamonds, 212
Dili, 180, 188, 195, 198, 199, 200
diplomacy, 3
DPKO, 120, 190, 191
dual key (Bosnia), xii, 151–3, 155, 172, 187
Dumbarton Oaks, 12
Dutch East Indies, 30, 178

Eagleburger, Lawrence, 86, 108
East Timor, xii, 10, 30, 73, 126, 169, 177–204, 208, 209, 218; *see also* Timor Leste
ECOMOG, 134, 135
Economic Community of West African States *see* ECOWAS
economic sanctions, 1
ECOWAS, 126, 134–5
 Military Observation Group *see* ECOMOG
Egypt, 25, 50, 61, 130
 and Suez, 21–3, 38
 and 1973 war, 34–8, 61
El Salvador, 58
enosis, 219
Eritrea, 95, 97, 101, 103, 129
Estonia, 141
Ethiopia, 8, 68, 95, 97, 101, 103, 104, 111, 129; *see also* Abyssinia
ethnic cleansing, 78–9, 141, 145, 147, 148, 151, 154, 157, 159, 165, 168, 225
Europe, 2, 3, 6, 7, 8, 18, 43, 60, 89, 98–9, 141, 148, 160, 171, 203, 224
 central, 83, 142, 168, 204
 eastern, 17, 38, 83, 142
 western, 142, 143
European Community, 144; *see also* European Union
European Security and Defence Policy, 136
European Union, 136, 149, 170–1; *see also* European Community
 Rule of Law Mission (Kosovo) 170–1
Evans, Gareth, 76

Falintil (East Timor), 179, 182, 194, 195, 199, 203
feudalism, 2
F-FDTL (East Timor), 195, 198, 199, 201
Fiji, 91
Finland, 170
first world war, 4, 7, 15, 21, 96, 130, 142
Florida, 111
Food and Agriculture Organization (UN), xi

Foreign Affairs, 207
Foreign Legion (French), 94
Fortna, Virginia Page, 208–9, 213, 214
France, xii, 4, 7, 8, 9, 10, 11, 13, 46, 112, 164, 186
 and Africa, 94, 101–2, 125, 136
 and Bosnia, 144, 148, 149, 150–1, 153
 and Kosovo, 163
 and Rwanda, 116, 121, 122–3, 125–6, 186
 and Suez, 21–3, 24
Francophonie, 94
Frelimo (Mozambique), 210
French Revolution, 4
Fretilin, (East Timor) 178, 179, 194, 196, 197, 199, 200, 201
Fukuyama, Francis, 44, 68, 90

G-8, 168
Gambia, 99
general assembly (UN), 12, 13, 16, 17, 18, 22, 28, 31, 72–3, 96, 170, 180, 217
 and the 'responsibility to protect', 78–80
Geneva, 5
Geneva Conventions, 16
Genocide, Convention, 17–18, 77, 130
Germany, 2, 9, 10, 14, 9, 141, 144, 163
 and Africa, 11, 96, 115
 Hohenzollern, 8
 Nazi, 8, 10, 17, 141, 142, 146, 149
Ghana, 118–19
global governance, 69–70, 215, 224
globalisation, xiii, 69–70, 73
Golan Heights, 34
Gorbachev, Mikhail, 42, 81
Great Lakes (Africa), 76, 114, 217
Greece, 9, 61, 142, 171, 219–20
Gromyko, Andrei, 34
Guinea-Bissau, 55, 95, 99, 135
Guinea-Conakry, 135
Gulf war (1991), 46–8, 54, 72, 84, 88, 108, 113; *see also* Operation Desert Storm
Gusmão, Xanana, 182, 194, 197, 199, 200–1

Habibie, B. J., 180, 181
Habyarimana, Juvénal, 116, 119, 121
Hague, the, 5, 43
Hammarskjöld, Dag, 22, 24, 25, 31, 35, 74, 121, 216
 and the Congo, 27
 death of, 28, 107, 121
 summary study, 24–5, 50, 64
Harvard University, 86
High Commission for Refugees *see* UNHCR
Holland, 9, 10, 30, 149, 153, 154, 189; *see also* Netherlands
Holocaust, 15
Howe, Admiral Jonathon, 110
Human Rights Council (UN), 43

human security, 43–4, 77, 82–3
Huntington, Samuel, 90
Hutus (Rwanda), 28, 98, 114–27, 196, 203

IDPs, 56, 57
IFOR, 155, 167
Iganatieff, Michael, 168
imperialism, 2, 3–4, 95, 99, 100, 115, 146,
    177, 218; see also colonialism
    cultural, 19
Implementation Force (Bosnia) see IFOR
India, 21, 23, 61, 103
Indian Ocean, 104
Indonesia
    and East Timor, 73, 85, 177–204
    and West New Guinea/Irian Jaya, 30–3, 61,
    218
interahamwe (Rwanda), 119, 125, 131
INTERFET, 183–9, 198, 202, 203
International Court of Justice (ICJ), 15–16, 43,
    97, 170
International Criminal Court, 43, 70
International Force forEast Timor see INTER-
    FET
International Labour Office, 15
international law, 3, 16, 17, 43, 48, 50, 77,
    151, 164, 170
International Law Commission (ILC), 17
International Monetary Fund, 182
International Security Force (Timor Leste), 200
Iraq, 11, 46–9, 72, 80, 81, 88, 90, 108, 109,
    161, 163–4, 224
Ireland, 91, 119, 186
Irian Jaya, 23, 216, 217–18, 219, 223; see also
    West New Guinea
Israel, 21
    and Lebanon, 36–7
    and Suez, 21–3
    and 1973 war, 34–7, 38
Italian East Africa, 103
Italian Somaliland, 103
Italy, 8, 9, 59, 103–4, 112, 142, 163
Izetbegovi , Alija, 147

Jakarta, 180, 182, 184, 185, 186, 187, 199, 203
Janjaweed militia (Darfur), 131
Japan, 8, 11, 14, 19
Java, 33
JNA, 143, 144, 147, 164
Joint Task Force in Somalia (US), 110
Jola, 99
Jordan, 11
Jordan, 35
Justice and Equality Movement (Darfur), 131,
    132

Kant, Immanuel, 68
Kasavubu, Joseph, 26–7

Kashmir, 20–1, 22, 60, 209
Katanga (Congo), 26–8
Kenya, 186
KFOR, 167, 173–4
Khartoum, 130, 131, 132, 133
Khrushchev, Nikita, 27
Kigali, 120, 121, 124, 125, 126
Kinshasa, 26, 28
Kissinger, Henry, 34, 179
KLA, 157–8, 162–3, 164, 170
Klagenfurt Basin, 9
Korea, 19, 78
    North, 19–20, 47
    South, 19–20, 186
Korean war, 19, 21, 22, 23
Kosovars, 156, 158, 164, 165, 167, 168, 172
Kosovo, xii, 10, 30, 72, 73, 80, 81, 113,
    155–71, 172, 173, 177, 187, 202, 208,
    209
Kosovo Force see KFOR
Kosovo Liberation Army see KLA
Kurdistan, 48
Kurds, 48
Kuwait, 46, 48
Kyrgyzstan, 225

Labor party (Australia), 184
Labour party (Britain), 81, 159
Latin America, 46, 58; see also South America,
    Central America
Latvia, 141
League for a Democratic Kosovo, 156
League of Nations, 4–11, 12, 13, 15, 16, 20,
    21, 31, 64, 122, 172
    covenant, 5, 6, 11
    mandate system, 10–11, 96, 115
    Permanent Court of International Justice, 5,
    8, 15
    secretariat, 5
Lebanon, 11, 23, 25, 29, 35, 38, 61
    civil war, 36–7
Leticia, 10, 30
Liberal party (Australia) 184
Liberia, 61, 101, 111, 126, 129, 134, 135, 136,
    208
Libya, 97, 101, 130
Lisbon, 95, 178
Lithuania, 9, 141
London, 22, 104
Loromonu, 199, 203
Lorosau, 199, 203
Lumumba, Patrice, 26–7, 63
Luttwak, Edward, 207–9, 212–13, 216, 225
Luxembourg, 10

Macedonia, 54, 62, 142, 164, 172
Mahdi Mohammed, Ali, 107
Malaysia, 184, 187

Mali, 108
Manchuria, 8, 122
Mediterranean, 144, 219
Melanesia, 30, 33
Middle East, 11, 25, 34, 37, 47, 75, 94, 95
military observation, xii, 23, 49, 53, 63, 64, 134, 214
Military Staff Committee (UN), 45, 47, 52, 59
Mill, John Stuart, 208
Millennium Report (UN), 73, 76
Milošević, Slobodan, 143, 144, 146, 147, 156, 158, 159, 161–6, 167, 168
MINURCAT, 129
mission creep, 102, 111, 161
Mitrovica, 168, 170
Mobutu, Joseph (Sése, Séko), 28
Mogadishu, 84, 102, 104, 107, 109, 111, 114, 188
  'effect', 133
Monroe doctrine, 62
Montenegro, 144
MONUA (Angola), 220
MONUC (DR Congo), 128–9, 136, 196, 217
Moscow, 20, 28, 47, 81, 167, 170, 173
Mostar, 148
Mozambique, xiv, 55, 57, 95, 101, 118, 137, 148, 178, 210–12, 222–3, 225
MPLA (Angola), 117, 210–11, 220, 221
Multinational Force and Observers (Sinai) 38
Multinational Forces (Lebanon), 38
Musaveni, Yoweri, 116
mutually assured destruction, 34

Namibia, 11, 57, 96–7, 117, 137, 220; see also South West Africa
Napoleonic wars, 4
Nasser, Gammal, Abdel, 21–3, 25
National Consultative Council (East Timor), 194
National Council of East Timorese Resistance see CNRT
NATO, xii, 26, 38, 46, 53, 61, 95
  and Bosnia, 149–55, 171, 187
  and Kosovo, 73, 80, 155–73
neo-partrimonialism, 100
Nepal, 91
Netherlands, 5, 178; see also Holland
  and West New Guinea, 30–3, 61, 218
Neutral International Force (Rwanda), 117
neutrality (of intervening forces), 23, 24, 27, 29, 75, 117, 153, 191, 215
New Guinea, 30, 218
New York, xiv, 59, 80, 107, 117, 120, 121, 143, 147, 169, 217
New Zealand, 187
NFZ, 149, 150
Nigeria, 94, 134–5, 136
Nile river, 21

Nobel Peace prize, 180
no-fly zone (Bosnia) see NFZ
non-aligned movement, 143
Nordic countries, 42, 81, 88
North America, 18, 89
North Atlantic Council, 165
North Atlantic Treaty Organization see NATO
Norway, 9, 89
Nuremberg trials, 17, 43

O'Brien, Conor Cruise, 107–8, 121
oil, 47, 212
ONUC (Congo), 23, 25–30, 63, 64, 216–17
ONUMOZ (Mozambique), 222
Operation Allied Force (Kosovo), 165
Operation Deliberate Force (Bosnia), 154, 166, 172
Operation Desert Storm, 47, 49, 108, 113; see also Gulf war
Operation Restore Hope (Somalia), 87, 108–9, 113, 123, 202
Operation Turquoise (Rwanda), xii, 125–7, 186
Organization for Security and Cooperation in Europe see OSCE
Organization of African Unity, 116
OSCE, 144, 158, 169
  Verification Mission (Kosovo), 158, 163, 164
Ottoman empire, 4, 8, 11, 145; see also Turkey

Pacific, 11, 183
Pakistan, 21, 23, 31, 61
Palestine, 11, 20–1, 22, 23, 29, 35–6, 60, 209
Papua New Guinea, 30, 184, 218
Paris, 22, 125, 126, 155
PDD25, 123
peace enforcement units (Agenda for Peace), 51, 52, 54, 59
peace-building, 53, 55, 57, 59, 74, 86, 134, 214, 219
peacekeeping, xi, 19, 20, 21, 23, 24–5, 26, 27, 29, 33, 36, 37, 51, 53, 60, 63, 64, 67, 71, 74–5, 87, 91, 95, 97, 106, 109, 119, 148, 154, 156, 171, 183, 186, 214, 215
  'Hammarskjöldian', 24, 49, 63, 64, 129, 148, 154, 171, 215
  'new', 60–4, 67
Pearl Harbor, 11
Pearson, Lester, 22
Pérez de Cuéllar, Javier de, 106
Peru, 10
Philippines, 184, 187, 190
plebiscites, 9–10; see also Referendums
Poland, 9
Portugal, 36, 95, 96, 101, 117, 210, 211, 220
  and East Timor, 176–7, 181, 186, 188, 192, 201

Presidential Decision Directive No. 25 *see* PDD25
preventive diplomacy, 24, 74, 216, 218
Princeton University, 5
Pristina, 166
Protestantism, 2
Putin, Vladimir, 81

Qana, 37

R2P *see* 'responsibility to protect'
Račak, 158, 164
Rambouillet, 158, 164, 166, 167, 170
Ramos-Horta, José, 180, 182, 200, 201
Rapid Reaction Force (Bosnia), 153
Reagan, Ronald, 36
Red Cross, 15
referendums, 10; *see also* plebiscites
Renamo (Mozambique), 210, 211, 212
Republika Srpska (Bosnia), 147, 149, 155
'responsibility to protect', 79–83, 87, 123, 125, 130, 154
    Commission, 74, 76–9, 82–3, 89, 123, 160–1, 165–6
Revolutionary United Front (Sierra Leone), 134
Rhodesia, 95, 211; *see also* Zimbabwe
Romania, 171
Romanovs, 8
Rome, 59, 104
Rome Statute (ICC), 43
Roosevelt, Eleanor, 18
Roosevelt, Franklin D., 7, 12, 13, 18
RPF, 116, 119, 121, 124, 125–7, 129
RtoP *see* 'responsibility to protect'
Ruak, Taur Matan, 195
Ruanda-Urundi, 115; *see also* Burundi; Rwanda
Rugova, Ibrahim, 156, 169
Russia, 8, 72, 81–2, 88, 122, 126, 141, 152, 172, 122, 126
    and Bosnia, 152
    and Kosovo, 158–71
    see also Soviet Union
Rwanda, xii, xiv, 11, 18, 42–3, 51, 57, 58, 73, 79, 98, 101, 102–3, 111, 114–28, 129, 131, 133, 137. 173, 177, 196, 202, 203, 208, 209
    CNN effect in, 83, 85, 86
    genocide in, xiv, 28, 54, 55, 59, 61, 72, 75, 85, 87, 102, 154, 195, 217
Rwandan Patriotic Front *see* RPF

Saar, 10, 30, 64, 172
Sadat, Anwar, 50
Saddam Hussein, 46, 48, 54, 161
Sahnoun, Mohamad, 106–7, 110, 112, 121
Santa Cruz massacre (East Timor), 180, 199

Sarajevo, 145, 147, 149, 151, 153, 155
Saudi Arabia, 61
Savimbi, Jonas, 211, 212, 220
Scandinavia, 2
Schleswig, 9
Scott, Ridley, 111
second world war, 5, 8, 14, 15, 19, 30, 43, 96, 103, 178
secretariat (UN), 45, 107
Security Council (UN), 12, 13, 14, 16, 18, 21, 22, 37, 72, 76, 81, 85, 103, 135, 207, 208, 213, 216, 219, 221
    and Bosnia, 148, 151–2
    and collective security, 45–6, 53, 54, 59, 164
    and the Congo, 26, 27
    and East Timor/Timor Leste, 183, 188, 197, 200
    and Korean war, 20
    and Kosovo, 160, 163, 164, 165, 169, 170, 172
    and Lebanon, 25
    and the 'responsibility to protect', 77–80
    and Rwanda, 122, 123, 125
    and Somalia, 106, 107
    veto in, 22, 56, 48, 78, 79, 162, 163, 164, 170, 173, 225
self-defence (in peacekeeping), 24, 27, 64, 71, 106, 109, 153, 214
self-determination, 5, 8, 10, 11, 15
Senegal, 99, 125, 135
Serbia, 57, 88, 142, 143, 172
    and Bosnia, 145–55
    and Croatia, 144–5
    'greater', 143, 156
    and Kosovo, 73, 81, 156–71
Shawcross, William, 128
Shevardnadze, Eduard, 81
Shia muslims, 48
Siad Barre, Muhammad, 104
Sierra Leone, 43, 61, 85, 101, 126, 129, 134, 135, 136, 161
Silesia, Upper, 9
Sinai, 38
Singapore, 184, 187
Sino-Soviet conflict, 81
six days war, 24
slave trade, 4
Slovakia, 141
Slovenia, 142, 143, 147
Smuts, Jan, 96
SNA, 107, 110, 111, 113
Solana, Javier, 165
Solomon Islands, 30
Somali National Alliance *see* SNA
Somalia, xii, 49–50, 51, 57, 59, 64, 67–8, 72, 76, 79, 95, 101, 102, 103–14, 129, 133, 135, 137, 148, 171, 187, 188, 195, 202, 203, 205, 208, 209

CNN effect in, 83, 86, 87, 102, 104, 108, 109
and Rwanda intervention, 117, 118, 119, 121, 122, 123, 124, 125, 127, 128
Somaliland, 104
South Africa, 11, 78, 96–7, 133, 135, 210, 211, 220, 221, 223
Union of, 96
South America, 10; see also Latin America
South West Africa, 96; see also Namibia
South West Africa People's Organization see SWAPO
sovereign equality, xiii, 89
sovereignty, xiii–xiv, xvi, 2, 7, 16, 31, 51, 67, 69–74, 76–7, 79, 82, 87–90, 130, 132, 159, 165, 167–8, 170, 183, 183–4, 215
Soviet Union, 13, 22, 25, 42, 43, 47, 49, 62, 89, 117, 126, 142, 220
and the Congo 26, 27–8
and Korean war 19–20
and Middle East, 36, 38
end of, 81, 88, 102, 141
see also Russia
Spain, 9, 171
Srebrenica, 74, 154, 158, 208
Stalin, Joseph, 12, 143
Sudan, 72, 82, 97, 101, 129–33
Sudanese Liberation Movement, 131, 132
Suez, 21–3, 25, 29, 32, 60–1, 209
Suharto, 178, 181, 182
Suhrke, Astri, 191–2
Sukarno, 30, 31, 218
Sukarnoputri, Megawati, 197
Sunni (Iraqi), 48
Supplement to An Agenda for Peace (1995), 55–6, 58, 59, 60, 64, 83
supranationalism, xiv, 2
SWAPO, 96–7
Sweden, 9, 10, 22, 89, 91, 119, 135
Switzerland, 5, 45–6
Syria, 11, 25
and Lebanon, 36–7
and 1973 war, 34–7, 61

Tanzania, 11, 43, 95, 116, 121
Taylor, Charles, 134
Tel Aviv, 34
Thaçi, Hashim, 170
Thailand, 184, 187
Thant, U, 31, 32, 34
The Economist, 72
thirty years war, 2, 4
Tiananmen Square, 44
Timor Leste, 177, 197–204; see also East Timor
Timor Sea, 204
Tito, Josip Broz, 142–3, 156
Togo, 11
Transcaucasia, 49

Troika proposal (UN), 28
trusteeship system (UN), 11, 96, 104
Truth and Friendship Commission (Timor Leste), 199
Tudjman, Franjo, 144
Turkey, 5, 8, 61, 110, 141, 156, 219–20; see also Ottoman Empire
Tutsis (Rwanda), 98, 114–27, 196, 203

UDT (East Timor), 178
Uganda, 95, 98, 101, 115, 119
Ukraine, 141
UN Aouzou Strip, Observer Group see UNASOG
UN Assistance Mission to Rwanda see UNAMIR
UN Civilian Police see UNCIVPOL
UN Disengagement Observation Force (Golan Heights) see UNDOF
UN Emergency Force see UNEF, UNEF-II
UN Force in Cyprus see UNFICYP
UN India–Pakistan Observation Mission see UNIPOM
UN Integrated Mission in East Timor see UNMIT
UN Interim Force in Lebanon see UNIFIL
UN Military Observer Mission in India and Pakistan see UNMOGIP
UN Mission in Central African Republic and Chad see MINURCAT
UN Mission in Congo see MONUC
UN Mission in East Timor see UNAMET
UN Mission in Ethiopia and Eritrea see UNMEE
UN mission in Kosovo see UNMIK
UN Mission in Sierra Leone see UNAMSIL
UN Mission in Sudan see UNMIS
UN Mission of Support in East Timor see UNMISET
UN Observation Mission in Lebanon see UNOGIL
UN Observer Mission in Liberia see UNOMIL
UN Office in Timor Leste see UNOTIL
UN Operation in Somalia see UNOSOM-I; UNOSOM-II
UN Operation in the Congo see ONUC
UN Preventive Deployment Force (Macedonia) see UNPREDEP
UN Protection Force (former Yugoslavia) see UNPROFOR
UN Transition Assistance Group (Namibia) see UNTAG
UN Transitional Administration in East Timor see UNTAET
UN Transitional Authority in Cambodia see UNTAC
UN Verification Mission for Angola see UNAVEM-I; UNAVEM-II; UNAVEM-III

UN Yemen Observer Mission *see* UNYOM
UNAMET, 181–3, 188, 201, 202
UNAMID, 129–33
UNAMIR, 114, 119–27
UNAMSIL, 161
UNASOG, 97, 98
UN–AU Mission in Darfur *see* UNAMID
UNAVEM-I, 97, 117, 221
UNAVEM-II, 117, 220–2
UNAVEM-III, 220
UNCIVPOL, 171, 200
UNDOF, 34–6
UNEF, (Suez), 22–4, 60
UNEF-II, 34–5, 36, 38
UNFICYP, 23, 218–19
UNHCR, xi, 56, 57, 195
Unified Command (Korea), 20
Unified Task Force (Somalia) *see* UNITAF
UNIFIL, 34, 36–7, 38
UNIKOM, 49
UNIPOM (India–Pakistan), 23
UNITA (Angola) 52, 117, 210–12, 220, 212, 221
UNITAF, 57, 84, 109–10, 113, 125, 202
United Nations charter, xii, 1, 12, 13, 14, 16, 52, 54, 71–2, 73, 75, 77, 78, 96, 109, 151–2, 162–3, 179–80, 186
  Chapter VII, 13, 44–7, 49, 51, 52, 109, 162, 163–4, 179, 186
  Chapter VIII, 52–3, 151–2
United Somali Congress, 107
United States, 3, 5, 6–7, 11, 12, 13, 42, 43, 44, 54, 62, 80, 88, 89, 117, 122, 124, 130, 141, 220
  and Bosnia, 149–55, 166
  Congress, 5, 6, 12
  Department of Defense, 109
  and East Timor, 178, 182, 187, 203
  and Iraq, 46–7, 164
  and Korean war, 19–20
  and Kosovo, 162, 163, 170
  and Lebanon, 25, 36, 38
  and Somalia, 57, 59, 68, 84, 86, 102, 104, 108–14, 122, 135, 187–8
  State Department, 109
  and Suez, 22
Uniting for Peace (resolution), 22, 78
Universal Declaration of Human Rights (UDHR), 18–19, 43
UNMEE, 97–8
UNMIK, 162, 167–71, 173, 189, 190
UNMIS, 130, 132
UNMISET, 193, 197–9
UNMIT, 200, 201
UNMOGIP, 21, 23

UNOGIL, 23, 25, 61
UNOMIL, 126
UNOSOM-I, 57, 106–8, 148, 202
UNOSOM-II, 110–13, 127, 187
UNOTIL, 198–9
UNPREDEP, 54, 172
UNPROFOR, 57, 145–51, 153–5, 171, 187
UNSF, 23 (West New Guinea), 31–3, 217
UNTAC, 62, 189
UNTAET, 188–96, 198, 202
  Office of District Administration, 190
UNTAG, 97
UNTEA, 23, 31–3, 189, 217
UNTSO (Palestine), 21, 23
UNYOM, 23
USSR *see* Soviet Union

Versailles, 9, 12
Vieira de Melo, Sérgio, 189, 191, 192
Vietnam, 83, 178
Vilna (Vilnius), 9

Waldheim, Kurt, 34
war on terror, 83, 90, 108
Washington, 12, 22, 47, 80, 102, 109, 110, 112, 122, 149, 154, 167
West New Guinea, 10, 30–3, 34, 61, 62, 64, 184, 189, 216, 217
West Timor, 178, 182, 188, 195–6, 198, 199, 203
Western Sahara, 101, 128
Westphalia, Treaty of, xiii, 2–3
Westphalian system, xiii, 2, 14, 24, 67–8, 89
Westphalianism, xiv, 7, 25, 33, 48, 51, 70, 87, 91, 159, 170, 215
  post-, xiii, 67–70, 87, 89, 215, 224
White House, 36, 109, 149, 150
Wilson, Woodrow, 4–5, 6–7, 12, 141
  and the Fourteen Points, 5
World Bank, 182
World Court, 8
world system theory, 99; *see also* dependency theory

Yalta Conference, 12
Yemen, 23, 61
Yudhoyono, Susilo, 199
Yugoslav National Army *see* JNA
Yugoslavia, 42–3, 54, 55, 57, 62, 72, 106, 118, 141–73
  Kingdom of, 142

Zagreb, 144
Zaire, 28, 102, 196; *see also* Congo
Zimbabwe, 78, 95, 211; *see also* Rhodesia